THE ART OF CHRISTIAN LEADERSHIP

By Rev. Jon Byler

Lancaster, PA, USA
GlobalDisciples.net

Dedication

This book is dedicated to pastors around the world, men and women with a heart for God, especially those who labor in parts of the world where there are few resources and learning opportunities. I admire your faith and your courage and pray that God will encourage you as you give Him everything you have! My prayer is that God will use you to raise up a new generation of leaders with Christ-like character, practical knowledge, and effective skills to lead others.

The Art of Christian Leadership
TABLE OF CONTENTS

Introduction

What makes an effective Christian leader? Many of us wrestle with this question. While I don't have all the answers, let me share my leadership journey with you.

By age 21, knowing that God had called me into full time Christian ministry, I began my preparation. After receiving my college degree in Christian Ministries, I sensed that my beautiful certificate had not fully prepared me for ministry, so I served for a year as an apprentice to an experienced church planter. That gave me valuable experience, but I was still a novice in leadership. In 1991 I moved to Kenya, East Africa to pastor a newly planted church. For the next five years I gave my heart and soul to that work, making my share of mistakes and enjoying some successes. The church grew from 30 to 250, and we also planted two other churches. During that time I was called to be an overseer, and for several years worked with 15 churches in that area. As I worked with these pastors I began to ask questions about leadership. I wanted to see all those churches doing well and growing strong, but some weren't. Of course, each pastor would give exciting testimonies about how God was blessing his church, but when visiting the church I saw the same faces as the year before! What was happening? What could be done to strengthen these churches? Why were some growing and others not growing? "If only these pastors could go to Bible school," I thought, "things would change." So I watched those who went to Bible schools. Some were helped, while others surprisingly came back worse! My question was still unanswered.

Next, I considered the environment. Perhaps some of the pastors were in difficult localities, with poor, uneducated people, hindering church growth. Then a close friend with no theological training went to a remote location to start a church. Within a few years he had a strong church and was planting others! Another of my theories was discarded!

Meanwhile, I continued to pour my life into leaders. I taught at a Bible school, started a Theological Education by Extension (TEE) program in the church, held leaders' seminars, and prayed with the pastors I was overseeing. Many of my questions remained unanswered. That some people can be leaders and others never make it in leadership must be a sovereign decision by an Almighty God about which I could do nothing!

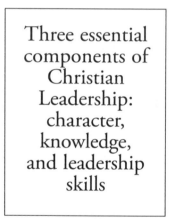

Three essential components of Christian Leadership: character, knowledge, and leadership skills

At that time I was called to work with Centre for Christian Discipleship, a ministry devoted to equipping leaders. In my study about leadership, I was particularly challenged and influenced by materials from Rev. John Maxwell. He taught me that "everything rises and falls on leadership"[1] and that leaders are not born, they are made. He gave me fresh hope that leadership can be learned and he provided practical resources and ideas that have shaped my teaching. Thanks, Rev. Maxwell!

With renewed vigor and fresh determination, I began to make a difference in the lives of leaders, first in Kenya through the Leadership Training Institute and now internationally.

In reflecting now on what makes an effective Christian leader, I have identified three essential components: character, knowledge, and leadership skills. Character deals with heart issues of motives, integrity, submission, the leader's

---

1. John C. Maxwell, *Developing the Leader Within You* (Nashville, TN: Thomas Nelson, 1993), viii.

relationship with Christ, family, etc. Knowledge includes a basic understanding of the Bible as well as self-awareness. Leadership skills are the skills that cause others to desire to follow the leader, and includes a wide range of skills such as knowing how to connect with people, communicating vision, setting goals and managing time well, understanding different people, equipping others, team building, managing conflict, etc.

Like the three legs of a stool, each is necessary for the leader to stand. Without knowledge a leader cannot communicate truth effectively, and he is unable to draw on the vast resources in God's Word to strengthen him. However, knowledge without character will lead to an arrogant, cocky leader who cannot sustain his leadership over time. Some leaders have both knowledge and good character but are ineffective as leaders since they lack leadership skills. They are wonderful people and love God deeply, but their churches will never grow to their full potential because they aren't good leaders. These areas are the *head*, the *heart* and the *hands* of leadership. David, the shepherd king, combined all three in a powerful way. With his *head* he knew God so well that he was called 'a man after God's own heart' (1 Samuel 13:14). The Bible also says of him, *"And David shepherded them with integrity of heart; with skillful hands he led them."* (Psalm 78:72)

In my ministry God has called me to focus primarily on two legs of the three-legged stool: character and leadership skills. This in no way implies a lack of respect for those whom God has called to devote their lives to equipping leaders with knowledge. They have an essential role in developing leaders and I value their contribution.

My book *The Heart of Christian Leadership* focuses on character. In it I explore issues of character such as motives, brokenness, servant leadership, authority, forgiveness, etc. These are issues that form us as leaders and areas in which

God needs to deal with us before we become skillful in the art of leading others. I consider that book to be a foundational book and strongly recommend that it be read first or at least simultaneously with this one. A brief summary is provided here.

This companion book focuses on leadership skills. I am confident that the principles outlined here will help any leader become more effective in calling others to follow. However, I would deeply regret helping leaders with weak character become more influential. Howard Hendricks states it clearly, "The greatest crisis today is a crisis of leadership. And the greatest peril of leadership is a crisis of character. Think about it, to give a person management techniques and leadership skills without integrity is simply to enable him to become a better rip-off artist." Again, I strongly urge you to deepen your character as you develop your skill.

Both books are written for those in leadership or aspiring to leadership in the church, especially for those in pastoral leadership. The principles however, are applicable to all Christian leaders at whatever level.

I pray that this book will be useful in your life, to make you a more effective leader in the church, your home and in society. Read, reflect and respond. Use the action assignments at the end of each chapter to allow the material to challenge your thinking and change your life. After it has changed you, it can be used to teach others! Individual lessons with student handouts can be purchased for this type of training. The following items from this book are available on our website (www.GlobalDisciples.net) or at the author's website (www.LeadersServe.com) to download and print:

Appendix A: My Identity in Christ
Appendix B: Time Evaluation Chart
Potential Leader Checklist
Personality Quiz

Acknowledgments

I want to acknowledge the special role several persons have played in my life to make this book possible.

First and foremost, I acknowledge the Lord Jesus Christ, the only perfect leader. As my Sovereign Lord, He is daily changing my life to become more like His. May He receive all glory and honor.

Second, I want to acknowledge my lovely wife, Loice. She has been used far more than she will ever know to make me more effective as a leader. Thanks, Loice, for your constant encouragement, tender rebukes and words of affirmation.

Finally, I want to thank all those leaders whose books and teachings have mentored me in my journey: John Maxwell, John Haggai, Bruce Wilkinson, Zig Ziglar, Neil Anderson, Ralph Mahoney, Rick Warren and others too numerous to mention. Wherever possible I have tried to give credit to the appropriate source. Much of the material in chapter six on priorities has been modified from Rev. John Maxwell's video presentation: *Priorities, the Pathway to Success*. To all who have greatly influenced my life and leadership "Thank you!"

Summary "The Heart of Christian Leadership"

The companion book, *The Heart of Christian Leadership*, lays the foundation for our focus on leadership skills. Read it first, if possible, but here is a brief summary.

Three essential components of Christian Leadership are: character, knowledge, and leadership skills. This book focuses on the first component, character, which determines our long-term success in Christian leadership. You can build short-term success on charisma and charm, but you cannot build a lasting work for God without solid character. Many leaders have extensive knowledge and effective leadership skills but fail because of character issues. Character is *the qualities and traits that make up a person, the core of your being, the heart of who you are.* When God chooses a leader, character is more important than competence. Followers also look for character because it produces confidence and trust, without which effective leadership is impossible. Character development, a lifelong process requiring much work, is achieved through our daily choices, especially through difficult times. There are no shortcuts. Building character requires time and patience.

Many kinds of leaders exist in the world. Some seek to please people, others strive for personal gain. Some have a genuine heart for people, others do not care. Some communicate, others dictate. Some help with the work, others give orders and watch. In Luke 22, Jesus taught His disciples that, unlike the world's concept of leadership which is based on authority, *His followers were to be servant-leaders.* In Luke 22:27 He told them: *"I am among you as one who serves."* Following His example, Christian leadership is characterized by service which means *giving*, not *getting*. The world says that "servant" and "leader" are opposites. But Jesus, the greatest leader in history, says you are to be a servant leader in order to change hearts and churches. The prime example of His leadership model is in John 13, as He washed the feet of His disciples, and taught them profoundly about their future leadership. He then went to the cross as the ultimate expression of sacrificial leadership. **In God's Kingdom, true power to influence comes as we serve.**

In the natural world a broken item decreases in value. In our spiritual lives, the opposite is true: the more broken we are, the more useful in the Kingdom. *Brokenness is an absolute surrender to the Lordship of Jesus Christ.* Jesus taught this in Luke 9:23-26, which begins: *If anyone would come after me, he must deny himself and take up his cross daily and follow me.* Here Jesus speaks of a depth of Christian experience few of His followers even consider. Jesus' call to self-denial is so radical that we often dismiss it as aimed only at a select group of followers, but He intended it for all of us. Brokenness and full surrender to His lordship requires death or denial of your *self.* You will experience the abundant Christian life only through this death which is a daily action. True revival comes as the fruit of broken and submitted hearts and lives and is tested in relationships. God does not hold you accountable for what others do to you, but for how you respond to them. Brokenness will revolutionize your life beginning at home where you show your true nature. It also greatly affects your leadership, enabling you to receive criticism without being defensive. A broken leader does not think too highly of himself, rejoices in the successes of others, is transparent with people, and serves others. These kinds of leaders are desperately needed in the home, the church and the world.

In Christian leadership, motives are as crucial as the actual work. The instructions of 1 Peter 5:1-4 exhort us to *Be shepherds of God's flock that is under your care, serving as overseers—not because you must but because you are willing, as God wants you to be; not greedy for money but eager to serve; not lording it over those entrusted to you, but being examples to the flock.* Christian leadership should never be forced or dictated, but should come from a clear sense of God's calling. Without this calling, Christian ministry quickly becomes an overwhelming burden and leads to burnout but with a calling the leader is energized by God's supernatural vision, and service becomes both exciting and rewarding.

This calling guards the heart against many wrong motives. The Christian leader's first motive is *to serve,* seeking to *give* rather than *receive.* This requires genuine love, looking out for others, being eager to see them prosper and grow. The second motive is *to show,* seeking to provide a model for others. This requires careful examination of your life to ensure that you are a worthy example. The third motive is *to satisfy,* seeking to please the "Chief Shepherd," the Lord Jesus. The greatest reward for a faithful leader is described in verse 4: *And when the Chief Shepherd appears, you will receive the crown of glory that will never fade away.*

Your words are powerful. They can encourage or discourage, speak the truth or lies, bring peace or tension. Since your "tongue" is such a powerful instrument, God is very concerned with your speech, especially since a leader's actions are magnified before others. Jesus wants His people to put away unwholesome talk as Paul commands, *Do not let any unwholesome talk come out of your mouth* (Ephesians 4:29). Unwholesome talk can be seen in many ways. Speaking lies can be done directly or by giving a false impression, by allowing others to believe something we know to be false, or even by "stretching the truth." Other unwholesome talk includes words spoken in anger, obscene language, foolish talk, coarse joking, talking too much, flattery, swearing, gossip, and slander. Positively, Jesus wants our tongues to build others up. Such edifying talk meets the needs of others and benefits the listener and is to be the *exclusive* talk of the believer. This seems impossible, but God has provided the way to change our tongue. This begins by confessing our sins and asking God to change our hearts which happens as we memorize and meditate on the Word of God. Make this your habit, and allow God time to transform your tongue.

Truthfulness is an area of our speech which greatly impacts our character and capacity to lead. Although truth is rare today the Bible clearly expects us to be truthful. Deceit, especially when a generational sin, is a powerful influence, but God can set us free. In the seeming conflict between speaking *truth* and expressing *love,* the exhortation in Ephesians 4:15 is to *speak the truth in love.* Truthfulness is difficult; lying is often much easier than telling the truth since it is part of our sinful nature and encouraged by our culture. Often we lie directly, but at other times we lie with exaggeration, deceptive words to our children, allowing false impressions, keeping silent when others are lying, or practicing deception in business. Truthfulness begins at home, in honesty with our spouse and in communication with our children. It is essential in our work, even when we are tempted to shade the truth to avoid losing business or our job. Leaders are held to a higher standard, and must carefully communicate truth, following three guidelines: 1) always give accurate information to people; 2) do not withhold information unless absolutely necessary; 3) take the blame instead of passing it on to others. Although it is difficult, the reward of truthfulness is *trust,* without which a leader cannot lead. Learning to be truthful leaders requires a personal commitment, confession of sin, asking God to change our hearts, memorizing His Word, and trusting Him to establish us in the truth.

A proper understanding of authority is essential to Christian leadership. Scripture teaches four major principles of authority. First, *God establishes authority,* begining in the home, then in the church, the government, and at work and school. Second, *God expects submission to authority,* respecting those over you and willingly supporting their leadership. This provides both protection and true freedom. Third, *God enables you to submit to authority,* receiving correction, admitting mistakes, being accountable, and showing true loyalty and respect.

Fourth, *God exemplifies submission to authority.* In the incarnation, Jesus the Son submitted to the Father, even to His death on the cross. The Apostle Paul called on his disciples to *follow me as I follow Christ.* In their submission, Jesus and Paul provide the perfect model for all Christian leaders.

Forgiveness is required of all Christians, especially those in leadership. We are commanded to forgive others, as God has forgiven us in Christ. Forgiveness is a choice we make, an act of our will, not our feelings. Unforgiveness affects us spiritually, physically, emotionally, and socially, crippling our lives as a heavy burden. Forgiveness begins with yourself, choosing to look at your past through the blood of Christ. Then it goes to the home, including your parents, spouse, and children. It extends to friends and associates, both Christians and non-Christians, and to those under your leadership. As Jesus taught, forgiveness is for everyone, for everything, and to be given as often as needed. There are at least five results of forgiveness: 1) reconciliation with God; 2) reconciliation with others; 3) Christian growth; 4) strengthened prayer life; and 5) freedom from negative emotions. In spite of the benefits of forgiveness, your flesh and your culture both resist forgiveness. Although your culture encourages *getting even* instead of forgiving, in Christ forgiveness is an integral part of the new life and the new culture you experience as you walk in obedience.

Many leaders have tended to put their Kingdom service above everything, including their family, but family leadership is a prerequisite for Christian leadership. Paul's instruction in 1 Timothy 3:4-5 gives these qualifications for the Christian leader: *He must manage his own family and see that his children obey him with proper respect. If anyone does not know how to manage his own family, how can he take care of God's church?* Family leadership therefore both precedes God's call to ministry and serves as a preparation for ministry.

Family should be the first priority, since God established the family from the beginning as the foundation of all society, including the church. In practice a strong family enables the leader to minister effectively and actually serves as the best validation of a leader's ministry. Making family a priority begins with time with your spouse, then with your children. Time with children should include both learning *and* fun. Investing significant time brings beautiful results both in your immediate ministry and in building strong leaders for the next generation. Loving family relationships provide strength in ministry and witness to the vibrancy of your Christian faith.

Many leaders focus on leading well but forget that in times of moving on to another assignment they should also leave well. In the process of leaving, it is essential to consider your motives, seeking godly counsel from others.

Examine your responsibility for leaving. Ask for blessing for those who remain, even when there have been disagreements or other problems. Leaving with integrity requires you to value relationships with all your brothers and sisters in Christ, but also to exit completely, leaving behind relationships and physical property that rightly belongs to the incoming leader.

Finally, begin your journey as a leader with the end in mind. The Bible reveals many leaders who started well but finished poorly through personal pride and failure to obey the Lord. Examining the lives of the biblical examples of Uzziah and Solomon reveal several reasons leaders fail to finish well. These include self-realization and pride, the distraction of success, forgetting God, writing ones own rules, finding ones primary identity in work or ministry and failure to deal with hidden sins. To finish the race with integrity requires humility, a clear goal to continually serve the Lord, keeping His Word, dealing with personal sin, keeping a proper perspective on life, recognizing your own vulnerability, and being accountable to peers who will encourage and exhort you. Follow the examples of Peter, James, John, Paul, and many contemporary leaders who have finished well. Be assured of God's victory as you walk humbly with Him, never assuming that strength today assures victory tomorrow. My prayer is that both you and I will finish well.

Summary by W. Lee Troup

Part One: Leading Yourself

"Be not angry that you cannot make others as you wish them to be, since you cannot make yourself as you wish to be."
- Thomas a Kempis

"Before we can conquer the world, we must first conquer the self. A leader is a person who has learned to obey a discipline imposed from without, and has then taken on a more rigorous discipline from within. Those who rebel against authority, and scorn self-discipline – who shirk the rigors and turn from the sacrifices – do not qualify to lead. Many who drop out of ministry are sufficiently gifted, but have large areas of life floating free from the Holy Spirit's control. Lazy and disorganized people never rise to true leadership. Thus, the progression of discipline in the life of a leader is as follows: First, he submits to discipline from without. By doing so, he develops discipline from within. When that is mature, he is then permitted by God to give discipline to others. He has become a leader."
-J. Oswald Sanders in SPIRITUAL LEADERSHIP

1

Chapter One
THE LEADER UNDERSTANDS LEADERSHIP

Peter rubbed the sleep from his eyes and pushed the covers away. As the early morning light poured into his window, he could hear the stirring of the neighbors as they prepared to leave for another week of work. Sitting up, he recalled the events of the day before, the first Sunday in his new church. Peter was pleased with his new appointment. The church assigned to him seemed just right for a recent graduate of Bible College. At the thought of college, he gazed at the beautiful certificate hanging on the wall. All his effort had been worthwhile. The people were already calling him "Pastor Peter," sweet words to his ear. He smiled as he recalled his sermon, a homiletic masterpiece that revealed his deep understanding of the Word of God. Everyone had complimented him on his delivery. One lady in particular couldn't seem to stop shaking his hand as she congratulated him on the message. What a thrill!

Then, as he recalled the afternoon board meeting, his smile turned to a frown. The elders had disapproved his plan to change the starting time of the service. Maybe they were annoyed because he had announced it in church without consulting them. They also didn't seem to appreciate his ideas about changing the style of the worship. Didn't they realize that he was the pastor and that God had called him to show them the way? Soon, he thought, they'll understand. With that, he put on his slippers and headed for the shower.

Like many church leaders, Peter had Biblical knowledge, a good heart and a desire to lead. But he had much to learn about leadership. He didn't understand the three foundational principles of leadership which are the focus of this chapter.

PRINCIPLE ONE: THE SIMPLICITY OF LEADERSHIP

What is leadership? If you ask 20 people, you will likely get 20 different answers. Many people consider leadership complicated and nearly impossible to define. True, the practice of leadership is an art that takes a lifetime to develop; however understanding the meaning of leadership is relatively simple.

> "Leadership is influence. Nothing more, nothing less."

LEADERSHIP IS INFLUENCE

A leader is one who knows the way and leads others to follow. A leader influences people, either for good or for bad. John Maxwell says it very simply, "Leadership is influence. Nothing more, nothing less."[2] This concise definition has helped millions of people to understand what leadership is.

Leaders change the direction of others' lives through words and example. They influence people to do things that they would not otherwise have done. They encourage, inspire and unite people for a common goal. Leaders are change agents in the world. Leaders influence!

---

[2] Maxwell, *Developing the Leader Within You*, 1.

LEADERSHIP IS NOT POSITION

If leadership is influence, it is not simply having a position. Peter didn't realize this. He assumed that his position of leadership would bring changes, and people would follow him. But since he hadn't influenced the elders, the stage was set for a common power struggle. While a position of leadership provides a platform from which to influence people, it does not guarantee true influence. Those who try to lead only from a position usually become dictatorial and govern by intimidation. These methods rarely produce long-term positive changes. This is not to say that position doesn't matter; some people will respect you and follow you for a time because of position, but that is actually the lowest level of leadership. If people follow you only because you're the boss, you're in deep trouble!

If true leadership is being a person of influence, many people in positions of leadership are not the top influencers of the group they are "leading." The true leaders of the group are those who influence the others.

Here is a simple way to identify the real leader. The person others listen to is the real leader. For example, in a church board meeting the chairman proposes painting the offices blue. A discussion follows, with some favoring blue and others green. Before a decision is reached, people will likely wait for one particular person to speak. After hearing his opinion, they all nod in agreement. That person is the real leader. Whether or not he holds the position or title, he has influenced the group. This would have been especially instructive to Peter, who was recently placed in a position of leadership.

Another way to spot the true leaders in a church is to ask, "Who would I go to if I wanted to start something in the church? To find out what is going on?" Write their names on paper. You have just listed key influencers in your church. They are leaders, whether or not they have a position.

4

This principle is simple, but has profound implications. In teaching this to many people, I watch them struggle with these ideas which are so contrary to what most have been taught. For many, this definition of leadership threatens their position! It is important that they understand there is nothing wrong with a position, but if you have to tell people you're the leader, you're not! So in the board meeting, if Peter bangs his fist on the table and declares, "Don't you know that I'm the pastor?" he is using his position, not leading.

In practice, many people are leaders without realizing it! The mother who influences her child to talk nicely is a leader. The teacher who guides a student to excel is a leader. The mature believer who helps a young believer learn how to pray is exerting a powerful influence. Clearly, leadership is not just for the select few at the top of an organizational chart; it is for all who make an impact in the lives of others.

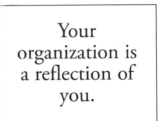

Your organization is a reflection of you.

Furthermore, since true leaders of a church or organization influence others, the group eventually will become like them. After you have been a leader for some time, your people will be more like you. If they are proud and arrogant, it's because you are proud and arrogant! If they are prayerful, it's because you are prayerful. **Your organization is a reflection of you.** This might give you great joy…or severe depression!

Finally, this principle teaches that true leadership in a church or other voluntary organization may in fact be the most demanding. In the business world when a boss demands something, it will likely be done because the employee knows that failure to comply might result in dismissal. The boss hires and dismisses at will. But in the church, this is different. The leader has only the power of influence. If people decide that they don't like you or the

5

church, they can simply walk to another church and you can't stop them! They will only stay if you influence them to stay. It is therefore imperative that church leaders learn and practice the art of leading through influence.

When you understand this principle you will ask yourself, "Whom do I influence, and how well?" And most importantly, "How can I increase my influence with people to help them grow to maturity in Christ?" Your greatest privilege as a leader is to influence and enable your followers to be more like Jesus and to influence others to become like Him!

Take a moment to think about your leadership. How much do you lead by influence? How much by position? What do you need to change?

PRINCIPLE TWO: THE SIGNIFICANCE OF LEADERSHIP

The simplicity of leadership might imply that leaders are not essential. The opposite is true: leaders are essential. They are desperately needed. Some might say that we don't need leaders, that everyone can do it on their own. They might be so disillusioned with poor leadership that they consider no leadership better than poor leadership. However, a quick look at a nation without leadership should convince them otherwise.

The world is crying out for leaders. Many nations are struggling with massive problems of poverty, debt and disease. The cry of the common man is for competent, caring leadership! People intuitively recognize that many of their problems are really leadership issues. Even an uneducated farmer knows that the sad state of the roads which hinders him from getting his produce to market results from poor leadership. We all recognize that with good leaders a nation will do well. Every family, every community, every group needs able leaders.

The church also desperately needs leaders. It is not difficult to start a church. With a good sound system and some money, I can go to many areas of the world, preach for a week, and gather people for a new church. I could start 52 churches a year. Why don't I do it? Because there are too few qualified leaders for the new church! We face a leadership crisis in the church worldwide and our evangelistic efforts must be matched by leadership development!

How many small groups does your church have? Why not more? I can predict your answer, "That's all the people we have. We are praying for more people." Wrong! You don't have more groups because you don't have prepared leaders. A good leader can enlist people to join the group. Your church will only grow as fast as its leadership develops.

LEADERS ARE SIGNIFICANT BECAUSE THEY MAKE THINGS HAPPEN

Without leadership, not much happens. Any gathering of people usually starts with people greeting each other and chatting. Sometimes they will sit down in anticipation. But nothing happens until the leader says, "Let's sing a song." People start singing, and things start happening.

Leaders make things happen by sharing ideas. Leaders provide ideas for action. They see potential where others are not looking, and initiate a plan of action. They look at problems and find solutions. They observe growth and say, "We could start a second service."

Leaders make things happen by giving direction. The leader says, "Let's begin with prayer" giving direction to the group. A pastor may say, "Let's have an evangelistic meeting" helping others see a goal and move in that direction.

Leaders make things happen by giving motivation. Without leadership most people become discouraged. They require leaders to motivate and direct them by having a worthy vision and communicating it effectively. They encourage people and keep the morale high. This motivation is crucial to strong leadership and must be done on a continual basis.

LEADERS ARE SIGNIFICANT BECAUSE "EVERYTHING RISES AND FALLS ON LEADERSHIP"

Under good leadership, organizations, nations, and churches grow strong. With poor leadership, everything declines. Look at the Children of Israel in the Old Testament. Every time they had a good king, they prospered. Under poor leaders, they went down spiritually, physically and morally. As we have already observed, "Everything rises and falls on leadership."

This principle is true in the church today. What will cause your church or organization to grow? The economy? The pastor's education or theology? The financial capability of the congregation? These may affect growth, but they are not the primary cause. **ONLY ONE THING HINDERS THE GROWTH OF YOUR ORGANIZATION . . . LEADERSHIP!** You can never build a church higher than your ability to lead people. You can never lead people to a level higher than you are. You are the "LID" of your organization. Your people will not go beyond you. That's why we say that the church is "under your leadership."

> You are the "LID" of your organization.

People naturally follow strong leaders they respect. Therefore, if you are a number "5" as a leader, it will be difficult to lead "6's" and "7's." But if you attain a higher level, you'll attract higher levels of people as well as greater numbers. I know that these are painful truths. You want to blame something or someone else for the size of the group that you are leading. Resist that temptation and evaluate yourself. I have observed the growth of many churches. The new church grows quickly at first, then begins to plateau. It may stop growing at 40, 110 or 800 people. But almost every church reaches a level at which it stops growing. What is happening? The church has grown to the level of the leader. It has hit the "lid" and growth stops. The chart below illustrates this principle. The only way for a church to grow more is for the leader to grow and learn how to influence more people.

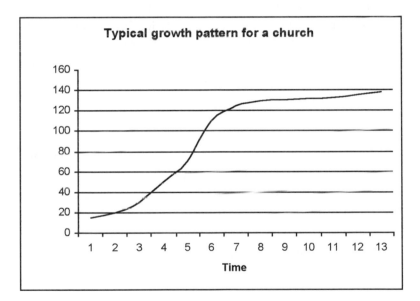

If this is too hard to accept, let me share my experience in my first church. I began with faith and enthusiasm, and worked hard. God blessed us, and the church grew. When the church reached about 250, we reached a plateau. I kept working hard, but when the growth wasn't there I rationalized, "We are now growing more spiritually than numerically." Only after leaving the church and reflecting could I see what had happened: the church had reached my "lid." I was only able to lead 250 people and stopped growing. I determined never again to stop growing! As I led the Center for Christian Discipleship I was continually sobered to realize that if I stop growing the ministry will also stop growing. After several years I was called to be the senior pastor of a church with 800 members. Since "everything rises and falls on leadership" I resolved by God's strength to keep growing!

PRINCIPLE THREE: THE SERIOUSNESS OF LEADERSHIP

If you understand the first two principles, you are ready for the third: The Seriousness of Leadership. Your leadership capacity will determine the growth of your church or organization. Others are looking to you as God enables you. If you are going to be serious about leadership, there are two steps you need to take.

STEP ONE: START GROWING AS A LEADER

Since "everything rises and falls on leadership" personal growth in leadership is essential. Think about it: you are the leader; others follow. If they are outgrowing you, they become the leader! Your growth determines not only how far you go, but how far your people go. There are three things you can do to start growing.

Realize that leadership can be learned

All who desire to grow can improve their leadership skills and their effectiveness in the Kingdom of God. Leaders are not born; they are made. You can learn to set goals, to communicate, to build relationships, and how to influence people! This book is dedicated to helping you develop leadership skills. When you practice these principles, you will grow in your capacity as a leader. Pause now and ask God to make you become an effective leader.

Recognize your growth potential

God has given you the potential to do great things for Him. He created you to lead. Think about what could happen in your life if you started growing

Desire in Christ all that He created you to be. Why settle for less! BE ALL THAT YOU CAN BE IN CHRIST! If you're not moving forward you're sliding backward.

Too many Christians settle for less than their best. They remain as followers or as weak leaders when they have the potential to be great leaders. Today I challenge you to begin fulfilling God's purpose for you. Rise up and be the leader He created you to be!

Resolve to grow!

Now is decision time! With all your potential to grow, not much will happen until you resolve to grow. The Irish have a saying, "You've got to do your own growing, no matter how tall your grandfather is."

Personal growth is your choice. No one can make it for you. You must be willing to pay the price. In order to grow, you must be willing to change. There

> "You've got to do your own growing, no matter how tall your grandfather is."

is no growth without change. Gail Sheehy writes, "If we don't change, we don't grow. If we don't grow we're not really living. Growth demands a temporary surrender of security."

This growing will stretch you beyond your comfort zone. You must think new thoughts and do things differently. At times this will be painful and difficult. As Ronald Osborne observes, "Undertake something that is difficult; it will do you good. Unless you try to do something beyond what you have already mastered, you will never grow."

HOW CAN YOU GROW? CONSIDER THE WORD G-R-O-W:

Get a passion to grow
Read
Organize your life
Work at what you learn

G-GET A PASSION TO GROW

Ask God to light a fire in your soul that will give you a passion to grow, to keep reading, thinking, changing and learning. Become a life long learner. This passion to grow is not in competition with others but a struggle within yourself to be all that God created you to be. Stewart B. Johnson says, "Our business in life is not to get ahead of others, but to get ahead of ourselves—to break our own records, to outstrip our yesterday by our today."

This passion to grow is your pursuit of excellence. You must ruthlessly evaluate yourself as you grow. According to Coach Pat Riley, "Excellence is the gradual result of always trying to do better."

This passion to grow is a lifelong pursuit. If you are not growing, you are starting to die. A tree is either growing or dying. When it stops growing, it starts dying. Ray Kroc quipped, "As long as you're green, you're growing; as soon as you're ripe, you start to rot."

Do you have a passion to grow? Are you ready to persevere on a daily basis?

R-READ

One of the best ways to grow is to read. Reading is to the mind what exercise is to the body. What good book have you read lately? What new thoughts have you had? What new

insights into the nature of God? What have you learned about yourself that will help you be more like Christ?

One of the negative things about many of our schools is that they encourage reading mainly to pass the exam. Teachers should be giving us the desire and power to read. You can read! In preparation for your final "exam" of life, this is the time to read!

You're already a reader because you are reading this book. Keep it up and don't stop with this one! Books may cost money to purchase, but this will test your resolve to grow. Erasmus, one of the early church fathers, said, "When I get a little money, I buy books; and if any is left, I buy food and clothes." That's commitment to reading!

A good friend of mine told me, "It's bad manners to have more clothes than books." If we don't have money for books, why do we spend so much on clothes? If the outside looks good, make sure there's something on the inside!

Remember, "He who doesn't read good books has no advantage over the person who cannot read them." If you're not willing to read, you might as well be illiterate.

Find ways to get books. Join a library or borrow books, but don't miss opportunities to read.

O -ORGANIZE YOUR LIFE TO HAVE TIME TO GROW

Growth will take time. But you say, "I'm already too busy!" Examine your schedule and you will find that much of your busy-ness is trivial pursuit. The people you are leading demand so much from you that you don't have time for personal growth. Soon your well will run dry and you will have nothing more to give them. You must make personal growth a priority. Maybe the best thing you can do for your people is to take some time to read a book, attend a seminar, or listen to a tape that will help you grow. You will get new insights and be refreshed to continue leading them. Stop saying, "When I get time." You already have all the time you will ever have!

Use a few minutes between meetings to read a chapter of a book. Listen to a tape as you are driving. Do whatever you need to do to organize your life to grow!

W-WORK AT WHAT YOU LEARN

Your goal is not to accumulate knowledge, but to use your learning to help others. The old saying is "Practice what you preach!" As you read and learn, write down one action that will change your life, and put it into practice.

Then teach others what you are learning. Share with your spouse or a friend. Develop a lesson to teach those who are under you. If you don't utilize what you are learning, your growth will just be intellectual. Our world already has enough intellectuals!

The choice to grow is yours. Make this choice today. It will forever change your life!

STEP TWO: START GROWING OTHER LEADERS

Once you start growing, you can focus on growing other leaders. As you see the difference that growth makes in your own life, think of that growth multiplied many times in helping others to grow. Harvey Firestone, the founder of Firestone Tire and Rubber Company, observed, "It's only as we develop others that we permanently succeed."

Many leaders who are insecure in their position try to protect it. They want to be the only one that can meet the needs of people. They fear sharing their power with others. This reveals a poor self-image, which must be dealt with by the Spirit of God!

In reality, one of the best ways to build a church or organization is to develop its people. As you begin to grow, seek followers to develop as leaders. These leaders will attract their own followers and you will have both leaders and followers!

As a leader, your job is to develop other leaders. Many pastors feel that their responsibility is to do all the work of ministry, whereas God has called them to *"prepare God's people for works of service"* (Ephesians 4:12). Your primary calling is to develop others to do the work of serving.

Only leaders will reproduce other leaders. This does not happen by accident but because you deliberately plan for it

It takes time to develop other leaders. The "Pareto principle" states that 20% of the people in your church will produce 80% of the results. A wise leader will identify these 20% and devote priority time to these key people. This investment of time into their lives will build them up and make them more effective leaders. Sometimes, however, these people are already active and have their own agendas, and don't come looking for assistance. In addition, pastors, because of their own insecurities and lack of training, spend much of their time with the other members who seem to have greater needs. How much of your time do you spend equipping others to do the work of the ministry? If you will begin to devote your time and energy towards personal growth and developing leaders, your church will become a vital, growing body.

CONCLUSION

In this chapter you have learned several foundational principles of leadership. .
- The simplicity of leadership....
    Leadership is influence, not position.
- The significance of leadership...
    Leaders are significant because they make things happen.
    Everything rises and falls on leadership.

15

- The seriousness of leadership....
    Start growing as a leader, and growing other leaders.

Having learned the basics of leadership, you are ready for action! Complete the action assignment before continuing with the rest of the book.

ACTION ASSIGNMENT

1. In this chapter you learned that "Leadership is Influence." Think of the group that you lead. Whom would you approach to start something in your group? (List two or three people and your reason for considering them.)

a.

b.

c.

Before this lesson, did you recognize that these people were leaders in your group?   How can you improve your relationship with them?

2. Reflect on the statement, "Everything rises and falls on leadership." Give an example from your own experience of how this statement is true.

What does this statement mean for the people you lead?

3. How many people are you now leading? How many would you like to lead? What will need to change if you are to lead more people?

4. You learned that leaders provide ideas, direction, and motivation. On a scale of 1-10 (with 10 being perfect and 1 being not at all) how well do you...

_____ initiate ideas?

_____ identify potential leaders?

_____ direct the people you lead?

_____ motivate your followers?

_____ set a godly example?

5. Look at the acrostic for the word "GROW." Choose one of the areas that was a challenge to you and explain how you were challenged.

6. What specific steps will you take as a result of this chapter?

When will you do it? (Put the date or indicate if you have already started.)

Chapter Two

THE LEADER'S POTENTIAL

Take a moment to dream. What is the most that you can see yourself accomplishing in life? What can God accomplish through you in a year? In the next 20 years? If you had 50 pages to write about your potential in all areas of life, how many pages could you fill?

Most of us have limited vision of what God has placed within us. We accomplish far less than we could, because we fail to see our true potential.

John Maxwell says that most people use only about 10% of their potential. Those who use as much as 25% are called geniuses.[3] Wow, what could happen if we lived up to our potential?

> Most people only use about 10 percent of their potential

Before learning how to reach our potential, we must understand what potential is. The dictionary describes

---

[3] John C. Maxwell, *Be All You Can Be* (Colorado Springs: Chariot Victor Publishing, 1987), p. 29.

potential as "existing in possibility...something that can be developed or become actual; capable of becoming actual."

Author and speaker Myles Munroe says potential is, "Dormant ability... reserved power... untapped strength ... unused success... hidden talents ... capped capability....all you can be but have not yet become...all you can do but have not yet done, how far you can reach but have not yet reached, what you can accomplish but have not yet accomplished. Potential is unexposed ability and latent power."[4]

Potential deals with our future. We all have tremendous potential in Christ, but most of us struggle to realize our true potential.

Our problems in relation to our potential are largely due to faulty vision. We don't see things clearly. This chapter will focus on four things that we need to see properly in order to fulfill our potential in Christ.

SEE GOD PROPERLY

Sometimes we don't discover and use our potential because our view of God is faulty. What do we need to recognize about God?

GOD IS THE SOURCE OF POTENTIAL

All potential already exists in God. Before God created anything, He possessed within Himself the potential for everything! In creation, He simply spoke into existence what was within Himself. He had the potential to create birds, and He did. He had the potential to create mountains, and He made them! The same is true for plants, animals, stars, and human beings.

Because God is the source of potential, He is a God of possibilities. Consider these verses:

---

[4] Myles Munroe, *Understanding Your Potential* (Shippensburg: Destiny Image Publishers, 1992), p. 1.

- *"For nothing is impossible with God."* Luke 1:37
- *"However, as it is written: "No eye has seen, no ear has heard, no mind has conceived what God has prepared for those who love him."* 1 Corinthians 2:9
- *"Now to him who is able to do immeasurably more than all we ask or imagine, according to his power that is at work within us,"* Ephesians 3:20

All potential comes from God. He is the source of everything.

GOD IS THE GIVER OF POTENTIAL

God is not only the source of potential but He also gives potential. He could have kept it all to Himself, but as a loving creator He chose to share it. He gives us three things that enable us to have potential.

God gives us life

I'm alive as I write these words. And as you read them, you also are alive! This life comes from God. John 1:4 says, *"In him was life..."* Our life is a reflection and extension of His life. Because He has potential within Himself and gave life to us, we also have potential.

All life has potential. Munroe points out that within every tree seed is a forest. Think about a corn seed. Look at it carefully. What do you see? "Just a seed," you might say. But look more closely. In that corn seed is the potential to produce other corn seeds. Given the right conditions, that seed can produce 800 seeds. If these 800 are planted again they can produce 640,000 seeds in the second season, 512,000,000 in the third season and by the fourth season one seed has the potential to produce 409 billion seeds. That's 60 for every person alive! That single seed has the potential to feed an entire nation, even the world!

If God has placed within one small seed the potential to feed the world, what has He placed within you? Surely your potential is far greater than the small seed which can easily be kicked aside and trampled! The seed cannot think or plan, it cannot dream or imagine, and it cannot act on its own but you can do all these things.

As long as you are alive, you have potential! And since you are spirit, not only a body, you will live forever. It will take forever for you to develop your full potential!

God gives us minds

God also gives us our minds, filled with potential. Our minds are fantastic instruments of God's creation. With our minds we think, dream, and create. We can envision things

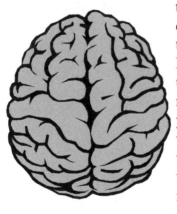

that have never been done. We can create mental pictures with the potential to become reality. Before anything happens through us, we must conceive it in our minds. Look at the room around you. Someone "saw" it before it was. The builder, the architect, the owner all visualized it before the first stone was laid! Their minds had the potential to conceive what is now visible.

Our minds are powerful, particularly if we are in Christ. 1 Corinthians 2:16 tells us, *"For who has known the mind of the Lord that he may instruct him? But we have the mind of Christ."* This reality releases tremendous creative power within us to fulfill His purpose.

The Bible makes it clear that we are what we think. Proverbs 23:7 says, *"For as he thinks in his heart, so is he..."* (NKJV) Our thoughts shape who we are!

No wonder there's such a spiritual battle going on for our minds. The enemy wants to control the mind because he understands its power. If he can make us think small, we will remain small. If he can convince us that we are poor, we will remain poor. If he can deceive us that we can never accomplish much, we won't!

According to Henry Ford, "Whether you think you can or think you can't — you are right." Read that again!

So, a significant step towards developing our potential is changing our thinking habits. The way we think will either make us or break us. The scripture informs us about our thoughts:

- *"All of us also lived among them at one time, gratifying the cravings of our sinful nature and following its desires and thoughts. Like the rest, we were by nature objects of wrath."* (Ephesians 2:3) In our old life we followed not only the actions, but also the thoughts of the world. Upon conversion, many people leave behind the old actions but keep thinking the same thoughts! Our thinking must change.
- *"Therefore, holy brothers, who share in the heavenly calling, fix your thoughts on Jesus, the apostle and high priest whom we confess."* (Hebrews 3:1) We are to focus our minds on Jesus, to think what He thinks.
- *"For the word of God is living and active. Sharper than any double-edged sword, it penetrates even to dividing soul and spirit, joints and marrow; it judges the thoughts and attitudes of the heart."* (Hebrews 4:12) Our thoughts are being judged by God's Word.
- *"Finally, brothers, whatever is true, whatever is noble, whatever is right, whatever is pure, whatever is lovely, whatever is admirable—if anything is excellent or*

23

praiseworthy—think about such things." (Philippians 4:8) We can choose to think on the right and positive things.

Since God gave us our minds and the power to control them, we must learn to think His thoughts. Memorizing and meditating on scripture is essential. Our minds are powerful but they are also slaves. Our subconscious mind will believe whatever it is programmed to believe whether true or false. You can use this to your advantage by speaking the truth to yourself continually until your mind believes it. Psychologists call this "self talk" which is simply speaking to yourself the things that you want your unconscious mind to begin to accept as truth.

"My Identity in Christ" (see *Appendix A*) is designed for this. It contains powerful statements of truth about your relationship to God and your potential in Him. Some statements may not sound true at first, but keep saying them until you believe them. Try saying it aloud morning and evening for 30 days and you will see a change in your thinking. Some call this "brainwashing" and in a sense it's true. Our brains need *washing* with the truth of God's Word! God has given us our minds; it is crucial that we use this wonderful gift to fulfill His plan.

God gives us ability

God not only gives us life and minds, but also the ability to do great things for Him. Consider the following verses.
- *"Now to him who is able to do immeasurably more than all we ask or imagine, according to his power that is at work within us"* Ephesians 3:20
- *"I can do everything through him who gives me strength."* Philippians 4:13
- *"It is God who arms me with strength and makes my way perfect. He makes my feet like the feet of a deer; he*

*enables me to stand on the heights. He trains my hands
for battle; my arms can bend a bow of bronze. You give
me your shield of victory; you stoop down to make me
great. You broaden the path beneath me, so that my
ankles do not turn over."* 2 Samuel 22:33-37

God is the giver of all our ability, a great resource. But
some of us don't believe we can do great things. We see God
as all-powerful, but forget that
we are created in His image! We
believe in His ability; but confess our inability! In thinking we
can do nothing, we deny God's
power to do great things. We
sing, "He is able" and then say,
"I can't!" It doesn't work that
way! If He is able, we are enabled through His strength.

GOD IS THE JUDGE OF POTENTIAL

God has invested great potential in us, and is keenly
interested in what we will do with it. Romans 14:12 reminds
every believer, *"So then, each of us will give an account of
himself to God."* He will judge us not only on the basis of
what we have done, but also could have done!

The Parable of the Talents in Matthew 25:14-30 teaches
us that God holds us accountable for all He has given to us.
We can either fulfill our potential or hide it. But God will
judge us.

What a tragedy when we do not reach our God-given
potential! Maxwell states, "One of the greatest sins we commit against God is not reaching the potential He has placed in
us."[5] What would it be like to get to heaven and God asks you
what you have done. He listens intently as you list your
accomplishments, teaching Sunday School class for 10 years,
leading 30 people to Jesus, and guiding 10 people to maturity

---

[5] Maxwell, *Be All You Can Be*, 37.

in Christ. Then He responds, "My child, those things are good. However, I gave you the potential to lead 300 people to Me, to write lessons for Sunday School and to bring 100 people to maturity in Me. If only you would have grown to the potential I gave you." What a moment! Sadly, too many believers die with unfulfilled potential. Munroe says that the richest place on earth is the graveyard, because of all the potential buried there. Books never written, songs never composed, achievements never reached are all buried under the ground.

This should motivate us to develop all the potential that God has placed in us. Jesus could say at the end of his life, *"I have brought you glory on earth by completing the work you gave me to do."* (John 17:4) Jesus, the perfect Son of God, set the example for us by fulfilling all of His potential. Although we cannot attain perfection, He enables us through the Holy Spirit to glorify God, the Father as we develop what He has put within us!

This is especially crucial for leaders. When we fail to develop our potential, it affects not only us, but those we influence!

Dear friend, if God were to call you today and ask, "How much of the potential I placed in you have you used?" what would you answer? 20%? 50%? 80%? None of us could say 100%, but let's strive towards that goal.

Recently I asked myself that question. My answer? 50%. Then I asked myself, "What do I need to change to reach my potential?" Four things came to mind: time management, physical health (diet and exercise), self-image, and willingness to take more risks. I am seeking to change these things. The things that hold you back may be different, but I challenge you to examine yourself and set new goals for your life.

SEE YOURSELF PROPERLY

What do you think about yourself? What kind of person are you? Are you important or insignificant? Are you someone who can accomplish great things for God? The way you see yourself affects greatly the way you will use your potential. You need to see yourself as God sees you, nothing more and nothing less. Otherwise God will not use you as He intended. When you view yourself according to the Word of God, you will begin to have a proper view of your potential. There are three "truth declarations" that will help you see yourself properly:

TRUTH DECLARATION ONE:
"I am uniquely created by God"

Psalm 139:14-16 reveals, *"I praise you because I am fearfully and wonderfully made; your works are wonderful, I know that full well. My frame was not hidden from you when I was made in the secret place. When I was woven together in the depths of the earth, your eyes saw my unformed body."* God's works are wonderful, and you are one of His works! Say aloud, "I am wonderful!" Say it again! This may sound strange, or even seem like a lie, but according to God's Word, it is true!

God formed you just as He wanted you to be. Yet, many people don't see themselves as wonderful creations of God. They consider their nose too short or too long; or lament that they come from the wrong nation or people. Many live in a world of "if only's" and "could have beens." "If only" my parents had educated me. "If only" I had more money. If I'd married someone else, I "could have been" successful.

You need to accept by faith what God has given you. He made you unique! There is no one like you, with your ability and your potential. God doesn't create trash! Therefore, you are "somebody" in the Kingdom! He created you uniquely and desires you to succeed!

TRUTH DECLARATION TWO:
"God has a plan for my life."

God not only created you as an individual with wonderful potential. But also He thought about what you could do; He planned your individual potential. Knowing that He has a plan for you should be a great motivation to develop your potential.

David said to God, *"All the days ordained for me were written in your book before one of them came to be."* (Psalm 139:16) Books are written about special people and God has written one about you! Imagine God's book in which are written all His plans for you. He has a page that indicates what He wants you to do today, and a page for tomorrow and each day of your life. What a special book! Although you cannot see it with your eyes, as you walk with Christ you can learn His plan for you. This chapter is a part of His plan to help you discover what He wants you to know.

Jeremiah speaks of God's good plan when he says, *"For I know the plans I have for you," declares the LORD, "plans to prosper you and not to harm you, plans to give you hope and a future."* (Jeremiah 29:11) Take a few moments to meditate on what this means for your life.

Paul reveals that God's plan for us is to *"put on the new self, created to be like God in true righteousness and holiness."* (Ephesians 4:24) God plans for us is to become like Him, to be daily transformed into the image of Christ! This is a lifelong plan of growth and character development.

These verses make it clear that God has a specific plan for you, a plan only you can fulfill. Since you are unique, His plan is specific for you. You have potential to do things that your brother doesn't have.

When this truth sinks deep into your spirit, you may feel convicted that you have not understood or followed God's plan for you in the past. The enemy may have messed with God's plan for your life to this moment, but I have good news for you: "Yesterday ended last night!" Today is the first day of the rest of your life! Take a minute (or a month!) to dream about what God has planned for you. He may have called you to lead many to Christ; or to discover a cure for AIDS; perhaps to write books, plant churches, or lead the nation. He

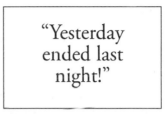

"Yesterday ended last night!"

may plan for you to teach, serve in a children's ministry, or be a powerful intercessor. God's plans for you are undoubtedly much greater than you could ever imagine.

Henry Ford, the automaker, observed, "There is no man living who isn't capable of doing more than he thinks he can do."[6]

Ford's boyhood friend and inventor Thomas Edison said, "If we all did the things we are capable of, we would literally astound ourselves."

Think of God's plan; use your imagination! What can God do with you? He has a plan, a great one, just for you. Trust Him and begin to realize your potential!

Meditate on these words by Myles Munroe, "What I see when I look at you is not all you are. It is only what you have become so far. Your potential is much greater than what you are right now. What you will become is much more than we could ever believe now. You are somebody because you came out of God, and He leaked some of Himself into you."[7]

> ## TRUTH DECLARATION THREE:
> ### "I can develop my God-given potential."

How exciting to realize that God has created you as an individual and has a wonderful plan for your life. This third declaration, however, makes potential become reality. You

[6] Henry Ford, quoted in The Success Journey, p. 14.

[7] Munroe, *Understanding Your Potential*, 23.

must grow in order to reach your potential. To accomplish this, you must first discover your potential and then develop it.

DISCOVER YOUR UNIQUE POTENTIAL

To discover your unique God-given potential, you must know yourself intimately. You might not want to look that deeply, but you will not otherwise know who you can become. If you think this will make you proud, consider Paul's words, *"For by the grace given me I say to every one of you: Do not think of yourself more highly than you ought, but rather think of yourself with sober judgment, in accordance with the measure of faith God has given you."* (Romans 12:3) Yes, you can easily think too highly of yourself, and that is pride. But Paul exhorts you to think of yourself "with sober judgment."

What should you know about yourself? As a Christian you should know four things about yourself.

1. Know Your Gifts

Your spiritual gifts are crucial to understanding your potential. God gives you His gifts in order to achieve His plan for your life. Peter says, *"Each one should use whatever gift he has received to serve others, faithfully administering God's grace in its various forms. If anyone speaks, he should do it as one speaking the very words of God. If any-*

one serves, he should do it with the strength God provides, so that in all things God may be praised through Jesus Christ. To him be the glory and the power forever and ever. Amen." (1 Peter 4:10-11)

Your spiritual gifts provide a key to unlock your potential. If you have the gift of teaching, you have the potential to become a great teacher!

You need to recognize your gifts and begin to develop them for God's glory.

If you don't know your spiritual gifts, I suggest that you read my book, "Use that Gift," or a similar book.

2. Know Your Personality

Tim LaHaye has written extensively about the topic of temperament or personalities. He defines temperament as "the combination of inborn traits that subconsciously affect man's behavior."[8] Temperament affects all you do without your awareness. It makes some people talkative and others quiet; some active and others analytical; some outgoing and others shy. Some who write on personality identify four major temperaments: Sanguine, Choleric, Melancholic, and Phlegmatic, with unlimited combinations of the four. The sanguine and choleric are considered outgoing, or extroverted personalities. The sanguine is the talkative, life-of-the-party kind of person who makes friends easily. The choleric is the natural leader who knows what he wants done and how to do it. He is the world changer! In contrast, the introverted or shy personalities are the melancholic and phlegmatic. The melancholic is very gifted, neat and organized. The phlegmatic is the most easy-going, quiet and peaceable. Each of the temperaments has its own strengths and weaknesses. We will examine personalities in more detail in chapter nine. Understanding them is a key to knowing yourself and understanding others.

3. Know Your Strengths

Know the areas in which you excel. Everyone has strengths of character, ability, and personality. Discover where you are strong. Be grateful for what you do well; it is God's gift to you! Honestly acknowledging and nurturing

---

[8] Tim LaHaye, *Why You Act the Way You Do* (Wheaton: Tyndale House Publishers, 1984), p. 23

your strengths is not necessarily pride, just as knowing your weaknesses is not necessarily humility. When you have identified your strengths, you will be able to focus on them and develop them.

4. Know Your Weaknesses

Even as you must know your personal strengths, you must also know your weaknesses. Each person has weaknesses which need to be faced and understood. Some of your "weaknesses" are sin, like anger and unforgiveness. These you need to confess and repent of. Other weaknesses may not be sin, but you need to recognize and seek to overcome them. Perhaps you are not a good administrator. This is a weakness, not a sin, but if it keeps you from reaching your full potential, you need to work to change. At the same time, many weaknesses are not worth spending much time and energy to correct. We can more profitably build on our strengths.

Knowing your spiritual gifts and your personality should provide insights on your strengths and weaknesses. Your spouse or good friend can also help you gain understanding, if you are willing to listen humbly. J. Oswald Sanders offers this advice: "The first step toward improvement is to recognize weaknesses, make corrections, and cultivate strengths."[9]

WORK AT DEVELOPMENT

When you recognize your potential and know yourself well, you can begin to work at development. This is where many miss the road. They get excited about potential and start to dream of doing great things for God and of changing the world. Unfortunately, they never wake up and get busy! Reaching your potential requires a lifetime of self-discipline and trust in God. Potential will always be unrealized until it is developed and implemented.

---

[9] J. Oswald Sanders, *Spiritual Leadership* (Chicago: Moody Press, 1994) p. 109.

Some "spiritual leaders" sit around and pray for God's blessing. They wait for "breakthroughs," for something supernatural to happen in their lives. They wander through life; wondering why their churches don't grow. why people don't follow them, why others are succeeding. They are unwilling to pay the price for greatness.

The key to releasing your potential can be expressed in one word: growth. Maxwell says, "You can reach your potential tomorrow if you dedicate yourself to growth today."[10] Keep growing, and your potential will be released. If you stop growing, your potential is limited.

Myles Munroe expresses this masterfully:

"Everyone has the capacity, potential and raw material to become a leader by the design of the creator." However, "most of us are mere products of our environment, lacking the will to change, to develop and maximize our potential and become who we really are.... Most people live their lives walking around in borrowed postures, spouting secondhand ideas, trying desperately to fit in rather than stand out."

"Our world today is suffering a leadership vacuum, but you can change it. You have within you the ability, capacity and power to become a change agent in this generation. Don't wait for someone else to take responsibility for the future. You do it now! Rise up from the seat of the follower, and enter the school of leadership, for it is God's will that you lead others to their full potential in Him. Settle for nothing less than your best."[11]

We may look at those who have done great things for God and say, "Wow! They made it to the top. God really blessed them." Yes, God has blessed them, but they succeeded because they were willing to develop their God-

---

[10] John C. Maxwell, *Failing Forward* (Nashville: Thomas Nelson, 2000) p. 93.

[11] Myles Munroe, *Becoming a Leader* (Bakersville: Pneuma Life, 1993) pgs. 35, 40, 170.

> "Either read or get out of the ministry!"
> -John Wesley

given potential. They didn't start out where you see them today. Great evangelists began witnessing to a handful of people; great speakers spoke first to 10 or 20 people who endured their faltering words. No one is born great; but everyone is born with the potential to serve God, some to achieve great things for Him. Motivational speaker Zig Ziglar quips, "Remember, grave diggers are about the only people who start on top - and they always end up in the hole."[12]

Evangelist and author Leonard Ravenhill tells the story of tourists in an old village in Europe. One of them asked an elderly villager, "Have any great men been born in this village?" The old man replied, "Nope, only babies."

If you want to develop, start making a plan for your personal growth. Reading this book is a good beginning, and any growth plan will surely involve strategic reading. It may also involve going back to school, listening to tapes, attending classes, setting goals, attending workshops, and the like. There is no excuse for you to remain where you are! You can accomplish much more for God! Get moving and develop your potential.

Accepting these three truth declarations will transform the way you see yourself. Review them often, repeat them aloud, and display them until they are part of you. Repeating "My Identity in Christ" in *Appendix A* will also help to see yourself as you are.

SEE SUCCESS PROPERLY

A third thing you need to see properly to develop your potential is *success*. Developing your potential means

---

[12] Zig Zigler, *See You at the Top* (Gretna: Pelican Publishing Company, 1982) p. 315

becoming a successful person. But success is a difficult concept to describe. What does it mean to be successful? How can you know if you are a success? Is it being able to buy a big house and having a shiny new vehicle? Is it the size of your salary?

Properly understanding success requires two crucial steps.

STEP ONE: UNDERSTAND WHAT SUCCESS IS

Many people have a distorted view of success, seeing it as a destination. In *The Success Journey*, John Maxwell argues that success is not a destination but a journey. When students graduate from the university we might call them a success when they receive the degree. But that is only the recognition of success. Real success meant staying up at night poring over the books struggling to learn what they needed to know to pass their exams. Real success involved the financial sacrifices enabling them to reach their goal. They were successful in the journey.

Maxwell defines success as "knowing your purpose in life, growing to reach your maximum potential, and sowing seeds that benefit others."[13] Let's examine this definition closely:

Knowing your purpose in life

You cannot be a success unless you accept God's call for your life. Why has He created you? What work has He gifted you to accomplish before you die? God has created you as a unique person with unique potential. Discover His plan for you, and you will know your purpose in life. This step may take a week, months, or years, but you will never become fully successful until you have understood why God created you. Then His plan will become your vision, and give you focus and direction in life, bringing true success.

---

[13] John C. Maxwell, *The Success Journey* (Nashville: Thomas Nelson, 1997) p. 11.

Growing to reach your maximum potential

Success requires growth. Maxwell says, "The only true measure of success is the ratio between what we might have been and what we have become. In other words, success comes as the result of growing with our potential."[14]

How can you grow as a leader? Follow these three steps.

Step One: Choose to grow

Growth doesn't happen just because you're breathing; it's a deliberate choice. It takes time and effort. Many people believe they are growing because they are alive. This is self-deceiving! Maxwell states, "You can be young only once, but you can be immature indefinitely. That's because growth is not automatic."[15] You can choose today to grow, or you can choose to stay where you are.

Step Two: Change to Grow

Growth always produces change. It is impossible to grow and remain the same! Many people don't grow because they're not willing to change. They won't consider new ideas and new ways of approaching life. They continue doing what they have always done. Their favorite song is "I shall not be moved." But while they sit, the rest of the world is moving. Times are different now than 10 years ago. The church desperately needs mature leaders who think creatively, are willing to change, and determine to replace things which are no longer effective. God's Word, our only rule of faith and practice, never changes, but appropriate methods and strategies for reaching the world constantly change. Leaders must be alert to what is obsolete, and develop new ways to fulfill God's purpose for their generation.

---

[14] Ibid., 14.

[15] Ibid., 100.

Maxwell shares these helpful insights:

"When the horse is dead, dismount."

"When you always do what you've always done, you'll always get what you've always got."

"Most people are funny; they want to get ahead and succeed, but they are reluctant to change. They are often willing to grow only enough to accommodate their problems; instead, they need to grow enough to achieve their potential."[16]

Take a moment to ask, "What have I changed recently?" Be specific. Name one action or attitude that has changed. Remember no change, no growth. Rick Renner writes, "If your church, ministry, or organization doesn't have to deal with the challenges of growth, it is a signal that something is drastically wrong."[17]

Step Three: Continue to grow!

When you choose to grow and are changing, you must continue to grow. Never stop growing. After growing for a time, you might become tired or discouraged. Having reached a new level, you might be tempted to settle back and enjoy your accomplishments. Beware! The greatest enemy of success is success. You relax and feel like you have arrived! You have passed the course! This is a dangerous moment, because when growth stops, decay begins. Author Eugene Habecker reminds us "The future truly belongs to the learning, not the learned."[18]

If you are still rejoicing in yesterday's successes, you're not successful! There is more for you to do today and tomorrow.

---

[16] John C. Maxwell and Jim Donavan, *Becoming a Person of Influence* (Nashville: Thomas Nelson Publishers, 1997) p. 26.

[17] Rick Renner, *Who is Ready for a Spiritual Promotion?* (Tulsa: Rick Renner Ministries, 2000) p. 143.

[18] Eugene Habecker, *Rediscovering the Soul of Leadership* (Colorado Springs: Victor Books, 1996) p. 27

When Spanish composer-cellist Pablo Casals was in his final years, a young reporter asked him, "Mr. Casals, you are ninety-five years old and the greatest cellist that ever lived. Why do you still practice six hours a day?" Casals' answer? "Because I think I'm making progress." What a man! 95 years old and still growing!

"The future truly belongs to the learning, not the learned"

The church is in a leadership crisis because we don't have enough disciples who are learning and growing. The difference between leaders and followers is not primarily in *gifting* but in *growing*. Those devoted to learning and growing become leaders simply because they rise above average. Suppose in your church two men, George and Sam, become believers on the same day. George, eager to learn, starts growing. He attends seminars, reads books, and asks questions. His life changes rapidly. Soon the pastor notices this growth and invites George to be an usher. A year later he is still growing. The pastor asks him to be a deacon, and after serving for two years, he is called to be an elder. Soon he is called to be the elder leading a newly planted church. As the leaders gather around George to pray, Sam thinks to himself, "Wow, George is really anointed. I wish I had the call of God in my life in that way!" Is it the call that is missing? No! Sam simply didn't grow and develop to be all that God wanted him to be. In contrast, George kept growing and became a leader.

Myles Munroe began his adult life as a school drop out. Determined to finish his education, he completed high school, went to college for a bachelor's degree, and finally earned a master's degree. He now writes and travels around the world speaking and challenging people to develop their potential. He became successful by choosing to grow, changing to grow, and continuing to grow. You can follow these same steps! Start now to become the person God intended you to be.

Sowing seeds that benefit others

An important way to cultivate success is to sow seeds that benefit others. Here the Christian's definition of success differs from the world's. The world defines success primarily by one's performance, even if he never helped another person succeed. But a follower of Christ cannot be successful without becoming a blessing to others.

Jesus said, *"For even the Son of Man did not come to be served, but to serve, and to give his life as a ransom for many."* (Mark 10:45) *"Whoever wants to become great among you must be your servant..."* (Matthew 20:26)

Jesus led His disciples into the arena of action, preparing them to serve others and change the world for the glory of God. Maxwell shares this thought, "The Christian has to say that to be a success, I must contribute to the welfare of others. To put it another way, to be all I can be, I need to help you be all you can be."[19]

This view of success really challenges your motives. Why do you want to grow and develop? Is it just to benefit yourself, or to serve others? Is your primary desire to get or to give?

Take a moment to reflect on your life. By this Christian definition, how successful are you? Are you doing all you can to benefit others? How much more could you benefit others if you would reach your full potential?

STEP TWO: DEVELOP CHARACTERISTICS OF SUCCESSFUL PEOPLE

What makes some people succeed while others fail? Studies on this question identify several common characteristics of successful people. This list, while by no means comprehensive, will provide useful insights.

---

[19] Maxwell, *Be All You Can Be*, 26.

1. SUCCESSFUL PEOPLE HAVE A POSITIVE ATTITUDE

A primary characteristic of those who succeed is a good attitude. They view life as positive. They smile in the face of adversity and keep going. Zig Ziglar well stated: "It's your attitude and not your aptitude that determines your altitude."[20] People with negative attitudes don't go far in life.

W. W. Ziege said, "Nothing can stop the man with the right mental attitude from achieving his goal; nothing on earth can help the man with the wrong mental attitude." Our attitude is a powerful factor in our lives and we have the power to change it.

How is your attitude? Is the glass half full or half empty? Do you see the potholes or the asphalt? Do you notice the roses or the thorns? Your attitude is part of you! You can change it!

2. SUCCESSFUL PEOPLE HAVE CLEAR GOALS

People who succeed don't arrive at their destination by accident. They have determined to set goals and achieve them. They plan each day, week and month to make good use of their time. Do you have written goals in life? Do you plan your schedule or wait for life to happen? Where do you want to be next year? Five years from now? Maxwell asserts that while less than 5% of people write their goals, 95% of those who write them, reach them![21] What a powerful incentive to write your goals!

The Greeks have a proverb, "Before you can score you must first have a goal." Many people are running around the field of life with no idea of where they are heading. Successful people have learned to set and achieve their goals.

---

[20] Zigler, See You at the Top, 92.

[21] Maxwell, Be All You Can Be, 28.

3. SUCCESSFUL PEOPLE WORK HARD

Success requires people willing to work hard to reach their objectives. They are not afraid of effort. Too many people wait for the "big break" when success will fall in their lap. They pray for miracles but don't go after them.

The scripture describes Hezekiah's key to success, *"In everything that he undertook in the service of God's temple and in obedience to the law and the commands, he <u>sought</u> <u>his God</u> and <u>worked</u> wholeheartedly. And so he prospered."* (2 Chronicles 31:21) Hezekiah balanced his seeking of God with hard work. He succeeded.

Radio commentator Paul Harvey said, "You can always tell when you are on the road to success; it's uphill all the way." People who coast through life are always going downhill!

4. SUCCESSFUL PEOPLE PERSEVERE

People who succeed don't quit. They believe the old saying, "if at first you don't succeed, try, try again." They stick to their goals. They don't take "no" for an answer. People who don't succeed find excuses about why they fail. They take difficulty as a sign that God has called them elsewhere!

Thomas Edison, the inventor, is a great example of perseverance. He tried over 10,000 experiments before he got the light bulb to work. If he had

> The only person who can stop you from becoming the person God created you to be is you.

stopped at 9,999 we might still be lighting candles! Edison said, "Many of life's failures are people who did not realize how close they were to success when they gave up."

Conrad Hilton, a successful hotel executive, echoes this thought: "Success seems to be connected with action.

Successful people keep moving. They make mistakes, but they don't quit."

Have you given up on something lately? Try, try it again! Put the saying on your wall, "Winners never quit and quitters never win."

5. SUCCESSFUL PEOPLE TAKE RESPONSIBILITY

Successful people refuse to blame others for their actions. They take responsibility, and are willingly accountable.

They are not like the young man in a job interview. The prospective boss inquired, "Are you responsible?" The young man replied, "Yes, I'm very responsible. At my last job when anything bad happened, my boss said that I was responsible!" Successful people readily accept responsibility. Agricultural scientist George Washington Carver noted, "Ninety-nine percent of failures come from people who have the habit of making excuses."

Successful people control their own worlds. This does not leave God out of the picture, but acknowledges the tremendous freedom and responsibility God has given. You are the only one who will determine whether or not you will develop to become the person God created you to be.

Do you take responsibility for your life? Have you made a mistake for which you blamed someone else?

SEE FAILURE PROPERLY

Finally, if you are to develop to your full potential, you must know how to understand and face failure. Every successful leader has experienced failure. Overcoming failure is important to achieving true success.

Fear of failure is a great impediment to developing our full potential. We hesitate to attempt great things for God, fearing we will fail. What if we aim to win 1000 souls for Christ, and only win 500? Is that failure? Many times we don't try new things because the last time we failed. No one has taught us how to "fail successfully." Maxwell's book *Failing Forward* has helped me greatly in seeing failure properly. He says, "The difference between average people and achieving people is their perception of and response to failure."[22]

Management expert Ken Blanchard observes, "Success is not forever and failure isn't fatal."[23] We must not let failures hinder the potential God has placed within us. Let's learn together how to see failure properly. Since everyone fails, let's look at each letter of the word FAILS.

FIND A NEW DEFINITION OF FAILURE

What is failure? How do you view yourself when you fail? Do you see a failure as a mistake made by an intelligent person or as an indication of a failed person? Tim Elmore reminds us, "Failure is an event, not an identity."[24]

Failure is an **event**. It is something that happens, not who you are. There's a huge difference between saying, "I failed" and "I'm a failure." A failure does not make *me* a failure.

Failure is a part of **life**! I fail, you fail, and everyone fails. The Bible says, *"All have sinned and fall short of the glory of God."* (Romans 3:23) We preach it to sinners, but somehow don't admit that we are human and humans make mistakes. You have failed, you are failing, and you will fail in the future! But you are not a failure! Don't let fear of failure keep you from doing all that God wants you to do. Learn how to cope with it and move on.

The devil uses your failures to make you feel like a failure. He is notorious for keeping records of mistakes and

---

[22] Maxwell, *Failing Forward*, 2.

[23] Ken Blanchard, *The Heart of a Leader* (Washington: Eagle Publishing, 2002) p. 18.

[24] Tim Elmore, *Mentoring: How to Invest Your Life in Others* (Kingdom Publishing House, 1995) p. 148.

uses them quite effectively. The next time he reminds you of how you have failed, remind him of his greatest failure, thinking that he could keep Jesus Christ in the grave!

ACCEPT RESPONSIBILITY FOR YOUR FAILURES

To see failure properly, learn to accept responsibility for your failures. When you fail, don't look for someone to blame.

Blame is as old as the first failure! Adam and Eve invented blame and passed it on to us! Remember what happened after they sinned? When God asked them what happened Adam said, "It was the woman." Eve said, "It was the snake." Only the snake had no one to blame! No one would take responsibility for their sin.

We must stop the blame game. There are two common targets of blame that need to go.

Stop blaming others

Blaming others is so common. Most of the excuses above are pointed at others. Parents blame children; spouses blame each other; the government blames the donor countries, and the cycle goes on and on.

Pastors often moan, "The members aren't praying, the giving is low, the area is difficult, my people are poor, I have one bad member who influences all the others." You are the pastor; take responsibility and stop blaming! Take responsibility for your church, for its financial status, and for its spiritual vitality. Leadership demands responsibility.

Maxwell says that if you have been a pastor for three years or more, every problem in the church is your problem. It's not the bishop or overseer, it's not the people, it's you!

When you blame others, you remove yourself from responsibility. Unwittingly, you also remove yourself from the authority of leadership because authority and responsibility are two sides of the same coin. You cannot have authority without responsibility.

Stop blaming your past

Blaming the past is a common way of dealing with our failures.

"I didn't have a good education."

"My parents were poor."

"I was mistreated as a child."

"Someone gossiped about me."

"The pastor did…"

Okay, it happened. Get over it! The past is past, so move on with life. Many people in mid-life are still moaning about their past. It will do no good to keep blaming things in the past that you cannot change. In fact it is self-defeating.

Remember the good news, "Yesterday ended last night!" It's finished. Your past can't defeat you. Your future is here. Your potential is waiting. Stop looking backwards.

The great Apostle Paul had much to put behind him as he determined to fulfill his high calling in Christ. He gave this testimony in Philippians 3:13 *"Brothers, I do not consider myself yet to have taken hold of it. But one thing I do: Forgetting what is behind and straining towards what is ahead, I press on toward the goal to win the prize for which God has called me heavenward in Christ Jesus."*

What did Paul need to forget? He had really failed God in the past, to the point of murdering Christians. But Paul looked forward instead of backward, and accomplished great things for God.

Many great leaders have had to deal with terrible pasts. Joseph was jailed and cruelly mistreated for years but came out as one of the strongest leaders in the Bible. He overcame idol worship, prostitution, lying, favoritism, and murder to become Pharaoh's governor in Egypt. Moses was a murderer who became Israel's great leader. David, a common shepherd boy, became the great king of Israel and a man after God's own heart. Peter, an unschooled fisherman before he met Christ, became a great leader in the early church.

Einstein, expelled from school for being stupid, went on to become a brilliant thinker! John Newton was a vulgar sea captain in the slave trade. After his remarkable conversion he wrote "Amazing Grace, how sweet the sound that saved a wretch like me..." Nelson Mandela was jailed for years, but came out without blame and led his nation.

INVESTIGATE YOUR FAILURES

While it is necessary to be freed from our failures, it is useful to investigate them so that we can learn from them. An honest look at our mistakes should make us wiser!

Dr. Ronald Niednagel quipped, "Failure isn't failure unless you don't learn from it."

H. Stanley Judd said, "Don't waste energy trying to cover up failure. Learn from your failures and go on to the next challenge. It's okay to fail. If you're not failing, you're not growing."

American playwright William Saroyan spoke to this issue when he said, "Good people are good because they've come to wisdom through failure. We get very little wisdom from success, you know."

Successful leaders continually ask "What can we learn from this?" There are several things we should learn as we investigate our failures.

1. Learn what went wrong

Identify the cause of the failure. If the crusade failed, was it publicity, lack of prayers, or lack of planning? If you lost money on a deal, what happened? Until you identify what went wrong you cannot fix it. Too many people keep repeating mistakes because they never look at what went wrong.

John Foster Dulles, a former American Secretary of State noted, "The measure of success is not whether you have a tough problem to deal with, but whether it is the same problem you had last year."

Learn what went wrong so that you don't repeat your mistakes.

2. Learn what needs to change

Learning what went wrong puts you on the road to success. Next you need to learn what to change.

View your errors the way Thomas Edison did. He said, "Failure is the opportunity to begin again more intelligently." He knew what he was talking about. He failed in thousands of experiments before he invented the light bulb. His workers would tell him, "We've tried 10,000 things and they failed." His reply, "No, we haven't failed; we have learned 10,000 things that don't work!" Failure is a chance to start again and change what you are doing, not repeating the same mistake. Find what went wrong and change!

If you realize that you're failing as a husband (or wife), figure out what has gone wrong and make appropriate changes. Begin by apologizing (accepting responsibility) and changing your behavior. If the crusade failed, decide what you will do differently. If you chose a leader who turned out to be ineffective, decide what you should change the next time you choose a leader.

LEAVE YOUR FAILURES

After learning from your failures, you need to leave them behind and move forward. Don't let past failures keep you from future successes.

Austin O'Malley, an Irish

> "It's not whether you get knocked down; it's whether you get back up that counts."
> -Coach Vince Lombardi

sportsman, asserted, "The fact that you have been knocked down is interesting, but the length of time you remain down is important." Don't waste time wallowing in pity and shame. Get up and move on!

Author and speaker Ed Cole noted, "If you get up the same number of times you fall, you will be standing." Think about that for a moment! The real losers in life are those who fall and stay there. The winners get back up and keep going.

Can you let go of the failures of your past and move on? Tell yourself, "Yes, I did it and I have learned from my mistake. But it's finished and I'm moving forward."

Let your failures challenge you to greater things. Don't admit defeat. Try again. Find another way. Winners never quit and quitters never win. Move past your failures.

STEP OUT FOR MORE FAILURES!

The last step in dealing with failures is radical: step out for more failures. What a step! Make more failures? Yes, if you can get over your fear of failure and grow from your past mistakes, you should be ready to take more risks. The more risks you take, the more mistakes you will make, the more you will learn, and the more successful you will become. You need to make more mistakes by taking more risks!

Myles Munroe says, "The poorest of men are men without a dream. Don't be so afraid of failure that you refuse to try. Demand something of yourself. Failure is only an incident. There's more than the failure - there's success deep behind that failure. Failure is the opportunity to more intelligently begin again. When you fail, that is a great chance to start again. Learn from it and move on. Don't be paralyzed by the failure."[25]

The wife of Archbishop Mowll said, "The frontiers of the Kingdom of God were never advanced by men and women of caution." J. Oswald Sanders agrees when he says, "The great-

---

[25] Myles Munroe, *Understanding Your Potential*, 93.

est achievements in the history of missions have come from leaders close to God who took courageous, calculated risks. More failure comes from an excess of caution than from bold experiments with new ideas."[26] That's a challenge to me. I'm too cautious. I don't naturally take risks. I like to stay in my comfort zone. But I'll never develop my potential in my comfort zone. Maxwell challenges me to another level when he says, "If at first you do succeed; try something harder!"[27]

Former US Attorney General Robert Kennedy stated, "Only those who dare to fail greatly can ever achieve greatly." Dare to fail! Take some steps of faith this year, stretch to develop your potential! Do some things you've never done before. Don't be satisfied with the status quo. Stretch! Risk! Go for it!

Taking risks will produce some failure. Maxwell observes, "You see, the more you try, the greater amount of failure you are likely to experience-and the greater amount of success. I don't know about you, but I'd rather reach 90 percent of my potential with plenty of mistakes than reach only 10 percent with a perfect score."[28]

My goal in life is not "never failing." I am not seeking perfection, but production. If I am not failing enough, it's probably because I'm not attempting enough.

Too many of us are striving for the perfect score, cautiously hugging the shore of perfection when we need to launch out into the deep. Ships are not made for the shore, but to conquer the vast expanses of water. Likewise, we are not created for security. Set your face in the wind. Look towards the horizon. See the things that God wants to do with you. Step out of your comfort zone and find what God

---

[26] Sanders, *Spiritual Leadership*, 127.

[27] Maxwell, *Failing Forward*, 126.

[28] Ibid., 136

has prepared for you. I challenge you to fail while attempting great things for God!

Let's review our word "FAILS"

F ind a new definition of failure
A ccept responsibility for your failures
I nvestigate your failures
L eave your failures
S tep out for more failures!

CONCLUSION

Let's put the whole chapter together. If you are going to

Your potential formula: The way you see God + the way you see yourself + the way you see success + the way you see failure = your potential.

---

reach your potential you need properly to see God, yourself, success and failure. In other words, your potential formula looks like this:

Wrong vision in any area hinders your potential.

Take some time to complete the action assignment before reading the next chapter. It will take you several steps towards your potential! Make a copy of "My Identity in Christ" in *Appendix A* and begin saying it twice a day. May God bless you as you discover and develop your potential!

ACTION ASSIGNMENT

Evaluate the way you see each of the four areas of potential by answering the following questions. Answer the questions based on what you believed and did before this lesson.

1. How I see God
   a. God has given you your mind. Read and think about Philippians 4:8. What percentage of your thoughts obey this verse? What will you do to change?

   b. God is the judge of potential. If you were to appear before Him right now, what do you think He would say to you about how you used your potential?

   c. What percentage of your potential are you currently using?

   d. What keeps you from reaching your potential?

   e. What do you need to change in your life to increase that percentage? (Be specific)

2. How I see myself
   a. Write one paragraph on how you have seen yourself before this lesson. Answer the question, "What kind of person am I?"

b. To the best of your understanding, write your:

Spiritual Gifts

Personality (If you don't know the temperaments, what kind of person are you? Talkative? Outgoing? Shy? Bold?)

Strengths

Weaknesses

3. How I see Success
  a. What is your purpose in life? In other words, why has God created you?

  b. What are you currently doing to grow?

  c. What changes have you made recently in your life?

  d. What are you doing to benefit others?

Rate your success characteristics in the following chart. Place a mark for each characteristic from 1-7 with 1 being very poor and 7 being excellent, no improvement needed.

Characteristic	1	2	3	4	5	6	7
Positive Attitude							
Goals (know where you are going)							
Hard Work							
Perseverance							
Take responsibility							

4. How I see Failure

a. When you fail, do you typically see yourself as a failure or do you accept that you have failed? "I typically see myself as...

b. List 5 major mistakes you have made in your life. Mistake (describe briefly)

    1.

    2.

    3.

    4.

    5.

c. For which of the above mistakes have you taken responsibility? For which have you blamed others?

d. Think about blame. Who/what have you been blaming for your failures?

e. Choose one of the five mistakes above. Put the number of the one you have chosen. ___ Now answer the following questions about it.

1. What was your responsibility in the mistake?

2. What wrong action/thinking/behavior caused the mistake?

3. What did you learn from the mistake?

4. What changes have you made (do you need to make) in your life to avoid the same mistake again?

f. What area of risk is God calling you to take?

g. What fears keep you from taking that risk? (List all of them!)

h. Pray and ask God to deal with those fears and plan how you will take the risk. Mark here when you have done it.
_____

Write on another paper the potential that you believe God has given you. Include one paragraph for your personal growth and development, one for your job/career and one for your potential in ministry. (If your career is ministry, write only two but write plenty!)

Use the paper in *Appendix A*, "My Identity" for the next 30 days. Every morning and evening, stand before a mirror and read it aloud to yourself. Mark the boxes when you have done this and record here the number of days that you did it. _____

What was the result?

Chapter Three
THE LEADER AND VISION

Pause and think for a moment about a leader you greatly admire and are excited to follow. What about him or her is so attractive to you? (Don't keep reading until you have an answer!) You could likely give many reasons for following that person. Certainly one reason is that he knows where he is going in life. He has *vision*.

> Only 3-5% of pastors have a compelling vision.

You are called by God to develop your potential as a leader, so that others will want to follow you. For people to follow your leadership, you must know where you are going! Leaders are able to stand and say, "Let's move in this direction." What enables a leader to do this effectively? It's a quality called *vision,* without which you cannot lead. Maxwell calls vision the "indispensable quality of leadership."[29] Not everyone with vision is a leader; but every leader must have vision. Yet, many church

---

[29] Maxwell, *Developing the Leader Within You*, 139.

56

leaders can't clearly state their vision. Bruce Wilkinson says that around the world only 3-5% of pastors have a compelling vision. If this is true among the leaders, how many followers have a clear vision for their lives!

What is vision? What is its role in the life of a leader? Myles Munroe defines vision as "a glimpse of the end, a view of your purpose in life."[30] Wilkinson adds, "Vision is an internal picture, not of what exists, but what will be in the future." Notice the words used in these definitions: "glimpse, view, and picture." Vision involves our ability to look into the future to see what God wants to do in and through us. With our physical eyes we see things around us which we call our "vision." For a leader, vision is the ability to "see" ahead and recognize what the destination looks like.

All leaders should have a sense of what God is doing in and through them and a mental picture of their future. We can call this *personal* vision. Leaders must also have vision of what God wants to do through their group. This is a *corporate* vision.

Vision is what creates a fire within the leader. It is the fuel that enables him to relentlessly pursue his goals. Maxwell describes vision as "a picture of the future that creates passion within you today." This passion attracts others to follow when the vision is effectively communicated.

Sometimes we use the word "dream" to talk about vision. When Martin Luther King Jr. said, "I have a dream...." he was describing his vision for the future, not something he had seen in his sleep. He was a leader with vision.

Vision and goals are closely related, yet distinct. Vision is the end result, and goals are the steps to fulfill the vision.

Let's look more closely at what vision does for a leader. Vision provides three important ingredients: focus, force, and fortitude.

---

[30] Munroe, *Becoming a Leader*, 137.

VISION PROVIDES FOCUS

Vision enables us to keep our eyes focused on our purpose. It keeps us from being distracted by things that may  be good, but are not the best for us.

Two boys were trying to walk down a railroad track, carefully looking down at their feet. Each time they tried, they lost their balance and fell off. Finally they discovered that if they looked straight ahead, they could walk easily without falling off. Vision gives that focus, enabling us to walk confidently in the right direction without losing our way.

Proverbs 29:18 says, *"Where there is no vision, the people perish."* (KJV) The word *perish* actually means to live carelessly or to cast off restraint. Where there is no clear vision, people live aimlessly without a certain sense of direction and purpose. Without focus, precious resources like time, money, and spiritual gifts will be handled in a casual manner. Without vision your church is only a group of people *meeting* together but not *moving* together.

Vision focuses life to reach its fullest potential. A clear vision is like a magnifying glass. It takes the rays of the sun and focuses them on a blade of grass until wisps of smoke form and flames consume the grass. The energy of the sun has more power when it is focused, and vision focuses our lives to generate more power.

Vision energizes a leader and provides a powerful force

VISION PROVIDES FORCE

of energy. The leader receives strength from seeing where he is going, giving him power for the tasks necessary to fulfill the vision. An effective leader keeps his vision in his mind night and day. He dreams about it at night and during the day. He talks about it and acts upon it. The vision keeps him from getting tired. Good leaders are energetic. They are excited about the vision God has given them, and they work hard to see it happen.

The force created by the vision not only energizes the leader, but also gives strength to followers. They see the vision and the energy of the leader, and are encouraged to get involved in making the vision become a reality.

VISION PROVIDES FORTITUDE

Vision not only gives energy for the task, but fortitude and endurance, the ability to keep on going even when the going is tough. When obstacles face a person without vision, they lie down and go to sleep! But a leader with vision is not easily stopped. Even when things become difficult, vision keeps him going! He finds a way around the obstacles and keeps going until he accomplishes his dream. Vision provides "staying power." Leaders never quit, and their vision provides this quality of endurance.

It is no surprise then that vision is the "indispensable quality of leadership!" If you will make a difference as a leader, you must have vision and be able to get others to follow.

Nehemiah is a great example of a visionary leader, best known for his success in rebuilding the walls of Jerusalem around 445 B.C. The book by his name records the account of his clear vision for the work God had called him to do, and how he carried it out in spite of many obstacles. Nehemiah, living in a troubled time in Israel's history, was one of the Jewish captives in the Persian Empire. He had never lived in his ancestral home, but God planned for him to lead the building of the walls of Jerusalem.

Nehemiah received the report of the condition of Jerusalem. The wall that was to protect the city was broken down, and the people were living in disgrace. The news deeply affected Nehemiah, and he spent time fasting and praying about his ancestral home. Eventually he was convinced that he needed to take action, and he approached the Persian king with his plan.

A close look at Nehemiah's story reveals seven important "vision principles" that can make any leader effective for God.

VISION PRINCIPLE ONE:
VISIONS ARE BIRTHED IN PRAYER

"When I heard these things, I sat down and wept. For some days I mourned and fasted and prayed before the God of heaven." (Nehemiah 1:4)

Nehemiah's vision was birthed in prayer. He wept, fasted and prayed about the condition of his city. He was not happy with what he saw. His heart crushed by the need of his people, he cried out for God to do something about Jerusalem. Burdened to see change take place, his vision began to grow and he realized God was calling him to be personally involved in building the wall.

As Christian leaders we also need to get a burden for God's work. What is His vision for your life? For your church? For the ladies of the church? For the youth? For the lost?

In God's presence begin to pray about needs around you. Every genuine vision should result from a need that God calls us to meet. Visions are to meet needs, not of the leader, but of God's people. If a leader wants to build a large church or a program to meet his personal need for recognition, this is not a legitimate vision; God-given visions always focus on others.

Not every need that you recognize will become a burden for you and not every burden will grow into a vision. But some will grow in your spirit until you are convinced that God is calling you. You might see a needy child and think,

"Oh, someone should help that child," but within an hour you have forgotten about it. However, if it is a God-given vision, the burden will grow; the picture of that child will grow stronger until you are moved to act.

Every genuine vision for a Christian leader comes from God and is birthed in prayer. No one else can give you a vision; you can't find them at a Bible School or Seminary. In prayer you see your full potential and begin to understand what God is calling you to do. Prayer prepares your heart to feel the heart of God for a situation. Prayer enables you to surrender your own will to the plan of God and accept the personal cost to carry out the vision. Begin praying and asking God to give you the vision He has for your life. Don't stop praying until the vision is clear in your mind.

Your vision from God may come clearly with supernatural signs or in a dream. But often it comes slowly as you seek God and it becomes clearer that He has called you to do a certain work. In the process the vision should sink deep into your heart. Wilkinson states, "Vision is from the heart. It is only in the head you have an idea."

Paul Cho, pastor of the largest church in the world, was asked the secret of his success. He replied simply, "Pray…and obey." He had to hear God's direction, and then walk in obedience.

VISION PRINCIPLE TWO: VISIONS ARE PERSONAL

"If it pleases the king and if your servant has found favor in his sight, let him send me to the city in Judah where my fathers are buried so that I can rebuild it." (Nehemiah 2:5, underlining mine)

> God has a personal vision for you.

God had a personal plan for Nehemiah. He knew exactly what God wanted him to do and told the king that he wanted to go and rebuild the wall. This was not a vision for Ezra or anyone else. It was his personal vision.

God has a personal vision for you. You will not be called to accomplish the vision that God has given me, nor will I be responsible for your vision. Don't rely on following other peoples' visions. Get your own! God created you as an individual and his plan for you is unique. Your vision and someone else's might be similar, but make sure you have God's vision for your life. If you are a pastor, God wants you to do some things He calls every pastor to do. Still, His vision for you is unique, and your church will make a unique contribution to the Kingdom of God.

Does this mean that you can't support someone else's vision? Not at all! Many people will be called to support another leader's vision. Church members should embrace the vision of their leaders and help carry it out. However, you should be convinced that God's vision is for you to be right where you are, doing just what you are doing! You should make a conscious decision to embrace that vision and make it your own, not simply following because you have nothing else to do.

You may be called to work under someone else's vision for a time, as God prepares you to pursue your unique call. Don't see this as wasted time; God knows what He is doing.

Have you discovered what God's unique vision is for your life? He has a personal plan for you.

VISION PRINCIPLE THREE: VISIONS ARE SPECIFIC

"If it pleases the king and if your servant has found favor in his sight, let him send me to the city in Judah where my fathers are buried so that I can rebuild it." (Nehemiah 2:5)

Nehemiah knew that God had called him to a specific task—to build the wall at Jerusalem. He didn't say, "I'll go and help the people with their problems." He knew that his specific calling was to build the wall.

A leader must have a specific vision. A general calling such as "Glorify God" or "Seek first the Kingdom" won't produce much action. These are important desires, but not specific and measurable visions.

Paul was a great leader with a specific vision— to preach the gospel to the Gentiles. His vision was specifically focused on one group of people. He followed the vision and kept his mind fixed on where he was going. (See Acts 9:15; 26:19 and Philippians 3:14)

Seek a vision for your life that is specific. You may say that God has called you to be a pastor and your vision is to build a strong church. What does that mean? How will you know that you have accomplished the vision? What type of church is God calling you to build? What group of people is He calling you to reach? Be specific.

As a pastor I had a specific vision for the church I was building. God had called me to build a church that was growing numerically, but even more, where all members were involved and using their gifts. I wanted to see a giving church that was developing leaders continually. My vision called for a dynamic worship service, a strong choir, and active youth given good opportunity to develop their gifts to do something significant for God. I envisioned new believers being discipled and growing in their faith. My role as pastor was to be an "equipper" as presented in Ephesians 4:12, *"to equip God's people for works of service."*

My vision kept me going from early to late, meeting people, encouraging leaders, planning seminars, setting goals, preparing for church council meetings, and many other essential tasks.

Now as the coordinator of a ministry, I have different visions but still specific directions that I believe God wants to take us. Writing down the vision will help you to make it specific. Habakkuk 2:2 challenges us, *"Write the vision"* (KJV).

What is <u>your</u> specific vision?

VISION PRINCIPLE FOUR: VISIONS ARE LARGE

"I also said to him, 'If it pleases the king, may I have letters to the governors of Trans-Euphrates, so that they will provide me safe-conduct until I arrive in Judah? And may I have a letter to Asaph, keeper of the king's forest, so he will give me timber to make beams for the gates of the citadel by the temple and for the city wall and for the residence I will occupy?' ....So I went to the governors of Trans-Euphrates and gave them the king's letters. The king had also sent army officers and cavalry with me." (Nehemiah 2:7-9)

Nehemiah had a big vision. It would require massive resources, many people to do the work, and God's favor in order to be completed. Anyone who has constructed a wall around a small lot realizes that building a wall around a city is no small task!

Visions should be too big to do apart from God's help! If your vision can easily be accomplished, it is too small! It might only be a short-term goal, or it might be a dream that did not come from God that can be accomplished without him.

Andy Stanley, pastor of North Point Community Church says, "The task always appears out of reach. And the reason it appears that way is because it is. God-ordained visions are always too big for us to handle. We shouldn't be surprised. Consider the source."

Many church leaders have what I call "survival vision." Their main goal is to survive. Month by month, year by year, as long as they survive, they are contented. At the end of the year they say, "Thank God, we didn't lose any members this year; we have kept the faith!" That's not vision, that's surviving! Are you dreaming of surviving, or of changing your world for Jesus? Don't be a survivor, be an overcomer! For God's sake, make an impact on the world!

Jabez was a visionary. He prayed, *"Enlarge my territory."* He was not content to remain where he was; he longed to do more for God, and to expand his influence. (See 1 Chronicles 4:10)

I believe that our vision often is too shallow. We have a vision for preaching the word and seeing a few people saved. Many churches are doing this effectively. But I challenge you to get a vision that is bigger than the ordinary, something that only God can enable you to accomplish.

As soon as you start getting a big vision, you'll be reminded that there's no money! Don't give up the vision because you can't see any way the resources will be provided. If God is in it, He will provide the resources.

Ralph Mahoney says this about money and vision.... "The financial problem most church leaders and other leaders face arises because they don't know where they are going."[31] The biggest problem is not lack of money but lack of vision.

Money flows towards vision. Most people are not willing to give freely until they see the vision, accept the vision, and begin to work towards the vision. In many churches with limited vision the offering appeal is made, "Let's support the work of the Lord" or "Don't fail to give God His portion." Members give something, but they also leave the church with money in their pockets. In the afternoon they attend a large evangelistic meeting where the speaker says, "I want to reach the continent for Jesus! We plan to purchase a huge sound system that will result in the salvation of thousands of people who are now perishing in sin. If each of you will give 10 dollars; this will become a reality." What happens? They give the 10 dollars that they kept in their pockets at church! Why? They got excited about a vision!

Wilkinson points out that money is not a validator of the vision, but a test. In other words, don't look at available resources to determine God's will. Find God's will and then look for the money! "Provision" contains "vision."

---

[31] Ralph Mahoney, *The Shepherd's Staff* (Burbank: World MAP, 2002) p. 180.

This doesn't mean that it will be easy to get the money for the vision, but without a vision finances will always be a struggle.

Another resource that flows towards a vision is people. You may have a big vision and then realize that you don't have the people to make it happen. But big visions attract big people! Maxwell says, "Successful people stretch to the vision; unsuccessful people shrink from the vision."

How big is your vision? Is it big enough that it will take God to make it happen? Does it far exceed your current resources?

VISION PRINCIPLE FIVE:
VISIONS TAKE TIME TO DEVELOP

"I went to Jerusalem, and after staying there three days I set out during the night with a few men. I had not told anyone what my God had put in my heart to do for Jerusalem. There were no mounts with me except the one I was riding on. By night I went out through the Valley Gate toward the Jackal Well and the Dung Gate, examining the walls of Jerusalem, which had been broken down, and its gates, which had been destroyed by fire. Then I moved on toward the Fountain Gate and the King's Pool, but there was not enough room for my mount to get through; so I went up the valley by night, examining the wall. Finally, I turned back and reentered through the Valley Gate. The officials did not know where I had gone or what I was doing, because as yet I had said nothing to the Jews or the priests or nobles or officials or any others who would be doing the work.",

"So the wall was completed on the twenty-fifth of Elul, in fifty-two days." (Nehemiah 2:11-16; 6:15)

Nehemiah's vision took time to develop. He took time in prayer to develop the vision. He took time to speak with the king and to make arrangements for the journey to

Jerusalem. He took time to examine the situation before talking to the people. Then when the work began, it took only 52 days to build the wall.

Visions take time to develop. Don't think that just because God has given you a vision it will happen in a day. It will take time. You may need training and shaping. You may require more time praying and fasting. Others who are important to its success need time to accept the vision.

God may have to do a deep work in your heart so that you will fully accept His calling. In His time the vision will burn deeper in your heart and your passion will increase.

Years ago as a pastor, one of my visions was to have a church council that was generous with workers allowances! That may look selfish, but part of my vision as a missionary was to have the church generously support the pastor who would follow me. It took several years before they caught the vision. By that time, God was calling me to another place of ministry!

Time is also required to fulfill the vision. There is much to be done to make the vision a reality. It takes time to develop people, raise money, plan, communicate, and all the other necessary things. A big vision should keep us going for at least several years. Wilkinson says, "Vision that is powerful is a long-term vision." Some visions are not even accomplished in a lifetime!

> Visions are like babies; they can take months in the womb before birth and many years to develop to maturity!

Be patient with your vision and allow enough time to accomplish it. Visions are like babies; they take months in the womb before birth and many years to develop to maturity!

VISION PRINCIPLE SIX:
VISIONS MUST BE COMMUNICATED

"Then I said to them, 'You see the trouble we are in: Jerusalem lies in ruins, and its gates have been burned with fire. Come, let us rebuild the wall of Jerusalem, and we will no longer be in disgrace.' I also told them about the gracious hand of my God upon me and what the king had said to me. They replied, 'Let us start rebuilding.' So they began this good work." (Nehemiah 2:17-18)

Nehemiah now shares his vision with the people. He communicates the problem and his desire to build the wall. As he communicates the vision to the people, their hearts are stirred, and they agree to help him accomplish the task.

The vision must be communicated to others before it will become a reality. Vision begins in the hidden prayers of the leader, but in time must be shared with others. When the vision is communicated, people and resources will be mobilized to fulfill it. Many leaders stumble at this point, and don't effectively communicate the vision to others. The leader who can communicate his vision will do far more than the one who has a great vision but can't communicate it. Nehemiah's example shows us how to effectively communicate a vision.

FIND THE RIGHT TIME

Timing is crucial. Nehemiah chose the timing very carefully. He was in Jerusalem several days, and no one knew what he was doing. He did his homework, checking out the situation, and testing his theories before sharing the vision with others. Then he called people together and shared the vision. Before sharing the vision, it must be deep within the heart of the leader. He must be personally committed to the vision and prepared to pay the price. Before informing the people, the leader must have carefully thought out the plan of action be able to clearly spell out at least the first steps that are required. Nehemiah did this very effectively, and the results confirm his wisdom.

Once I was in a church where a baby had died the previous week because of negligence in the local hospital. Everyone in the church felt the pain of the loss. An elder proposed that the church should build a clinic to ensure that children wouldn't die needlessly. It was an excellent vision and the people were excited about it. If an offering basket had been ready, it would have overflowed! However, the vision died because of negligence. It had not been carefully thought out and there was no plan of action. The leadership of the church had not accepted the vision. The vision was right, but the timing was wrong. The result was failure of the vision.

Think carefully and pray about the right time to present your vision. Is it God's time? Has the vision matured in your heart? Are people ready to listen? Are you ready with a plan of action? Does the vision consume you? Have people bought into you as a leader before you ask them to buy into the vision? If you answer "no" to any of these questions, the timing may not be right yet to share your vision.

Think about which people should first hear the vision. Communicate the vision first to the leaders and later to the people. There are some key individuals in your group that need time to own the vision. They may also help to shape the vision and make it stronger and more focused. When they support the vision they will help you share it with others.

IDENTIFY THE NEED

Nehemiah identified the problem that existed in Jerusalem. *"You see the trouble we are in: Jerusalem lies in ruins, and its gates have been burned with fire."* What was he doing? He was identifying the need before he shared his vision. You may think that the need was obvious. However, the people had been living with the broken down wall for so long that they didn't even notice as they passed by it every day. They forgot that the piles of rubble were supposed to be a wall! Nehemiah had to point out the need to them before they could accept the vision.

As a leader one of your responsibilities is to point out needs. You will need to remind people that a building is needed; that the prayer meetings have not been well attended; that there are people with physical needs.

One of the temptations of leadership is to assume that people know their needs. As a pastor, I observed that members often started treating evangelistic crusades very casually. In spite of announcements encouraging them to attend, they didn't come. Upon reflection, I realized that we were talking more about the crusade than about those who were lost without Christ. I needed to remind people of the real reason for our crusades.

Every vision from God must meet a need. Again, the vision must be about people and their needs, not your need as a leader. Sometimes pastors want to be recognized so they embark on a big building program. They would never say it publicly, but their real motive is selfish. Be sure your vision is from the Lord, and that you communicate this to the people.

COMMIT YOURSELF

Notice what Nehemiah said, *"You see the trouble WE are in."* He didn't say, "You." A good leader always identifies with the problem and commits himself to the appropriate action. Don't call people to a work that you are not willing to do!

> **Don't call people to a work that you are not willing to do!**

Nehemiah didn't have to deal with the problems of Jerusalem. He could have continued serving wine to the King and eating roasted meat! But because he chose to make their problem his own, the people were willing to follow him.

SHARE THE PLAN

Nehemiah then shared his plan with the people, saying, *"Let's rebuild the wall."* He told them in detail who would do what aspect of the task. It is crucial that before you communicate your vision, you have a plan of action ready to share with the people.

Imagine what might have happened to Nehemiah if he didn't have a plan. What if they said, "Yes, let's do it, where do we start?" and Nehemiah replied, "Umm… let's see, I'm not really sure what we need to do, I'll have to consult with the masons!" That would have killed their morale and confidence in Nehemiah's vision and leadership.

CALL PEOPLE TO ACTION

After stating the problem and sharing his plan, Nehemiah called the people to action, *"Come, let's rebuild the wall."* Leaders call others to action. They are not afraid to ask for a commitment from the people. This is a tough moment, because it is now that the leader will find out who will accept the vision and follow. It takes courage and commitment to the vision to challenge the crowd and ask them to sign up. But until you are ready to take this step, nothing will happen. Not everyone will accept the challenge, but leaders look for people who are ready to accomplish the vision. Don't be afraid to ask people to enlist. If you have a good vision and have communicated it well, you won't be standing alone when you say, "Let's move!"

Author Mark Chironna summarized this well when he said, "Vision without action is merely a dream. Action without vision just passes the time. Vision with action can change the world."[32]

VISION PRINCIPLE SEVEN:
VISIONS WILL ENCOUNTER OPPOSITION

But when Sanballat the Horonite, Tobiah the Ammonite official and Geshem the Arab heard about it, they mocked and ridiculed us. "What is this you are doing?" they asked. "Are you rebelling against the king?" I answered them by saying, "The God of heaven will give us success. We his servants will start rebuilding, but as for you, you have no share in Jerusalem or any claim or historic right to it." (Nehemiah 2:19-20)

Opposition surfaced when Nehemiah shared the vision, and it continued throughout the building of the wall. It would be nice to think that when a leader has a good vision that will benefit people's lives, everyone will support him. Sadly, this is not the case. Movement produces friction. Any worthy vision will produce some resistance along the way. Expect opposition! If you are experiencing no opposition in your church, you are probably not going anywhere! Going in circles doesn't stir up anything but dust!

We cannot comprehensively deal with the subject of opposition here, but we can observe several key ways that Nehemiah dealt with opposition by looking closely at what happened in Nehemiah 4:7-23.

"But when Sanballat, Tobiah, the Arabs, the Ammonites and the men of Ashdod heard that the repairs to Jerusalem's walls had gone ahead and that the gaps were being closed, they were very angry. They all plotted together to come and fight against Jerusalem and stir up trouble against it. But

---

[32] Mark Chironna, *Breaking The Boundaries of The Possible* (New Kensington: Whitaker House, 1996).

we prayed to our God and posted a guard day and night to meet this threat. Meanwhile, the people in Judah said, "The strength of the laborers is giving out, and there is so much rubble that we cannot rebuild the wall." Also our enemies said, "Before they know it or see us, we will be right there among them and will kill them and put an end to the work." Then the Jews who lived near them came and told us ten times over, "Wherever you turn, they will attack us."

Therefore I stationed some of the people behind the lowest points of the wall at the exposed places, posting them by families, with their swords, spears and bows. After I looked things over, I stood up and said to the nobles, the officials and the rest of the people, "Don't be afraid of them. Remember the Lord, who is great and awesome, and fight for your brothers, your sons and your daughters, your wives and your homes."

When our enemies heard that we were aware of their plot and that God had frustrated it, we all returned to the wall, each to his own work. From that day on, half of my men did the work, while the other half were equipped with spears, shields, bows and armor. The officers posted themselves behind all the people of Judah who were building the wall. Those who carried materials did their work with one hand and held a weapon in the other, and each of the builders wore his sword at his side as he worked. But the man who sounded the trumpet stayed with me.

Then I said to the nobles, the officials and the rest of the people, "The work is extensive and spread out, and we are widely separated from each other along the wall. Wherever you hear the sound of the trumpet, join us there. Our God will fight for us!" So we continued the work with half the men holding spears, from the first light of dawn till the stars came out. At that time I also said to the people, "Have every man and his helper stay inside Jerusalem at night, so they can serve us as guards by night and workmen by day." Neither I nor my broth-

ers nor my men nor the guards with me took off our clothes; each had his weapon, even when he went for water."

HE KEPT THE VISION

The most significant thing that Nehemiah did in dealing with opposition is that he refused to be distracted. He kept the vision in spite of all the challenges. He never considered stopping the work to deal with the opposition.

Nehemiah didn't take the threats personally; realizing that others were opposing him for their own selfish interests. He realized that the attacks were not against him, but against his God-given vision.

HE ADJUSTED THE PLAN

Although Nehemiah refused to give up the vision, the opposition forced him to adjust the plan. He had to have half of his people standing guard, while the others continued building. He was willing to modify the plans as long as they kept working on the vision.

HE ENCOURAGED THE PEOPLE

Nehemiah, as all great leaders, dealt with opposition by encouraging the people. He spoke words of encouragement when he said, "Don't be afraid of them...." He kept reminding them that God was on their side, helping them focus on the task rather than the opposition. When opposition comes, people get discouraged, and a strong leader is needed to keep the morale high.

He also encouraged them by his presence. He stayed with the people and carried his weapon with him.

CONCLUSION

As you have looked at the life of Nehemiah, I trust your heart has been stirred to look ahead and discover the specific vision God has for your life.

What is your vision? What has God created you to do in life? That's a BIG question; one that deserves a serious response. Take time to think and pray about what God wants you to do. Use the action assignment to help you clarify your vision. Work at it until you can write your vision statement, and then start moving!

ACTION ASSIGNMENT

Work through the process of getting a vision for your life. Your goal is to be able to write down your vision for life and ministry. Use Maxwell's suggestions and the sample vision statements to assist you. But remember, your vision is yours!

MAXWELL'S SUGGESTIONS FOR GETTING A VISION[33]

Look **within** you. What is your passion? What is your feeling? What do you get excited about doing?

Look **behind** you. What have you learned? Who are you as a person? What positive results can you build on? Do people trust you? The way a vision is received depends much on who you are as a leader.

Look **around** you. Are people ready for the vision? Do they sense a need? You can't run too far ahead of people.

Look **ahead** of you. What is down the road? What is the big picture? What are the long range plans?

Look **above** you. What does God expect from you? Most important, what is God's vision for your life? God has given you tremendous gifts and potential; it is up to you how you develop them and use them for His glory.

Look **beside** you. What resources do you have? What is available in your church or community that you have to work with? At what level are your people?

SAMPLE VISION STATEMENTS.

(These are given as samples to help you establish and organize your own vision. Notice that vision statement is a broad, long-term expression of what God has called you to do.)

- My vision is to develop leaders. God has called me to develop myself to the highest potential to equip other

---

[33] Maxwell, *Developing the Leader Within You*, 145-149.

leaders through training, providing resources to them, encouraging them and mentoring them.

- My vision is to build the church in which I am the pastor to its highest potential. God has called me to "equip the saints," with every member actively involved in using his/her gift in the church. I envision a church that is aggressive in evangelism while having a serious discipleship ministry. We will focus on. ...(meeting the material needs of the poor in our community, calling men to the church, worship/music ministry, developing cell groups, etc. In other words, what will be the specific focus of your church?)

- My vision is to be an intercessor. I believe God has called me to develop the gift of intercession and to encourage others in the church to pray. I will do that through promoting seminars and workshops on prayer, beginning in our local church and then spreading to other churches in this nation.

- My vision is to work with children. God has called me to develop our children's ministry to its highest potential. I will develop my own gifts by taking advantage of any training opportunities and reading books on the same. I will promote numerical and quality growth in the church by committing myself to pray for the ministry, recruiting other teachers, organizing seminars for training, organizing activities for the children such as camps and competitions.

- My vision is to assist the needy in our society. God has given me a vision of developing an interdenominational ministry that will focus on enabling people to develop job skills and find suitable employment.

- My vision is to enable women to reach their fullest potential in Christ. God has called me to establish a ministry in our church denomination that will minister to the unique needs of women. We will emphasize the power God has given to women, finding their identity in Christ, and dealing with the things that intimidate them. We will hold seminars in every district of our church and establish women's chapters in every local church.

After prayer and thinking through the above notes, write clearly the vision God has given you for your life.

I believe God has called me to:

_____

_____

_____

_____

_____

_____

Chapter Four

THE LEADER AND GOALS

Vision provides the picture of where you are going, but that is not enough to achieve your dream. The leader needs goals to put the vision into action. Goals are simply a set of specific steps to achieve the vision. Someone has said, "Goals are dreams with a date." Vision provides the big picture; goals are shorter-term measurements of how we are reaching our vision. We must build steps (goals) to reach our target (vision). (See diagram) As God blesses us and we succeed in one goal, our faith increases and we are ready for the next.

If I ask you, "Where do you want to be five years from now?" your answer will tell me your vision. But to know your goals I will ask, "How will you get there?"

One vision produces many goals. A church pastor may have a vision to build a church of 600 people that is active in church planting. Many specific goals will be required to fulfill that vision.

Nehemiah had a vision, to see the wall standing in Jerusalem. But to implement that vision he had to achieve several goals. First, he had to see the king and get his

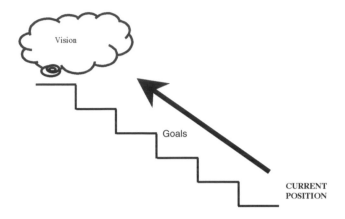

approval. Then he had to acquire supplies and make a journey. Finally he had to sell the vision to the people, organize them to work, and deal with opposition. All of these were steps needed for Nehemiah to fulfill his vision.

As an overseer of more than a dozen churches one of my visions was that we would be "sending" congregations; to see beyond our own boundaries and plant churches in other regions. In time we planned to plant a church in Western Kenya. It took a year of planning and setting goals before the vision became a reality. Before we shared our vision with people, we set goals about sending a team of "spies" to view the place we wanted to go. We had a goal of raising money for the outreach and when the church would actually be established. It took hard work before the vision was accomplished, but at last we succeeded.

> "The instant you set a goal a light goes on in your future."

Your vision must be clear and specific. Then your goals will enable you to accomplish this vision. Write down your goals. Make a plan, with a calendar showing when you want to accomplish those goals. Estimate the cost. Think about how it will be done. Visualize it in your mind. Get to work and reach your goals. This is the work of a leader! Jim Paluch, a motivational speaker states, "The instant you set a goal a light goes on in your future."

This chapter will guide you in setting good goals and making them work.

GOALS SHOULD BE S.M.A.R.T.

Effective goals have certain characteristics. Once you learn the fundamentals of setting goals, it will not be so difficult to make and reach worthwhile targets. Each letter of the word "S.M.A.R.T." stands for one characteristic of effective goals: Specific; Measurable; Attainable; Relevant; Transferable.

SPECIFIC

Effective goals must be specific. Vague goals won't work. Nehemiah didn't say, "I'll go to Jerusalem and see what needs to be done." or "I'll improve security." He was specific, "I will build the wall around Jerusalem."

Your goals should be specific. If you say, "I want to grow" that's a good desire, but it's not specific. In which area do you want to grow?

MEASURABLE

For a goal to be helpful, it must be measurable. Goals need <u>numbers</u> and <u>dates</u> to be effective. You should be able to know at the end of the specified time whether or not you have reached your goal.

Your goal may be specific, for example, "I want to grow strong in faith." However, how will you know if you are strong in faith? It is not measurable. It will be measurable when you say, "Each month I will read a book on faith." At the end of the month you can very easily know if you have reached the target.

Another person may say, "I will win souls for Jesus." That's a great desire, but not a measurable goal. It becomes measurable when he says, "I will win 100 souls for Jesus this year." He will know at the end of the year if he has reached his goal.

Making a goal measurable is difficult. Although not technically difficult, it is emotionally difficult because in putting dates and numbers to your goal you fear failure. IT IS BETTER TO MISS A GOAL THAN TO NOT HAVE ONE! While there's a chance that you will miss your goal, it will make your target clear. Those who never have measurable goals don't have to worry about missing. They are like Charlie Brown in "Peanuts" where he is throwing darts. Wherever the dart lands he runs and draws a circle around it. Lucy comes and says, "Charlie Brown, that's not the way you play darts." He replies, "I know, but this  way I never miss!" Many people go through life this way. Since their goals were not measurable, they say at the end of a year, "We thank God for where He brought us!"

As a pastor I wrote measurable goals for each year. We always knew whether we had reached them or not, because they were measurable. I had a goal for several years to double our finances in the church. We had goals for the number of youth seminars. We had goals for outreach, the number of crusades, and to plant a church by a certain date. At the end of the year we could see what we had achieved and what we had failed to achieve.

In the area of physical development many pastors have a clear plan and have done well in goal setting. "We will replace the roof this year." But "equipping the saints" is harder to measure. A goal that people will "pray more" is difficult to measure, while "doubling the number at prayer meeting by summer" is measurable.

Test yourself to see if you have understood this principle. Read the goals below and mark the ones that are measurable.

a. _____ I will read my Bible.

b. _____ I will bring souls into the Kingdom.

c. _____ I will disciple new believers in the church.

d. _____ I will lose weight.

Did you mark any? *None* of the above goals are measurable! Let's make them measurable....

a. I will read two chapters of my Bible daily.

b. I will share Christ with someone every day.

c. I will go through 10 lessons of training with five new believers this year.

d. By December I will lose 10 pounds.

The key is to make sure that your goals have **numbers** and **dates**. A goal that is not *measurable* is *miserable*!

<u>A</u>TTAINABLE

Set your goals high, so that you must stretch to reach them. But make sure they are attainable. They should be realistic if they will work well. There are several things to consider as you set goals.

Look at *your resources*. These include available finances, people to work with and their abilities, your own level of leadership, and your strengths and weaknesses. Given your resources, is the goal attainable?

Look at *previous experience* for comparison. Don't try to jump from A to Z in one year. See how far you've come. Then set goals for the year.

In planning our budgets at the church, we made them realistic by taking the report for the last year or two. We could see how much the tithes had been, and how much we had spent on office supplies. From there we were able to look ahead and make a projection based on realistic faith. Balance faith with realism; make your goals high, but attainable.

Once I received a fund raising card from a pastor who was raising money for land. I asked him what his goal was and he said with great confidence, "We are targeting $7,000 in our fundraising." I knew that his church was small and asked him, "The last time you had a fundraising, how much did you raise?" He replied, "$450." I groaned inwardly because his goal was not achievable. His members were excited because he kept telling them "We are trusting God for $7,000." On the day of the fundraising everyone did their best and they raised over $1,100. Was that a good effort? It was a *great* improvement over the last event. But what happened to the people? They were discouraged and felt defeated.

If your goals are not attainable, you set people up for failure and discouragement. It will also be very difficult to motivate them another time to try again. Especially if you are just starting out on the goal setting process. Be sure to set goals that you are confident you can reach. Stretch people a little bit, and allow them to feel the joy of victory. This will give them courage to stretch further the next time. Nothing encourages faith like victory!

Also, look at *your ability to influence the outcome.* Make sure that the goal is **within your ability to reach**. You cannot make goals for others! I have had many students who said that their goal was for their spouse to be saved by the end of the year. While their motive is excellent, the goal is not attainable. They cannot ensure that their spouse will be saved by the end of the year since it is only God that can save someone. However, they can have a goal that is to pray daily for 15 minutes for their spouse's salvation. This is within their power and is an attainable goal.

RELEVANT

Your goals should also be relevant. Relevant means applicable, pertinent, or related to the purpose. Goals must be relevant to the needs of people. A goal to start a single mother's ministry, when you have no single mothers, would not be relevant. A goal to have a prison ministry in a place where there is no prison is likewise not relevant.

Your goals should be relevant to the vision you have. If your vision is to develop an intercessory ministry, several of your goals should relate to prayer. Some of these might be:
- To read a book on prayer each month
- To attend one seminar on intercession this year.
- To meet with the pastor by July to share my vision with him
- To form a group of five intercessors by September who will meet monthly for one hour of prayer.

TRANSFERABLE

Our goals should be clear enough so that they can be shared with others. They can join us in reaching the goal or simply hold us accountable to reach what we have stated.

To make your goals transferable, put them in writing. The simple act of writing them greatly increases the probability that you will reach your goals. As noted earlier, 80% of people who put their goals in writing accomplish them; 20% of those who don't write them achieve them!

Tell your goals to others. Incredible power is released when you publicly commit yourself to a goal. When you tell your spouse that you will get up

> "The people with whom you share your goals will play a major part in whether or not you reach the goals."

85

every morning at 6:00 a.m. for prayer, you can be sure that at 6:00 the next morning you will feel "encouragement" to get up! When you announce that you have a goal of leading 10 people to the Lord this month, people will ask you after one week, "How many have you won?" This provides great motivation to keep working to reach your goal. Zig Ziglar observes, "The people with whom you share your goals will play a major part in whether or not you reach the goals."[34]

If you adopt S.M.A.R.T. goals, you will have a good chance of succeeding. Take some time to do the action assignment, and set goals for your life and ministry. You'll be amazed at the difference it brings, and what it enables you to accomplish in life.

GOALS SHOULD BE FOLLOWED BY PLANS

Once your goals are on paper, you are ready for action! The next step is to begin planning how you will accomplish your goals. Plans are goals with shoes on them and will define what you need to do to accomplish your goals. Let's observe several principles of planning.

PLANNING INVOLVES ANSWERING QUESTIONS

When you begin planning, answer the following questions.

What? What money, training, people and other resources are needed to meet the goal?

When? When will the goal be accomplished? What needs to change in your schedule so that you can meet the goal?

Whom? Who will be involved? What is required in terms of personnel? Do they need to be trained to do the work? If so, who will do that and when?

How much? This question deals with the cost of those goals that require financial resources. Where will the

---

[34] Zig Ziglar, *Over the Top*, (Nashville: Thomas Nelson, 1997) p. 244.

money come from? Who will raise the money and how long will this take? What priorities need to be changed?

PLANNING NEEDS TO BE FLEXIBLE

Plans are made to help you reach your goal. Therefore, if a plan is not working, you can change the plan to something that will work. For example, your goal might be to exercise for 30 minutes every day. Your plan to reach that goal is to exercise early in the morning. However, you find that this doesn't work with the family schedule. So you change the plan to do it in the evenings while listening to the news. Your plan may change, but your goal remains.

When we raised money for our mission to Western Kenya we fell short of the targeted amount. We didn't change the goal, but modified our plans to work with a more limited budget.

We have already seen how Nehemiah modified his plans when opposition arose. He kept the vision and the goals alive, but changed his plans. Maxwell and Donavan write in *Becoming a Person of Influence,* "Set your goals in concrete, and write your plans in sand."[35]

PLANNING CLARIFIES PRIORITIES

When you begin making plans you will realize you can't do everything at once. You may have to decide whether to hold a crusade, or plan a seminar first. Or the issue might be whether to spend money on books first, or to enroll in a training course. Which is most important for your vision? Which needs to be done first? These are questions of priorities.

If we fail to prioritize, we try to do too many things and not well at any. If you are planning for your organization ask, "Of all the things we are doing, what is the one thing we cannot abandon?" That is your top priority and should be foremost in your planning. If you then ask, "What

---

[35] Maxwell and Donavan, 146.

is the next most important thing that we do?" you will find your second priority. Continue and you will have the priorities of your organization. Working on this will ensure that you do not waste time on secondary issues.

PLANNING SHOULD BE FOLLOWED BY WORK

To achieve our goals we must be willing to work. Vision and goals look good on paper, but nothing happens until we start working on them. This takes discipline, effort, and sweat! Nehemiah's wall building required much work. Nehemiah 4:21 says, *"So we continued the work...from the first light of dawn till the stars came out."* That's a long day! The Biblical workweek was six days, probably 11-hour days. That's 66 hours! Too many people start thinking about overtime pay as soon as it's 5:00, but successful people realize what is required to reach their goals. People with a vision learn how to work to make it happen. Myles Munroe says, "Some people have visions without the will to bring them into reality. They dream but they don't wake up!" They talk about how nice it would be to have a big church or a successful business. They may pray for God to enlarge their congregation, but they aren't willing to pay the price to make it happen. This is not to minimize the importance of prayer; it is crucial. Remember Cho's formula, "Pray..., and obey." There is a time for prayer and a time for action.

GOALS MUST BE EVALUATED

Nehemiah evaluated his work. The scripture says, *"After I looked things over..."* (Nehemiah 4:14) He was checking on the progress of the work, to see if they were still on track. A leader is always looking over the work, evaluating, checking to see how things are going, and looking ahead.

Good evaluation is essential to successful goal setting. We must ask tough questions. Are we still on the right track? Have we gone astray? What problems have come up, and how can we deal with them? Did we succeed?

Don't expect to succeed without evaluation. Even when the goal is accomplished, sit down and evaluate. What helped us succeed? What could be improved?

Many people avoid evaluation, unwilling to admit to having fallen short. It might mean acknowledging that the crusade was not as "successful" as we told people. It forces us to acknowledge that the church is not really growing. It is painful when we have not reached our goals, but evaluation will help us grow in wisdom and do better the next time. Evaluation may also reveal that we have more than met our goals and give an opportunity to celebrate our success!

Your evaluation may indicate that you are well on the way to reaching your target. This may be the time to set a higher goal. Mahoney suggests that when you reach 80% of your goal; start planning for the next. If you have 30 people plan for 60; when you get to 48, start working for 90. Evaluation will help you know when it is time to set new goals.

Effective evaluation helps you set and reach goals. It gives you more confidence as a leader, and your followers grow in their confidence in you. Each success encourages you to move on to greater things with God.

CONCLUSION

There is a deliberate progression. Vision comes first and provides the direction. Goals should then be set, and plans made to reach them. Then it's time to do the work, and finally to evaluate what has happened.

One of the best ways for you to grow in leadership is to put these things into practice. It will require much prayer and effort, especially if you have not been doing it.

Pastors, it is crucial that you do this with your church council, board or leadership group. After affirming your vision, set goals. When you have agreed on the goals, start planning. This means getting a calendar for the year and making sure that all activities in your goals have a place in the calendar. Then start planning for individual goals to happen. When this is in place the work can begin. The same principles apply for leaders of other organizations.

Vision, goals, and plans are practical steps to take in our ministry. In no way do they replace prayer and our spiritual foundation in the Word. You must have the foundation of a heart for God and commitment to His Word. But prayer and Bible study without specific steps of action will not make you fruitful in ministry.

It's time for action. Go through the action assignment and set your goals. Don't move on to the next chapter until you have done this exercise. May God give you His direction as you proceed.

Remember: Establish vision, set goals, and make plans to accomplish great things for God!

ACTION ASSIGNMENT

1. Set goals

Think about your own life. What goals are needed to help you reach your vision? Use the sample goals on the following pages to help you see what S.M.A.R.T. goals will look like.

Think of the following areas. What goals do you have in each of them? Set at least three goals in each area. Make sure they are S.M.A.R.T. goals.

    a. Personal life. What are your goals for spiritual growth? What are you doing to grow? In what ways are you getting input in your life? Do you need more exercise? What goals do you have in your profession or career?

    My personal goals:

    1.

    2.

    3.

    b. Family life. How much time should you spend with your wife? husband? children? What are you doing to lead and train your children in the Lord?

    My family goals:

    1.

    2.

    3.

    c. Ministry. Where do you want your church to be five years from now? What are your goals for the following groups/areas? Choir, ushers, elders, deacons, small groups, youth, parents, outreach, teaching. If you are not a pastor, look at the area you are involved in, and set goals that you can reach.

My ministry goals:

1.

2.

3.

2. Review your goals

Make sure that they are S.M.A.R.T. Do you have a number and date with each one? Will you know for sure if you have reached it or not? Is it an attainable goal?

3. Share your goals with someone

Write them out, and put them where you can easily see them on a regular basis.

SAMPLE **GOALS**

Look at the following sample goals to get ideas of what S.M.A.R.T. goals look like in different areas:

Personal Life: I will
1. Spend one hour daily in prayer and Bible reading.
2. Read one book each month on leadership.
3. Exercise for 30 minutes daily.
4 Read three chapters of the Bible each day.
5. Fast one day per week.
6. Enroll in a Bible training college by December.
7. Take guitar lessons once a week.

Family: I will
1. Spend at least one evening per week with my family. During this time (at least 30 minutes) we will read the Bible together and worship God.
2. Spend at least one day per month with my family for fun and recreation.
3. Meet daily with my wife for 20 minutes of sharing and prayer together.
4. Go through the discipleship lessons with my oldest son on Monday evenings.
5. Fast and pray one day per month for members of my family who are not saved.
6. Save $ _____ per month for a family project.

Ministry/work:
This will vary, depending on your personal involvement. A pastor in a local church could make the following goals for a particular year. A person who is not the pastor might be involved in one of these areas and develop more comprehensive goals in that area. Other professions can create goals related to their work.

93

1. MISSIONS/EVANGELISM

A. Plan three major crusades in the year.

B. Develop 2 other methods of evangelism, e.g. house-to-house, film ministry, etc.

D. Plant a daughter church by December

E. Start another ministry (hospital, prison, etc.) by October.

F. Have a mission's week to encourage missions in the church.

G. Equip the missions committee to be able to plan a crusade without the pastor's assistance.

2. FAMILIES

A. Hold two couples' seminars and at least two couples' fellowships.

B. Have two single parents' fellowships.

3. FINANCES

A. Meet the proposed budget of the church.

B. Have financial reports given to the church council monthly. Have a minireport given to the church after 6 months and a full report at the end of the year.

C. Have a series of teachings on finances.

4. PRAYING

A. Have an active intercessor's group that meets once a month to plan prayers in the church.

B. Hold prayer meetings every two months for the church leaders.

C. Hold a three-day prayer retreat this year.

5. SPECIAL EVENTS

A. Have two baptisms.

B. Hold one church retreat in August

C. Hold revival meetings twice.

D. Have Communion three times in the year.

E. Have a Mother's Sunday; Men's Sunday; Youth Sunday; and Visitor's Sunday.

6. TRAINING

A. Hold two leaders' seminars.

B. Establish a team that will follow up with new believers.

C. Teach a discipleship class twice in the year.

7. CHILDREN'S MINISTRY

A. Hold two Sunday School Teachers' seminars.

B. Develop a puppet ministry.

C. Have Sunday School presentations for Easter and Christmas.

D. Have a Children's Emphasis Week.

8. WORSHIP.

A. Develop musical skills in our worship team by having at least three persons enrolled in a training course.

B. Have a series of teachings on worship.

C. Have a praise and worship weekend.

D. Host a choir rally.

9. DEVELOPMENT.

A. Install new sound system.

B. Construct three temporary classrooms.

10. ELDERS

A. Hold a monthly teaching session with the elders.

B. Have at least two elders enrolled in some form of Bible training.

C. Appoint elders to be responsible for prayer cells, the worship service, finances, and discipleship.

D. Select three additional elders by the end of the year.

Other "ministry" goals for someone who is not a pastor could be to:

1. Start a ladies' prayer group in the church by November.
2. Share the gospel with at least one person each day.
3. Develop my evangelistic skills by attending two seminars on evangelism this year.
4. Start a team that will reach out to the Asians by _____ (date).
5. Develop a ministry that will reach the widows in our community by _____ (date).
6. Begin a discipleship group in my church with 10 members by _____ (date).
7. Meet with the pastor to discuss my vision this month.
8. Spend one week in prayer and fasting in January concerning this vision.
9. Organize weekend outreaches in at least 12 schools this year.
10. Plan an outing for the Sunday School children in October.

Chapter Five
THE LEADER AND TIME

How many times have you heard someone say, "I just don't have enough time!?" Time seems to always be in short supply.

When you begin to understand the potential God has given you; have vision of what God wants you to do in life, and have goals to fulfill your vision, it becomes crucial that you learn how to manage your time.

One of the keys for you to be effective in life and to accomplish all that God has for you is learning how to use your time well. I believe that most people could accomplish twice as much of eternal value with effective time management. (Even for those who already manage their time well, there is still room for improvement.)

When it comes to time management, there are three types of people:

    1. Some lack vision and are not busy enough. They <u>kill</u> time.

2. Some are busy doing the wrong things and need priorities. They <u>waste</u> time.
3. A few are busy doing the right things and deserve congratulations. They <u>use</u> time.

In which category are you? I try hard to stay in category three, but still find myself in category two much of the time. This chapter and chapter six are designed to help you achieve category three, which should be your goal.

THE IMPORTANCE OF EFFECTIVE TIME MANAGEMENT

Why is it important for us to learn to use our time well? There are several foundational truths that provide the foundation for time management.

TIME TRUTH ONE: TIME IS GIVEN EQUALLY TO ALL

This is a simple but profound truth. Every living person has the same amount of time every day: 1440 minutes! The president has the same amount of time as the teacher. The CEO of a large company doesn't have more time than you have. Yet, some people accomplish so much more with their lives than others! The secret lies in how they use their time.

Speaker and author Denis Waitley says, "Time is an equal opportunity employer. Each human being has exactly the same number of hours and minutes every day. Rich people can't buy more hours. Scientists can't invent new minutes. And you can't save time to spend it on another day. Even so, time is amazingly fair and forgiving. No matter how much time you've wasted in the past, you still have an entire tomorrow. Success depends upon using it wisely—by planning and setting priorities."

So many times we say, "I'll do that when I get time." What do we expect? Do we think that one day God is going to add another 30 minutes to our day? Or one year He will give us an extra week because of good behavior? It won't happen! We never shall have any more time. We have, and have always had, all the time there is. Stop saying, "When I get time." You won't get any more time! Stop praying for it!

TIME TRUTH TWO: THE TIME GIVEN TO US IS ENOUGH TO ACCOMPLISH THE TASK GIVEN TO US

God has a plan for our lives, and work He wants us to accomplish. The time He has given to us is His gift to us and is sufficient to do all that He requires of us. Why would He ever give us more work than time?

Jesus said, at the end of his life, *"I have brought you glory on earth by completing the work you gave me to do."* (John 17:4) He had finished his work! Jesus didn't do everything. He didn't preach to everyone, He didn't heal everyone, He didn't teach everyone. But He completed all the work assigned to Him! What a powerful statement! In order to say, "I completed the work you gave me to do" we must properly manage our time.

Notice that I did not say we have as much time as we want! But it is enough to accomplish what God wants us to do. We must learn to treat time like we treat money. I often ask people how many of them have all the money they want. Of course, no one says "yes." Then I ask them, "So, what do you do with what you have, since you don't have as much as you want?" They tell me that they have to budget the money. A budget simply prioritizes the limited resource, so that it is used very carefully. In the same way, time should be seen as a limited resource, to be used very carefully.

TIME TRUTH THREE: WE WILL BE HELD ACCOUNTABLE FOR THE WAY WE USE OUR TIME

Like every other resource God has given to us, He will demand an account of how we have used our time. Romans

99

14:12 says, *"So then, each of us will give an account of himself to God."* The parable of the talents in Matthew 25 also applies to time. God expects a return on His investment, and will judge us based on what we have done with that which was given us.

Our work will be tested to see what was genuine and what was wasted. (1 Corinthians 3:12-15) Wasted time will not pass the test.

Jesus said in John 10:10, *"The thief comes only to steal and kill and destroy; I have come that they may have life, and have it to the full."* This applies to many areas of life, including time. The devil will first try to keep you from being busy; if that fails, he will try to keep you busy with the wrong things. He hates people who have learned how to use their time effectively. He wants to steal God's gift from us. In stark contrast to the enemy's attempt to steal life from us, Jesus expresses God's plan for us to have a full life with purpose and enough time to accomplish all He desires for us.

No wonder the psalmist said, *"Teach us to number our days..."* (Psalm 90:12) He has a deep sense of the brevity of life, that each of our days is numbered. To "number our days" means to recognize that each day has a unique number, and once it is gone, it will not return. Today I am living in my day number 16,397. If God grants me a tomorrow it will be day number 16,398. When I realize that each day has a special value, I desire to live it to the fullest extent possible, and to use it to fulfill God's purpose for my life.

TIME TRUTH FOUR: TIME CAN BE USED EFFECTIVELY

Since God has given time to us, He will enable us to use it effectively. We can learn to control our time in order to bring glory to God and hear Him say, "Well done, good and faithful servant."

Ephesians 5:15-16 says, *"Be very careful, then, how you live—not as unwise but as wise, making the most of every opportunity, because the days are evil."* We are to live carefully, and make the most of every opportunity. The King James Version's "redeeming the time" conveys the idea of recovering lost time. The devil wants to steal it, and we are to get it back! Time is precious, and we should seek effective ways of using time that is now wasted.

Time, like money, can be budgeted or squandered. It can easily slip away, or it can be carefully allotted to fulfill our calling and vision. The difference between time and money is that when money is gone you might have a friend who will loan or give you some of his! But when you need more time, which friend can give you more?

Time cannot be recovered. Once it is gone, it is gone. But when used wisely, it will be multiplied for the glory of God!

THE BENEFITS OF EFFECTIVE TIME MANAGEMENT

What do we reap when we effectively manage our time? What benefits will come to our lives?

• INCREASED PRODUCTIVITY FOR GOD. DO MORE THINGS.

Effectively using our time will result in being able to do more for God. Looking at vision and goals, we realize how much there is to be done. How can we get it all done? Only through trusting God and effectively managing the time He has given us.

When we use our time wisely, we can accomplish much more for the Kingdom. Most of us could accomplish twice as much as we are now doing with effective time management. We can squeeze more into our days when we are managing our time. We can visit another person, read another chapter, win another soul, take better care of our bodies, and build a better marriage by using our time well.

Using our time productively is the only way we can develop our full potential in Christ. So many times we say, "I'll do that in the future when I get time." We fail to realize that "The future arrives an hour at a time." I have a note on my office wall that says, "In just two days tomorrow will be yesterday."

• MORE BALANCED PRIORITIES. DO THE RIGHT THINGS.

Effectively managing your time not only enables you to accomplish more in the same time, but also to do the most important things. You won't neglect your children for the sake of the church. You won't do a budget for the church, and fail to have one at home. You won't reach Saturday night and pray, "Lord, give me a message for tomorrow!" You won't neglect your body for the sake of the Kingdom! You will balance your priorities.

In teaching these principles, I use an illustration of an empty jar that represents our available time. Into this jar I begin putting fist-sized stones; each representing major activities that we do such as work, sleep, and ministry. When the stones have reached the top I ask, "Is the jar full?" A few will say "yes" but a keen listener will always notice the spaces between the stones that are not filled and say, "no." I proceed to add many small peas that fall in between the cracks of the large stones. While adding the peas I say, "With proper time management we can find time to do more things, time to visit a sick friend, counsel someone who needs help, or read a chapter of a book." When the peas have filled the jar I ask again, "Is the jar full?" By this time everyone says "no!" and they are right! There are still places between the peas where small grains of rice can fit easily. There is still time to write a note of encouragement, memorize a verse, or spend a few precious moments with our child. When the jar is shaken, more can be added.

This teaches the two benefits of effective time management. First, we can do much more than we imagined, if we manage our time effectively. Second, we should put our big pieces (priorities) in first. After the jar is filled with peas, it is impossible to find space for even one of the big stones. Our schedule should first include the most important things in our lives.

- INCREASED FREEDOM AND JOY IN LIFE. DO THINGS THE RIGHT WAY.

A third benefit of effective time management is increased freedom and joy in life. Too often we carry a big list of the things we haven't done, rushing from one activity to another and arriving late. We don't have time to stop and observe what is wrong, because someone is waiting to see us. Is this the "abundant life" Christ came to give? I don't think so. When I begin to live my life as God planned, I will be set free from the demands of other people, from being behind, and from being too exhausted to have time with my family. I can avoid burnout and procrastination! These are strong statements, and I'm still on the journey, but I believe they are true. God never planned for us to be worn out, burned out, or spaced out! He didn't create us to live under the cloud of regrets. He came to give an abundant life of joy and peace, which is possible as we organize our time!

Take a moment to reflect on your life. On a scale of one to ten, with one being totally disorganized and ten being the life that Christ lived, where are you now in managing your time? _____

STEPS TO EFFECTIVE TIME MANAGEMENT

Now, let's get to the practical aspects of managing your time effectively. How can you tame the "time monster?" These eight steps can revolutionize your life.

STEP ONE: RECOGNIZE GOD'S PLAN FOR YOUR LIFE

The first step in managing your time is to recognize the plan God has for your life and for every moment. He has plans for you today and every day. He knows what He wants you to accomplish this year, including rest, relaxation with your family, exercise, and the more "spiritual" things you do. Your use of time should reflect His plans. Psalm 139:16 says clearly, *"All the days ordained for me were written in your book before one of them came to be."* Wow! Wouldn't you like to look into that book! Since that is not physically possible, try to hear from God and to walk in daily obedience to His plan.

Until you believe that God's plan for you involves every moment of your life, you will not proceed far in the area of time management. Your goal as a Christian leader should be to order your life according to His plan.

STEP TWO: ESTABLISH PRIORITIES

Because your time is limited, you cannot do everything you wish to do. Therefore you need to set your priorities and stick to them.

In Matthew 6:33 Jesus says, *"But seek first his kingdom and his righteousness, and all these things will be given to you as well."* This is about priorities. Jesus is saying that if you focus on what is most important, the other things will take their proper place. The time God gives you is enough to accomplish the task He has given you.

> **What is "urgent" is not always important.**

Knowing our priorities enables us to be effective servants. Mark Porter writes in his book on time management, "Nothing is easier than being busy, and nothing is more difficult than being effective."[36] Successful people are always busy, but not all busy people are successful! The difference is that successful people have learned what is most important and focus on that priority.

---

[36] Mark Porter, *The Time of Your Life* (Kansas City: Walterick Pub, 1988) p. 94.

One of the most difficult aspects of managing your time involves choosing the best over the good. Many of your daily choices are not between good and bad, but between good and best! Luke 10:41, 42 tells the story of Mary and Martha. Both sisters were doing good things, but Jesus says, *"Mary has chosen what is better, and it will not be taken away from her."*

Choosing best over good is difficult. You must constantly strive to do the most important thing first. Many other things will crowd in and look urgent, but what is *urgent* is not always *important*. We can be busy with many things but accomplish little of value, because we fail to prioritize the most important things. Someone has said, "Don't spend a dollar's worth of time for ten cents worth of results."

Choosing the most important over the good involves learning to say "no." In *An Enemy Called Average* John Mason writes, "One of the best timesavers is the ability to say "no." Not saying "no" when you should is one of the biggest wastes of time you will ever experience."[37] It's not easy to say "no" when people place demands on you.

Jesus said "no" to many things in order to make time for the most important. There were times that He left the crowds to be alone with His Father or to take the disciples aside. He said "no" when called to attend Lazarus' burial, knowing that He would be misunderstood. When His brothers urged Him to go to Jerusalem for a major meeting, He told them that His time had not yet come. Are you able to say "no" without feeling guilty?

Overwork indicates being outside of God's will as much as laziness. Both are signs of poor time management. Some people burn out; others rust out! Line up your priorities with God's. If there are things you shouldn't be doing, take a step to be released. You may need to resign from some committees, or refuse some invitations, so that you

---

[37] John Mason, *An Enemy Called Average* (Tulsa: Insight Publishing Group, 1990).

can follow God's priorities. This step is so crucial that we will examine it in more detail in the following chapter.

STEP THREE: EVALUATE YOUR USE OF TIME

A significant key to effective time management is to find out what is happening with your time. You can't redeem time if you don't know where it is going! How can you make adjustments to your time if you don't currently know how it is being used? That's like trying to make a budget when you don't know how you spent money last month!

Here is a life changing assignment! Using the chart in *Appendix B,* track how you are using your time for the next two weeks. Record everything you do every 30 minutes. Yes, I'm serious! Complete the evaluation by following the instructions given in the action assignment at the end of this chapter. Evaluate where your time is being wasted, what you are doing that doesn't contribute towards your goals. Be prepared for a shock!

Socrates said, "Know thyself. The unexamined life is not worth living." Though painful, this will prepare you to make changes.

I encourage you not to read further until you have taken this significant step. It's for your growth, go ahead and do it!

STEP FOUR: TAKE TIME TO PLAN

The next step towards effective time management is to plan your time. Planning is what "separates the men from the boys" in time management! You may have the right vision and goals, but without proper planning you will never maximize your use of time. It takes time to plan, but Porter says that one minute spent in planning saves three to four minutes in execution!

Some Christians feel like planning is not very godly. "We should just follow the Spirit," they say. They quote Matthew 10:19, *"But when they arrest you, do not worry about what to say or how to say it. At that time you will be given what to say...."* Please note Jesus is talking here to martyrs, not preachers! Planning is spiritual! Note that God has plans for us (Jeremiah 29:11); Jesus planned (John 7:6; Mark 1:37, 38); and Paul planned (2 Corinthians 1:15-17). God planned the way of salvation before the foundations of the world were laid. (See Ephesians 1:4) He is a God that is still busy carrying out His plans.

Proverbs 14:15, says clearly *"...a prudent man gives thought to his steps."* He who fails to plan, plans to fail. Many times in managing our time we simply go with whatever happens, instead of taking charge and planning for what should happen.

Tips for planning

1. Use a "to do" list

A "to do" list is essential for time management. It is simply a list of the things that you need to do. You might have different categories ("home" "work" "church" "personal" "town") and then list what you need to do. As you complete different items, cross them off your list. Use your goals in making your "to do" list. Keep it with you, so that when you remember something to be done you can put it on the list.

> My "To Do" List
> • Buy shoe polish
> • Write to Mom
> • Visit Jane in the hospital
> • Write my goals
> • Call Sue

This will help you in practical ways. For example, if you keep a list, you won't think on your way home, "Oh, I forgot to pick up my coat!"

Your "to do" list can be a single sheet of paper, a notebook or an electronic organizer. The format is not crucial; the list is!

2. Use a date book

A date book is essential to keep track of appointments and other commitments. Without it you can easily forget to meet a certain person, or to attend a meeting. How many times have you met someone who said, "Where were you yesterday when we agreed to meet?"

When you have a date book, use it! Check it daily to see your commitments.

3. Set aside a time *daily* for planning

Daily planning has been one of the most useful things in wisely using my time. If I don't do this, I will fall victim to the "urgent" issues and the most important things will be pushed aside.

It doesn't matter if you do your planning in the morning or in the evening, but make a time to plan your day! Think about what is most important; check your goals to ensure that you are spending time on what is most important. Use your "to do" list to remember what you must do.

This planning may be for the next day, or a longer term. Try it for a week at a time, and when you are comfortable, begin planning for a month.

In your planning, allow time for the unexpected. Don't schedule every minute, or you will not be able to keep up and this will lead to frustration.

Organize "like things" together. For example, schedule a time to see people in your office, another time to visit, an hour or two to catch up on correspondence, even time to rest.

Remember, priorities first! This may include family time, time to read and reflect, time to study, or time to rest. Time management does not always mean doing more. We also need to plan times that we recharge our souls. This is the Biblical concept of the Sabbath rest.

Set the most important thing for the day and the second... then do them without interruption. This simple procedure can revolutionize your life!

STEP FIVE: DEAL WITH TIME WASTERS

When we evaluate our time closely, we will find many things that waste our time. Porter calls them time wasters, "an activity which is not as productive as another one we could be doing."

Look at your time assessment to find your time wasters. Look for things not associated with your goals. Consider what can be done more efficiently, in less time, or delegated to others.

Three common time wasters

1. Idle time

This is time not budgeted for anything, and lost. Many hours are wasted with idle time, waiting for transportation; sitting at a desk; standing by the roadside watching the cars go by, or chatting with friends. Good planning helps fill your schedule and greatly reduce idle time. Look closely at how to fill the minutes that are normally lost.

A sign in my office reads, "Maturity is revealed by what I do with my free time." What do you find yourself doing when your time is not scheduled?

2. TV

The television is a common time waster. You may sit down just to rest a bit, and before you know it 30 minutes have gone and another "good" program is coming. Soon you have spent hours in front of the screen, with nothing to show for the time spent. Recognize that the TV is  designed to keep you tuned in for the next show. It is amusement, which means "without thought." Unless you make a deliberate effort to control the TV, it will soon control you. Decide what you should watch and stick to it. Not everything on the TV is bad, but even the good can control you. If you can't control it, pull the plug and leave it off for a week. You'll survive…and maybe thrive!

3. People!

One of the greatest struggles in getting control of your time will be dealing with people. People are good especially for leaders who are in the people business. You must have time for people, but they will often consume time that should be spent doing other things.

People without goals in life don't mind taking 30 minutes of your time to chat! They sit and tell stories for a long time, and in the end you have accomplished nothing.

Even Jesus had to instruct his disciples, *"Do not greet anyone on the road!"* (Luke 10:4) Why? They had a mission, and Jesus knew that if they stopped to greet everyone along the way they would not accomplish it. Their mission was to minister to people, but greetings along the way would have distracted them from their priority. WE SHOULD NOT ALLOW OTHER PEOPLE TO FILL OUR SCHEDULE! God has a goal for us, and we should determine to do it. When this includes people, we should meet with them.

We are in the people business, but we must eliminate those encounters with people that are not productive. Some "interruptions" are God-given opportunities to minister to someone; others are time wasters. It takes wisdom to know the difference!

What can be done with people? Here are several suggestions that have helped me.

a. Schedule time to meet people

In your planning, include time to meet with people. The amount of time you plan will depend on what you are doing with people. Give time to people, but plan it.

If you are a pastor, announce the times that you are available to meet with people. As much as possible don't allow interruptions to your schedule. This will not always be possible, but even asking someone to wait five minutes while I finish a thought helps me, and may also help them to respect time better.

Perhaps you have set priority time to prepare a message for the Sunday service. As you are studying, someone comes who needs prayer for his marriage. You take time to pray with that person, and before you know it, the time has gone and you haven't prepared the message. You will now be praying to God in desperation on Saturday night, and when you preach on Sunday the people may say, "Today, pastor didn't have the anointing."

b. Encourage people to come to the point

When you meet with someone, encourage them to quickly come to the point. You may need to ask them, "Now, tell me, how can I assist you today?" Some time of greeting is good, but you need to help the person maximize the time you have given them.

c. Pray with them!

Praying with someone is important, not only to minister to their needs, but also to help manage time. When you are meeting with someone and have finished the initial greetings you can suggest, "Let's pray together as we begin." And then you pray, "Father, thank you for bringing us together today. Guide us as we share the issues that brought us together and give us wisdom as we talk." After the prayer, it should be easy for the person to get to the point of the meeting. Prayer always helps us get on God's agenda.

It may also be helpful to pray as you conclude the meeting, thanking God for what you have been able to share. If a need has been presented in the meeting, ask God to meet the need. This is not a manipulative technique, but it does help to control the usage of time.

111

It is not easy to know how to work with people. Keep asking God to give you wisdom to use your time well as you minister to others.

STEP SIX: DEAL WITH PROCRASTINATION

Procrastination is simply putting off things that need to be done. The result is devastating to us as leaders. We heap one on top of the other until we are overwhelmed with all the things that need to be done. Most of us have tasks like this, usually things that we hate doing! Your drawer is filled with papers that are unorganized, or you have a closet that hasn't been cleaned in months; the vehicle is overdue for a service or you haven't updated your financial records for a year. You have been intending to write a letter to your mom, or take your child out for a soda. But day after day goes by and these jobs just don't get done. What can we do? Ken Smith, in his wonderful book, *It's About Time*, suggests the following:
* Make a list
* Prioritize
* Move into action[38]

First, make a list of the things you have been postponing for a long time. Then decide which are most important. They may be the most urgent or the ones you dread the most! Schedule an hour each day to tackle an issue of procrastination, or put a time slot weekly to do these jobs. Start with the most urgent, and continue until they are finished. Often, these tasks don't take long to finish and what a great feeling to get rid of them!

STEP SEVEN: SEIZE THE MINUTES

People who effectively manage their time learn to seize the minutes. A minute seems small, only 60 seconds. But

---

[38] Ken Smith, *It's About Time* (Wheaton: Crossway Books, 1992) p. 59-61.

recognize this: if you learn to save 30 minutes per day you will add 182 hours to your year (that's more than one week!); in 40 years you will add 300+ days! How would you like to have an extra year in your life?

Learn the value of minutes. In only 10 minutes a day you can read the whole Bible in a year. With 15 minutes a day, you can read 25 books a year! Minutes are powerful! Learn to deal with minutes, and the hours take care of themselves!

Charles Colton says, "Much may be done in those little shreds and patches of time which every day produces, and which most men throw away."

Where do these wasted minutes come from, and what can we do with them?

• Waiting

Studies have shown that over a lifetime a person spends more than a year waiting! (In some countries it may be twice or three times that amount!) This happens minute by minute as you stand in line at the bank or the supermarket, or 10 minutes waiting for the bus. What can you do? Read a chapter of the Bible, memorize a verse, pray silently, witness to the next person in line, or think about a problem that you are facing and come up with a solution.

• Riding

Much time is spent in vehicles, either driving or riding. You can choose to watch the trees go by, or redeem the time and do something productive! You can read a book, memorize a scripture, learn another language, or study for the course you are taking! If you are driving, you can listen to a tape or CD that will stretch your mind and give you food for thought.

• In between other activities

We often find a few minutes between appointments, or between meetings. Those can be seized to file a paper, write a small note of encouragement, make a call, or even update your "to do" list.

- **In simple tasks that don't use our minds**
Driving, brushing teeth, cooking meals, and washing clothes are tasks that require your body but not much use of your mind. You can redeem that time to listen to a tape, memorize or meditate on scripture, or pray! Use the time you are cooking to chat with your daughter or call a shut-in.

Seize the minutes! Time is precious and you'll be amazed at how many "wasted" minutes you can use productively. Always carry reading material! I read many books a year and seldom spend more than 20 minutes at a time reading. Take your date book with you. When you have a few minutes, get it out and plan your week. Redeem the time!

STEP EIGHT: LEARN TO BE PUNCTUAL

Finally, practice being punctual. Habitually arriving late shows an unorganized life and disrespect of others' time. If a meeting involves 10 people and starts 30 minutes late, you have wasted 300 minutes (five hours!).

Timeliness strengthens relationships and honors God. Jesus said, *"Let your 'yes' be 'yes'"* (Matthew 5:37), which includes time commitments. Do you arrive at church on time? Can people expect you to arrive when you say you will?

It takes discipline to be on time. So many things can happen which you didn't anticipate. Once I had a sign in my office, "The only way to consistently be on time is to plan to be early." It's true and it helped me. (If you arrive on time and the meeting starts late, get out your book and seize the moment by reading!)

Let's review the steps to effective time management.

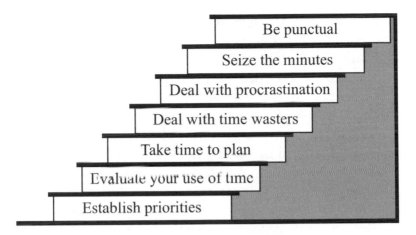

CONCLUSION

You can learn to effectively manage your time. Don't be discouraged about the past. The good news is that you have available in the future all the time you need, as you learn to use it wisely. Your life can literally be transformed, as you do the assignments and reflect on this lesson. Let me warn you, these assignments are tough! But they are guaranteed to produce results. You choose whether to simply read a nice chapter in a book or to really change. If you are ready for change, tackle the assignments. Hundreds of people have done them, and so can you!

Don't expect everything to change overnight. It will take time to break your habits and develop new ones. (It takes 21 successive days of repetition to develop a habit.) This is a journey and it begins now. The future arrives a minute at a time!

ACTION ASSIGNMENT
Part one (two weeks)

1. Photocopy the "Time Evaluation Chart" in *Appendix B*. Make <u>four copies</u> of each page for all the action assignments. For the next two weeks use the "Time Evaluation Chart" to record how you are spending your time. Carrying it with you is best. (Alternatively, record the times at the end of each day.) At the end of two weeks, review the record to find the hours you spent in the following areas. Write the number of the category in the box below, and then record each number for the totals. (Remember that each box represents 30 minutes, not one hour! There are five "night" hours that are not on your chart, don't forget them.) Divide by 14 to get the average number of hours per day. If fewer days apply, divide by the number of days (for example working days, or church attendance.) Some of the categories may not apply to you. If you are a pastor or full time church worker, you may want to further break down your hours into areas such as visitation, counseling, sermon preparation, and reading.

ACTIVITY	TOTAL HOURS (TWO WEEKS)	AVG. HOURS/DAY
1. Sleeping		
2. Eating/personal		
(Includes bathing, etc)		
3. Devotional time with God		
4. Work		
5. Travel	_____ /10 or12	
6. Cooking/meal preparation		
7. Ministry related time		
8. Church attendance		
9. Time with children	/2	
10. Time with spouse		
11. TV viewing		
12. Reading		
13. Physical exercise		
14. Others:_____		
15. _____		
Total hours		
Unaccounted for		

(Subtract total hours from 336 hours)

2. Evaluate the results:
   a. What were the greatest surprises from your evaluation?

b. Complete the chart below on all the areas that apply to you. Check your goals to see what you aimed to do in each area.

c. What are your most significant "time wasters?"

AREA	SPENDING TOO LITTLE TIME	ENOUGH TIME	TOO MUCH TIME
Personal devotions			
Time with spouse			
Time with children			
Time in ministry			
Time in physical exercise			
Sleep			
Time spent planning			

1.

2.

3.

d. What things are not helping you accomplish your goals and you need to say "no?"
1.

2.

3.

e. What things do you need to spend more time doing that will help you reach your goals and develop your full potential for Christ?
1.

2.

3.

ACTION ASSIGNMENT
Part two (One week)

1. Make a "procrastination list" below. List the five tasks that you know you need to do, but keep putting off. (These are not daily tasks like prayer, but jobs that you have delayed for some time.) In column two, prioritize them from one to five (one is most important and should be completed first. In column three, write the date and time that you will start on that task. In column four, mark when the task is completed.

	Task	Priority	Date/time	Completed
1.				
2.				
3.				
4.				
5.				

2. Take at least one hour to plan a weekly schedule. At the top of the "Time Evaluation Chart" write: "Weekly Plan." Use it to plan an entire week, writing down how you want to use every hour of your day. In many cases an activity will take several hours. Write the activity in the appropriate time slot, and draw an arrow to the time it is finished. Use your goals as you do this exercise to make sure that you are accomplishing them. Schedule a daily time for planning and put the procrastination items from #1 in your plan.

3. Track your actual usage of time as you did in the previous assignment, but for only one week. Use the "Time Evaluation Chart" and follow your plan.

4. Evaluate what happened compared with what you planned. Answer the following questions:
   a. What areas of your plan were the most difficult to accomplish?

   b. In these areas, do you need to put more effort into doing what you planned or do you need to adjust your plan to be more realistic? (You may have different answers for each of the areas identified in (a) above.)

5. Develop a "to do" list to assist in your planning. Put several categories (Personal, Family, work, church.) List what you need to do in each category. As you plan your daily/weekly schedule look at this list and determine which are priorities and must be done first. When you think of other things that you should do, add them to your list. Keep the list with you.

Mark here when you have made your "to do" list. _____

Congratulations! You are on your way to developing your full potential in Christ and accomplishing much more for His glory. Remember, change takes time. Keep working on the area of time management, and you will rise far above the ordinary!

Chapter Six
THE LEADER AND PRIORITIES

Pastor Richard looked exhausted. It had been a long day. He had planned to work on his sermon, but in the office he found people waiting to see him. After meeting with them he discovered that the electric bill for the church had not been paid, so he went to town to pay the bill. While in town he learned that a church member had been admitted to the hospital, so he hurried to see her before the end of visiting hours. He picked up the mail, and found several letters that needed a reply. When he got back to the office, he spent time answering them. Before he knew it, people were arriving for the Bible Study. He hurriedly scribbled his thoughts on paper and led the Bible Study.

After the Bible Study one of the men shared with him about a family problem, so he spent an hour with that family. As he walked home, he remembered that he had not yet prepared his sermon! He prayed quickly, asking God for divine intervention and hoping that like last week he would get a sudden inspiration before sleeping!

What is the cure for Pastor Richard's exhaustion? Like many pastors, he cannot be accused of being lazy. He is always busy, and has more things to do than can be accomplished. As a result, he frequently misses appointments or arrives late. He desperately needs help in establishing and living with priorities, so that he can be more effective with his time. Pastor Richard was busy, but not effective.

How do you decide what to do in life? How do you differentiate between the good and the best? Who determines what fills your calendar? These are questions of priorities and will be addressed in this chapter. Effective leaders have learned how to live by their priorities as a critical element of good time management.

Jesus is the best example of a leader who lived by priorities. He had a keen sense of what was most important at all times. He had time for prayer and ministry to people. At times He withdrew from the crowds, and at other times mixed freely with people. He never seemed rushed or behind schedule. He strode confidently towards His purpose at all times.

Consider again what Jesus said, *"But seek first his kingdom and his righteousness, and all these things will be given to you as well."* (Matthew 6:33) This well known verse is a verse about priorities. It teaches several "priority principles."

- PRIORITIES MUST BE KNOWN

Jesus teaches us in this verse what our priorities should be. Before we can do the will of God, we must know His priorities for us. Some things are of primary importance; others are secondary.

- PRIORITIES MUST BE SOUGHT

Jesus said, *"Seek first."* A life with proper priorities never simply happens. Keeping our priorities in focus takes deliberate effort. This requires seeking, the right priorities, and keeping our life focused on our priorities.

- PRIORITIES BRING RESULTS

Jesus says in this verse that when our top priority is truly number one, other good things follow. *"All these things will be given to you as well."* The opposite is also true: if we focus on number two things, we'll never get the number one things. For example, many people have succeeded in business but failed in their families. Their priorities weren't right, and they suffered for it.

With this foundation let's now look at the three "P's" of priorities: the purpose, the principle, and the path.

THE PURPOSE OF PRIORITIES

Learning to live by priorities does at least three things for us as leaders.

PRIORITIES KEEP US FOCUSED

When we know and practice our priorities, our lives will have a clear focus. We can see clearly how to follow our vision. Without a clear focus in life, we stretch in many directions at once. An octopus, with eight legs, can move in many directions, but unless all legs are moving in the same direction he won't go very far! Many people operate like an octopus, going in several different directions without a clear focus.

How focused is your life? Are you going in ten different directions? Are you trying to be a "jack of all trades and master of none?" Effective leaders do less and less things but learn to focus on what God has gifted them to do. They have learned to live by priorities which keep them focused.

PRIORITIES KEEP US PRODUCTIVE

In a leader's life, there's a big difference between activity and accomplishment. Activity is being busy but priori-

> There are two excellent ways to fail in leadership:
> 1. Do an equally good job of everything (all things are not equally important).
> 2. Do an excellent job of the wrong thing!

ties keep us busy doing the right things. Being busy does not always mean that we are accomplishing much.

Goals give us targets for life and keep us busy; priorities help us do the right things. We can easily waste our energy doing things that are of secondary importance. Misplaced priorities always lead to missed goals. Dr. Thomas Stevenin says that one way to fail in leadership is to do "an excellent job of the wrong thing!"[39]

Hard work is required for any successful leader; however, many leaders work hard doing the wrong things! It is good to work *hard;* it is critical to work *smart.* Being productive requires clear priorities that keep the most important things first.

PRIORITIES KEEP US BALANCED

We may have learned to focus and to be productive, but find that we are out of balance. While succeeding in ministry, we fail in our personal lives. We have a great budget in the office, but do not have one at home. We need balance. Well-established priorities are the key.

THE PRINCIPLE OF PRIORITIES

Pareto, an Italian economist, conceived the principle known as the "Pareto principle" or the "20/80" principle. His studies concluded that as a general rule 20% of the peo-

---

[39] Thomas J. Stevenin, *People Power: Tapping the Spirit of Quality Performance & Service in Your Organization* (Chicago: Northfield Publishing, 1996) p. 140.

ple controlled 80% of the wealth. This principle applies not only in economics but in many areas of life. Note these examples.

Work   20% of the people do 80% of the work.
Finances   20% of the people give 80% of the money.
Growth   20% of the people bring 80% of the growth.
Leadership   20% of the people make 80% of the decisions.
Products   20% of the products make 80% of the profit.
Time   20% of your time brings 80% of the results.
Reading   20% of the book gives 80% of the content.

Maxwell applies the Pareto Principle to priorities in this way: *20% of your priorities will give you 80% of your production, if you spend your time, energy, money, and personnel on the top 20% of your priorities.* So, when we truly know our top priorities and focus on them, our results will greatly increase.

In other words if you list your top 10 priorities in their order of importance and focus on the top two, you should achieve 80% of your goals. Conversely, if you work very hard on the other eight activities, you will only get a 20% return. This is illustrated in the following chart:

The Pareto Principle

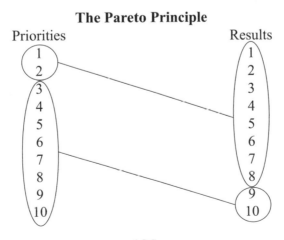

The principle is very simple, but raises the obvious question, "What should my priorities be?" and "How can I focus on the top 20 percent?" We will answer these questions by looking at "the path to priorities."

THE PATH TO PRIORITIES

CHOOSING PRIORITIES (THREE "R'S")

The first step towards putting the Pareto Principle into effect is to choose our priorities. Maxwell suggests three "R's" to help in this process.

1. Requirement

First, look at what is required of you. For your priorities at work, look at your job description. Certain things are required. If you are a pastor, ask yourself, "What do I have to do that no one else except me can do?" This work cannot be delegated to anyone else. Whether or not you enjoy it; you have to do it.

2. Return (results)

Second, ask yourself, "What things bring the greatest return to my organization?" Look objectively at the vision and goals, and ask what you do that gives the greatest benefit to the organization. Certain activities really help the church or organization to grow; other things produce very little.

3. Reward

The final area deals with your own enjoyment of what you do, and answers the question, "What gives me the greatest satisfaction?" What do you really like doing in your job? What puts a spark in your eyes?

When you answer these questions you can identify your priorities. If something shows up in all three areas, you are

126

in good shape. That action should be a high priority for you. If you get many different answers, you are in trouble! If something is required of you, but doesn't bring a high return, see that it is delegated, or the time reduced as much as possible. If something brings a high return, but is not required or enjoyed by you, consider whether you are in the right place! If something is rewarding and you love to do it, but it is not required and doesn't help the organization, you need to reduce the time you spend on that item. For example, when I was the director of a ministry to leaders, I looked at these three "R's" and discovered that I loved to do administration, but it didn't produce great returns for the organization. I needed to adjust my schedule to spend less time on administration.

Let me illustrate how this process works with my own example. As senior pastor of a large church, here's what my "Three R's" chart looked like:

Requirements. My major requirements: Providing vision and direction (leadership), preaching, and developing leaders.

Return. The things which bring the greatest return: Providing leadership, teaching (preaching), writing, developing leaders and administration.

Reward. The things I most enjoy: Providing leadership, teaching, developing leaders, administration, and writing.

Notice several things that are common in these lists. Leadership (setting the vision and direction of the church), preaching (or teaching), and developing leaders show up as three areas of priority for me. This means that I should spend 80% of my time in these areas.

Just as significant is what is not there. Counseling and visitation, for example, are not on the list. That means that I should not spend much time in those areas. They are not bad things, but if I spend large amounts of my time in these areas, the church will not grow as much. If I were the only pastor in the church, these areas would have higher priority.

Your items will be different, but mine will clarify the process. When you do it well, you should be able to identify the priorities in your work.

Stop now and do the worksheet in *Appendix C* before you continue with the next step.

CHECKING PRIORITIES

After choosing your priorities, it is time to see how closely they correspond to your life. Check your current schedule by doing a time evaluation, and examine how you make decisions.

1. Do a time evaluation

The purpose of a time evaluation for priorities is to answer the question, "How much of my time is spent in high return areas?" Find out how much you are spending on high priorities, and how much on low priorities. Look at the people you spend time with. Are they in the top 20% of your organization? Use Appendix *D* for this exercise. The recording part of this exercise is the same as when you recorded your activities for time management. This will take one week. But don't ignore it; it can change your life!

2. Look at your organizational style

Another way to check your priorities is to look at how you organize your time. How do you decide what to do today? Maxwell lists five different organizational styles...

- **Urgent**-Loud things first.

Many people decide what to do based on what is making the most noise! The department that is crying receives the attention. The church member who insists on seeing you gets the appointment. This is living by the old saying, "The squeaky wheel gets the grease."

- **Unpleasant**-Hard things first.

Some people look at the things to be done and choose the most difficult or unpleasant things first. Their goal is to get the least desirable activities out of the way, and enjoy the rest of the day! Unfortunately, the unpleasant tasks may not always be the most important ones.

- **Unfinished**-Last things first.

Others plan their schedule by doing first what was left undone the previous day. This is questionable planning. If an item was of little importance yesterday, it is likely of little importance today. If you have a good vision and goals, some things on your "to do list" will never get done!

- **Unfulfilling**-Dull things first.

Other people look at their list, and decide to do the dull things first. They hope to finish the boring work and then do what is enjoyable.

- **Ultimate**-First things first.

When you organize your schedule with first things first, you are truly living out your priorities. Whether they are dull or hard, making noise or not, you do what is most important first. This should always be your goal.

Which of these styles best describes your decision-making? Most likely you naturally follow one of these patterns. Identifying your style will help you know what you need to change.

CHANGING PRIORITIES

It's not difficult to choose our priorities or to check them, but now comes the difficult part, changing! Change is not pleasant, but without change we'll never grow. Maxwell says, People change only when they <u>hurt</u> enough to <u>have</u> to! They <u>receive</u> enough that they are <u>able</u> to![40]

I don't know how badly you are hurting, but my goal is to help you learn enough that you want to change and give you enough that you are able to change! There are two major areas that we need to look at when changing priorities: our schedule and our organization.

Prioritize your schedule

Your schedule should reflect your priorities. Four tips to prioritizing your schedule.

• Be in control of your schedule

Are you in control of your schedule, or do others determine how you spend your time? Don't answer without thinking carefully. Many people's schedules are actually controlled by others. Do you decide what to do each day, or do you allow events to unfold and determine what you do? The former US Secretary of Defense, Donald H. Rumsfeld said, "Control your own time. If you are working off the in-box that is fed to you, you are probably working on the priority of others." The "in-box" may be a paper, or an unexpected visitor or problem that arises in the course of the day.

The issue is not will my calendar be full but who will fill my calendar.

Strong leaders are always busy. The main question is whether they determine their schedule, or allow others to determine it. Maxwell quips, "The issue is not will my calendar be full but who will fill my calendar."

---

[40] John C. Maxwell, *The 17 Essential Qualities Of a Team Player* (Nashville: Thomas Nelson, 2006) p. 122.

This is tough for servant leaders! It is a paradox that I should serve others, yet retain control of my schedule. True, if I control my calendar for my selfish interests, it would not be right. However, if God has a plan for my life, and will hold me accountable, I need to be serious about controlling my schedule. When I sit at my desk and wait for people, I am a reactor, not a leader. I should plan time in my schedule for people, but not allow people to determine my schedule. I should decide when to meet them, instead of always going by their schedule.

• Be willing to say "No"

To prioritize our schedule, we have the will and courage to say "no." This is not as easy as it seems. When people come with a worthy request, it's difficult to say a firm "no." Mark Porter suggests a profound reason for this, "We may find it difficult to say no because we care too much about what people think, and not enough about the Lord's priorities for our lives."[41] Ouch! It may be painful for you to acknowledge this truth, but it will be the beginning of being set free from the demands of others. Read that quote again and ask where it applies to you!

Many times we say "yes" to many things and don't have enough time to do all the things we promised to do. We end up "stealing" time from our family or sleep to meet our commitments. Or we end up doing a half-hearted job instead of our best. Speaker and consultant Merrill Douglass offers wise advice, "For most people, saying yes is easy; deciding when is tough. Just remember, you'll never run out of work, but you'll often run out of time. Therefore, never agree to take on a job without first considering when you will be able to do it."[42]

---

[41] Porter, *The Time of your Life*, 11.

[42] Merrill Douglass, *Success Secrets* (Colorado Springs: Honor Books, 1997) p. 45.

If you would learn to succeed at maintaining priorities in your schedule, you must learn to say "no!"

• **Determine to choose the best over the good**
Oswald Chambers, in his classic book My Utmost for His Highest, wrote, "Very few of us would debate over what is filthy, evil, and wrong, but we do debate over what is good. It is the good that opposes the best." He's right on target. The choices I face each day are not whether to take a drink at a bar or witness about Christ. That would be an easy decision. My tough choice might be whether to spend time writing a chapter in a book that will benefit many or preparing a message that will also benefit many! My struggle is choosing the best over the good.

This is the struggle Mary and Martha had. They had two choices: cooking for Jesus, and listening to Jesus. Both were good. In fact, if Jesus was coming to my house I would be honored to cook for him! But for that time, listening to Jesus was the best choice!

You can't do everything that is good. You simply won't have enough time. Therefore, you must be willing to let some things remain undone, or delegate them. You must release some things, if you are going to stick to your priorities. Consider these quotes:

"God will only move me to bigger things if I let go of some of the little things!" -Bruce Wilkinson

"The art of being wise is the art of knowing what to overlook." -William James

"Don't be afraid to give up the good to go for the great." -Kenny Rogers

- **Plan your schedule based on priorities**

Stephen Covey in his book *The 7 Habits of Highly Effective People*, writes, "The key is not to prioritize what's on your schedule, but to schedule your priorities."[43]

If you would succeed in living by your priorities, you must put them in your schedule. Start determining your schedule based on priorities.

Three steps to planning with priorities.

Step 1: Decide what needs to be done

Look at your commitments. What have you committed yourself to do? What is required? This means you are choosing the best over the good.

Maxwell suggests dividing tasks into the following categories:

- High importance/high urgency - do it first
- High importance/low urgency - set deadlines and work into routine
- Low importance/High urgency - delegate if possible
- Low importance/low urgency - delegate or delete

Step 2: Decide how long it should take

Once you have concluded that something should be done, decide how much time it should take. If it is a meeting, how many hours should it take? If it is to prepare a message, how much time do you need to prepare? When deciding how long something should take, use your best judgment. Look at the past, and see how long it has taken before. Push yourself to complete it quickly, but be careful of unrealistic time estimates.

For example here are some of the tasks that are on my calendar and the time assigned to them:

---

[43] Steven Covey, *The 7 Habits of Highly Effective People* (New York: Simon & Schuster, 1989) p. 161.

Task	Time
1. Look at issues raised at the church council meeting	1:30
2. Prepare for a leaders' seminar	1:00
3. Meet with youth leader	1:00
4. Evaluate the Sunday service	1:00
5. Writing	3:00
6. Administration	2:00
7. Meet with pastors	3:00
8. Prepare for pastor's meeting	0:30
9. Reply to letters	0:30
10. Meeting with church council	2:00
11. Prepare for council meeting	1:00
12. Clear inbox and prepare schedule for week	1:00
13. Meet with administrator	1:00
14. Review committee reports	1:00
15. Prepare sermon for Sunday service	4:00

Step 3: Decide when you will do it

The final step is to simply decide when you will do the task, and put it in your calendar. Assign it to the right day or hour. Look at your list of tasks like mine above, and note any deadline. Then look for the best time to complete the task. As you do this, keep in mind your own preferences and working rhythms. I think best in the morning, and move administrative items, meetings, and appointments to the afternoon. Find out what times work best for you to do certain tasks.

The key here is to fill your calendar with the things you have determined are your priorities. Keep in mind that you also need to schedule times to meet with people. Determine when you will have time available to meet with them, and stick to this as much as possible.

This process can be used on a daily, weekly, or monthly basis. You can start with a simple plan of spending 10 minutes every morning to prioritize your day and plan your schedule. When you are comfortable with this, try to do a week at a time and then move towards a monthly time of planning.

Warning: This process is not easy, but it will change your life!

Prioritize your organization

The principle of priorities applies to individuals and organizations. Look at your organization and determine the priorities.

Before you can determine priorities, you must know your purpose of existence and what you value most. This is most often stated in your "Statement of Vision," "Core Values," or "Statement of Purpose." If you have not yet determined your purpose for existence, take the time to clarify this. Once your purpose or vision is clear, you can evaluate and prioritize the whole organization by looking at three different areas.

• Prioritize the programs

List all the things you do in your organization. (This can be teaching, prayer, evangelism, worship, providing materials, selling books, and the like.) How do you determine your priorities? Ask yourself, "Which bring the greatest return to our organization?" Rate the top three in that column, starting with the greatest return. Ask the following questions. "Which are closest to the heart of the people?" "Which are closest to the heart of the pastor?" "Which are closest to the heart of God?" (You are likely biased on this one, but try your best!) Use this chart as an example of how it might look. Each column should have three numbers only giving the top three priorities from the perspective of the column heading.

	Greatest return to the organization	Closest to the heart of people	Closest to the heart of the pastor/top leader	Closest to the heart of God
1. Small Groups	2	2	3	3
2. Lunch meetings		3		
3. Bible Study	3		2	
4. Youth meeting				
5. Evangelism	1		1	2
6. Worship		1		1

After you have done this exercise, review the results. Look particularly for any program with numbers in all or most of the spaces across the columns. This will indicate a high priority area. In our example, this would include small groups and evangelism. The next highest are Bible Study and worship. It's more difficult to evaluate these, particularly since "God" puts highest priority on worship! In a case like this, you need to ask yourself, "Are my priorities in line with God's priorities?" If not, serious prayer and repentance are needed!

When the pastor has a high priority in an area that the people don't, it usually indicates a need to share the vision with the people. If the people highly value an area that the pastor doesn't, something needs to change. Maybe the pastor is in the wrong church, and should change! If the program is not significantly bringing a good return to the church, but is valued by the people (like lunch hour meetings in our example), the pastor needs to wisely continue it, but not commit key people or resources.

As you work through your own scenario using the instructions in *Appendix E*, you should be able to clearly determine the priorities of your church. An individual or a group can do this.

- **Prioritize the people**
   Next, look at the people in your organization. For each key leader, fill the "Three R's" chart to determine what

he/she should be doing. This is especially crucial for the senior pastor. Look also at the lay people. List the top leaders in your church/organization, and their spiritual gifts. Also list the ministry in which they are involved. Does the ministry line up with the gift? Do you have key leaders in priority ministries? If not, start making the necessary changes. Use *Appendix F* to help complete this exercise.

- **Prioritize the Money**
Now that you have looked at your programs and people, take a look at the budget. Look at the programs you have already evaluated and examine how much money is going towards each one. (For this exercise you don't need to examine administrative expenses (salary, office expenses, etc.) Ask yourself if 80% of the budget is going to the top 20% of the programs? Are you putting the best resources where it will make the most difference? What changes do you need to make? Use *Appendix F* to complete this exercise.

This chapter is not easy to apply, but it can radically change the way you serve God. Remember that establishing and maintaining priorities is a journey, not an event. The sooner you get started, the further you will go! Start today, make some changes, keep reviewing, adjusting, and making the tough choices. Don't get discouraged when you fail. Get up and try again! And remember, "The main thing is to keep the main thing the main thing!"

ACTION ASSIGNMENT

Use Appendix C, D, E, and F to put this lesson into practice.

Part Two: Leading Others

"He that thinketh he leadeth and hath no one following him is only taking a walk!"

-Rev. John Maxwell

"Leaders of Christian enterprises tend to be spiritually qualified but organizationally illiterate. The problem is, leadership requires both the head and the heart."

-Hans Finzel

Chapter Seven
THE LEADER
AND PEOPLE SKILLS

After a long day, I finished teaching the Bible study, locked the church and headed home, eager to eat with my family. Opening the door, instead of seeing my children I found the house full of church members saying "surprise!" My wife, Loice, had succeeded in planning a surprise birthday party for me.

An even bigger surprise came when Loice invited different people to share something that they appreciated about me. I have long forgotten most of what was said, but I will never forget the voice of Faith, a shy young girl, and the leadership lesson she taught me when she said, "I like the way he smiles at me."

Her words penetrated deeply into my mind. *Smiling? I didn't even know I smiled. What about my great sermons and teachings and the other things I did as a pastor? Didn't she care about all those things? How can a smile make that much difference?*
I have often reflected on the lesson Faith taught me that night: that one of the most important skills that a leader

needs is the ability to relate well with people. Leaders are in the people business and must continually develop their ability to work well with others. We can be called, anointed, and qualified, but unless we work well with people we won't succeed as leaders. Remember that leadership is influence and the only power we have to influence people is when they choose to follow us. Effective people skills will cause people to desire to follow our leadership. This chapter will focus on developing skills in relating to people. Get ready for some surprises about what will make you more effective as a leader. Each of us has the potential to develop these skills to a higher degree in our life.

A foundational concept for developing people skills comes from Jesus' words: *"so in everything, do to others what you would have them do to you..."* (Matthew 7:12) This is not only the "golden rule" of life, but the "golden rule" of leadership. Our goal must be to treat others as nicely, politely, and considerately as we wish to be treated.

Note that it does not say to do to others *what* they do to you, but what you *would have them* do to you. Effective people skills means treating others the way we would like to be treated, which is usually better than people treat us.

Before we look at eight specific skills that will draw others to us, let's examine three core principles about people skills.

PRINCIPLE ONE: THE WAY WE RELATE TO PEOPLE EITHER ATTRACTS THEM TO US OR REPELS THEM

People will follow someone that attracts them. Some people are like magnets, they attract others to them. Other leaders are like porcupines, whenever you get close they cause pain!

Think about a close friend, someone with whom you enjoy fellowship. Why do you enjoy being around them?

Take a moment to identify several reasons you like to be with them.

What reasons did you think about? I doubt if you listed their degrees or certificates, the way they look or how much money they have. You likely thought of their love for you, their humor, the way they encourage you, their positive attitude, or similar things. Those are the things that draw us to others.

To be effective as leaders, we need to attract people. Leadership is influence, but we cannot influence those who do not follow us. We need to be the kind of people that others respect and desire to follow. Many times, even unconsciously, our character and actions drive people away rather than drawing them to us. We need to learn people skills. Our goal is not to be people-pleasers, bending to their every whim, but to influence them to become more like Jesus. We must be careful to practice people skills, not to manipulate others but to strengthen them.

PRINCIPLE TWO: EVERY ENCOUNTER WITH A PERSON REFLECTS CHRIST AND OUR ORGANIZATION

When meeting people our goal should be that they have a positive experience with us and with our church or organization. As a Christian leader I represent Christ and my organization/church in every encounter with people.

When someone walks in the door or talks to me on the phone or contacts me by email, they don't meet my "organization," they have an encounter with me. Every contact either positively or negatively impacts them and their attitude towards my organization. My words, expression, language, and attitude all communicate something to others. The same is true for people you meet. Your organization or church is not an institution— it is people. When potential members come to visit they do not meet the "church," they meet you. The way you interact with them will influence them to stay or to leave.

141

PRINCIPLE THREE: LEADERS ARE IN THE "PEOPLE BUSINESS"

People are our business. Everything we do relates to people. Even in our administrative tasks we are in some way relating to people. As leaders it is easy to think that our business is talking, counseling, casting vision, building an organization, etc. Remember that our business is building people, and how we relate to them makes a great difference.

People will follow us based primarily on their desire to do so, not based on our theology, doctrine or who sits on our board of directors. The primary difference between churches is not theology, but the way people are treated and the atmosphere created by the leader. This is not to ignore doctrinal or administrative differences, but most people do not choose a church based on theology. Remember, Faith taught me that my smile touched her more than my doctrine.

EIGHT KEYS OF EFFECTIVE PEOPLE SKILLS

Let's turn our attention to what we can do to build strong relationships with people. Some of the eight keys are matters of the heart that flow out of our relationship with Jesus; others are skills that can be mastered with effort.

1. A GENUINE LOVE FOR PEOPLE

Without genuine love for people it is impossible to be an effective Christian leader. This is the most important principle of being a leader others will want to follow. The common saying is true: "People do not care how much you know until they know how much you care."

Jesus said that the second greatest commandment after the one to love our God is to *"Love your neighbor as yourself."* (Matthew 22:39) This is God's number two concern for each of us, to love others. Christian leaders must have a primary motivation of love as they serve people.

A genuine love for people provides "warmth" in our relationship. Everyone wants to be loved and will follow a person they believe loves them. They take challenges and even rebukes from a person who loves them. This love is not something we can manufacture or fake; it must come from our hearts.

What happens when a leader loves his/her people? Peter tells us, *"above all, love each other deeply, because loves covers over a multitude of sins."* (1 Peter 4:8) A leader that loves his people can make many mistakes and still people will follow him. If you don't genuinely love people, make one mistake and that will be the end of your ability to lead!

What are some characteristics of genuine love?

Love Focuses on Others

Paul instructs us, *"Each of you should look not only to your own interest, but also to the interests of others."* (Philippians 2:4) *Self* focuses on me; *love* focuses on you!

We all love ourselves. We think our story is the most important and our children are the most special. Christ-like love enables us to look beyond ourselves and focus on others. Effective leaders love people and want to hear their stories, look at their pictures and to know what God is doing in their lives. They recognize that talking about themselves will never attract others!

Love Gives

Love is not self-seeking (1 Corinthians 13:5) but looks to give to the other person. Genuine love is not seeking what we will get out of the relationship, but what we can give to others to build them up. Love gives time, money, encouragement, and support to others. Giving reflects the love of God. *"God so loved the world that he gave."* (John 3:16)

How can we develop a love for others? Love is not a skill to be practiced, but an attitude to be fostered. We

143

must get closer to the heart of God and ask Him to transform our hearts to be like His heart. We should confess
selfishness and pride and ask His love to flow through us,
making a conscious effort to focus on others in conversation. As we focus on the needs of others we find our love
beginning to grow.

While there are no easy steps, learning to know more
about people often helps in loving them. Understanding
their background, temperament and gifts will go a long way
to really know them. If you are having a difficult time loving a certain person, take time to listen to their story. Find
out their experiences in life. You may learn something
about them that will enable you to understand them and
help you love them from your heart.

2. GENUINE HUMILITY

A second character trait of a leader who is effective with
people is genuine humility. Proud leaders cannot expect
others to follow them willingly. Followers may respect their
position but not their disposition! Even God doesn't want to
be around proud people! Peter tells us, *"God opposes the
proud, but gives grace to the humble."* (1 Peter 5:5)

A humble leader attracts others to himself because he is
genuine. Humble people don't put on a mask and pretend
to be what they are not. Humble people can laugh at themselves and don't seek to be on top all the time.

Genuine humility will be shown in three ways:

Admitting Mistakes

A humble person can admit his/her mistakes. I fail, you
fail, and we all fail in some areas. John reminds us, *"If we
claim to be without sin we deceive ourselves and the truth is
not in us."* (1 John 1:8) Can you admit your mistakes to your
wife? Can you confess them to the church? If you have
never confessed wrong to those that follow you, your abili-

ty to lead is weakened! They can see your mistakes. The only issue is whether or not you will admit them.

A Willingness to be Corrected

What is your response when someone tries to correct you? Do you even allow others to correct you? Do you become defensive and give excuses? Can you accept criticism and look to find if there is truth in it before you throw it away? The writer of Proverbs says, *"...Whoever loves discipline loves knowledge, but he who hates correction is stupid."* (Proverbs 12:1) If we are right, we need not fear criticism. If we are not right, we should be grateful to receive correction.

A Desire to Serve Others

Humility is expressed in service to others. Are we willing to serve, or do we want to be the "big man?" Jesus served and calls us to follow in His steps. He said, *"Even the Son of Man did not come to be served but to serve and give his life a ransom for many."* (Mark 10:45)

We tend to think that serving others will lessen their respect for us but the opposite is true. When the people talked to Rehoboam they asked him what kind of leader he would be. After listening to the young advisors the elders said profound words to the king, *"If today you will be a servant to these people and serve them and give them a favorable answer, they will always be your servants."* (1 Kings 12:7) The history of Israel would have been very different if Rehoboam would had agreed to serve the people.

The heart of a servant is attractive. The higher your position, the more important this principle becomes. Serve others, give your life to them and they will be attracted to you. Demanding positions, titles and power do not impress people. They are not drawn to you because of your nice suit and tie. But *genuine* humility will draw them like a magnet.

Pretense of humility will never work. People will quickly see through your hypocrisy.

How can we develop in this area of humility? This is a matter of the heart and spiritual growth, but several actions can help:

- **Memorize scriptures dealing with pride/humility**

  There is nothing like the Word of God to change us and to help us realize how much God hates pride. (See Proverbs 6:16,17; 1 Corinthians 4:7; 1 Peter 5:5,6; and Romans 12:3)

- **Commit yourself to admit your mistakes**

  Make a commitment that when you realize that you have made a mistake you will admit it. Learn to say, "I was wrong." These are not easy words to say but remember what John says, *"If we claim to be without sin, we deceive ourselves and the truth is not in us. If we confess our sins, he is faithful and just and will forgive us our sins and purify us from all unrighteousness. If we claim we have not sinned, we make him out to be a liar and his word has no place in our lives."* (1 John 1:8-10)

- **Be accountable to someone in your life**

  Accountability to someone can help keep leaders humble. This person could be a spouse, a fellow pastor, or another leader, but find someone with whom you can be accountable. Share with them your weaknesses and your desire to grow, and ask them to check on you. James provides a powerful and often overlooked instruction, *"Therefore confess your sins to each other and pray for each other so that you may be healed. The prayer of a righteous man is powerful and effective."* (James 5:16)

3. GRACIOUS SPEECH

One of the key tools leaders use with others is their tongues. *"The tongue has the power of life and death, and those who love it will eat its fruit."* (Proverbs 18:21) Your tongue will literally draw people to you or send them away!

The Bible says of Jesus, *"All spoke well of him and were amazed at the gracious words that came from his lips."* (Luke 4:22) Our goal should be to be like Jesus as Peter reminds us, *"If anyone speaks, he should do it as one speaking the very words of God."*(1 Peter 4:11)

What are the characteristics of gracious speech? The first three come from Ephesians 4:29, *"Do not let any unwholesome talk come out of your mouth, but only what is helpful for building others up, according to their needs, that it may benefit those who listen."*

Gracious Speech is Controlled

"Do not let any unwholesome talk come out of your mouth..." (Ephesians 4:29) We must learn to control our tongues. A tongue out of control is not a Christ-like tongue. We have to stop unwholesome talk: lies, gossip, slander, exaggerations, flattery, and other sins of the tongue. Although it is difficult, a leader must control his tongue. Our ears are not made to shut, but our mouth can open and close!

Gracious Speech is Helpful

"helpful for building others up...that it may benefit those who listen..." (Ephesians 4:29) All speech should be helpful for others. It should build, not destroy. *Every* word should be a blessing to the listeners. If not, it is not gracious and godly speech.

Gracious Speech Focuses on the Needs of the Other

"according to their needs." (Ephesians 4:29) We have already seen that one expression of love is to focus on

147

others. We can have this focus with our tongue as well. Whatever I say should meet a need in your life. If you need encouragement, I should encourage; if you need a rebuke, I should rebuke; if correction is needed, I should give words of correction. My speech should not be a reaction to my feelings but a response to your needs.

Gracious Speech Speaks the Truth

"Therefore each of you must put off falsehood and speak truthfully to his neighbor." (Ephesians 4:25) Lying is one of our most common sins of speech. Many people, including leaders, lie casually and think nothing of it. Whatever will benefit us or make us look good is acceptable whether or not it is true. Consider these verses:

Proverbs 12:19, *"Truthful lips endure forever, but a lying tongue lasts only a moment."*

Proverbs 12:22, *"The Lord detests lying lips, but he delights in men who are truthful."*

Matthew 5:37, *"Let your 'yes' be 'yes' and your 'no,' 'no'; anything beyond this comes from the evil one."*

To be effective in leading people nothing is more important than your word. When you say you will be there, be there! When you say you will pray for someone, pray for them! When you promise to give, give! When you make a pledge to bring something, bring it! When you give a report of the meeting, don't exaggerate!

In confrontation it is often difficult to stick with the truth. It is easier to "beat around the bush," use vague language, and fail to get to the point.

Gracious Speech is Spoken in Love

"Instead, speaking the truth in love..." (Ephesians 4:15) Truth should be tempered with love. Whatever we say should be communicated with love to the other person. This is especially crucial in speaking something that the other person

148

may have difficulty receiving such as a correction or rebuke. We must make sure that we are speaking the truth in love.

Gracious Speech is Positive

Our speech should always be positive. Proverbs 16:24 says, *"Pleasant words are a honeycomb, sweet to the soul and healing to the bones."* This doesn't mean that everything we say must be pleasing to the other person but our speech should have an overall positive tone. Focus on the good, emphasize the positive. Encourage the good you see in people. Compliment them for a job well done. Thank them for the way they have given.

Too many leaders are in the habit of being negative! They are fault finders, regularly criticizing, and chastising. Change that habit! It drains life from others. Start focusing on the positive.

Gracious Speech Uses Kind Words

Another characteristic of the gracious words that Jesus used is that they are kind. Consider these verses from Proverbs:

Proverbs 12:18, *"Reckless words pierce like a sword, but the tongue of the wise brings healing."*

Proverbs 12:25, *"An anxious heart weighs a man down, but a kind word cheers him up."*

Our speech should use words that bring healing and lift people. Our tongues should be skilled in using 'kind' words.

Three underutilized "kind" words.

• **"Please"**

Be generous with this word. It changes demands to requests. "Could you please send this letter?" sounds so much better than "Take this letter for me... and do it quickly!"

- **"Thank you"**

These are two words that cannot be used too often. We all like to be thanked. Saying "Thank You" shows appreciation and values people. Thank the person who sells you groceries, cooks your food, sweeps the floor, or arranges the chairs. Thank your spouse for the 'small' things they do, and thank your children when they serve you. To you I say "Thank you for reading this book." If you didn't read it, my writing would be wasted!

- **"I'm Sorry"**

"I'm sorry" should be frequently used. Make sure it is a sincere apology, not a casual remark. Leaders sometimes must apologize even when they are not the one directly responsible for the mistake. If it occurred under your leadership, accept responsibility and ask for forgiveness. For example, your secretary might have made a mistake in the bulletin. Apologize without making the secretary look bad. You can say, "I'm sorry for the mistake in the bulletin."

To develop people skills, these words must become a regular part of your vocabulary. Use them until they become a habit. If you did not grow up speaking this way, it might be difficult to change, but you can learn to use these words. And you can teach your children so that they will learn to use them naturally as they grow.

Gracious Speech is Sometimes Silent!

Sometimes gracious speech is silent! Ecclesiastes 3:7 cautions, *"There is a time to be silent and a time to speak."* We can avoid much damage by simply keeping quiet, especially when we have nothing good to say. For many, the first step to having gracious talk is simply to talk less! Not saying wrong things about people only requires silence.

4. A POSITIVE BELIEF IN PEOPLE

Leaders recognize a powerful principle: <u>People live up to our expectation of them.</u> If a leader believes that someone can do something and communicates that to them they will do their best to live up to that expectation. If we tell them that they will fail, they likely will. Our expectation of people greatly affects our ability to lead them. People love to follow a person that believes in them, affirms them, and builds them up. Give people opportunities to be successful and encourage them in it. They'll blossom in their own performance, and they'll think you're a great leader!

Do you focus on people's strengths or weaknesses? Do you see the best or the worst in people? Do you see them for what they are or for what they can become?

A positive belief in people is expressed through affirmation and encouragement. *"Therefore encourage one other and build each other up, just as in fact you are doing."* (1 Thessalonians 5:11) An effective leader will affirm and encourage people.

When I think about the people that I love to be around I think of one of my dearest friends. He is a great encourager and whenever I am around him he affirms me and builds me up. I'll travel a long way just to be with him. Everyone loves to be around people who believe in them.

Our belief in people will be expressed in our actions and words. A small note can change a life. We can all learn the art of affirmation and encouragement. Give people 20 words of encouragement for every word of criticism. People will not thrive under criticism. Yet, many pastors and leaders continually try to beat and berate their people into obedience. Our view of people can be changed with concentrated effort to see the positive. Make a habit of seeing the best in people. Communicate it to them. At first it may seem artificial but it will become natural to you with practice.

How Can We Become Encouragers?

- **Make a conscious effort to look for the good in people.**

Take a paper and write down the name of a person you lead, especially someone you find it difficult to see positively. List several positive things about that person. Don't stop until you have at least 4-5 positive things about them. Focus on strengths.

- **Don't allow yourself to criticize without affirming.**

Sometimes leaders must correct or rebuke followers regarding things that need to be changed. Remember that no one enjoys being corrected. When this is needed, do it in the best possible way by using an "affirmation sandwich." An affirmation sandwich is affirmation plus correction followed by another affirmation.

Suppose your worship leader, Jim, chose a song that was not appropriate for the service. Call him and correct him with an affirmation sandwich. *"Jim, thanks so much for your commitment to lead us in worship. I appreciate all the time you put into preparation and leading. There is one concern that I have about a song that you used in the last meeting and I want to talk about that."* (Give additional correction or discussion needed.) *"Thanks, Jim, for your time. I want to say again how grateful I am for your leadership on our worship team and believe that with these improvements you will be an even greater blessing to our congregation."* Using this approach gives the best chance that your concern will be heard and that the focus of your communication remains positive.

5. CONTROL OF OUR EMOTIONS

Leaders interact with many different people in diverse situations. Some of these interactions will be positive while others will be negative. The test of our ability to relate well with people comes with the unpleasant ones; the difficult encounters, the times when someone is angry with us or accuses us of unfairness. Leaders will be tempted to respond in like manner with anger, bitterness, rudeness, etc. But Peter, the quick tempered disciple, calls us to a higher level when he says, *"do not repay evil with evil or insult with insult, but with blessing, because to this you were called."* (1 Peter 3:9) It is not easy for a leader to keep his/her emotions under control. One of the most difficult emotions to control is anger. Consider the following verses about anger:

"In your anger do not sin. Get rid of all bitterness, rage and anger, brawling and slander, along with every form of malice. Be kind and compassionate to one another, forgiving each other, just as in Christ God forgave you." (Ephesians 4:26, 31, 32)

"A gentle answer turns away wrath, but a harsh word stirs up anger." (Proverbs 15:1) Our response will either bring solution or explosion!

"A hot-tempered man stirs up dissension, but a patient man calms a quarrel." (Proverbs 15:18)

"A fool shows his annoyance at once, but a prudent man overlooks an insult." (Proverbs 12:16) When people annoy us, do we show anger? Do we change our tone of speech and begin debating with them? Or calmly overlook the insult?

"Better a patient man than a warrior, a man who controls his temper than one who takes a city." (Proverbs 16:32)

While anger is a common emotion, these verses clearly teach that it needs to be controlled. We often think or say, "He made me angry." This implies that we are not responsible for our anger; it is the fault of the other person. The Biblical position is that we are responsible for our responses. We cannot control how others treat us; however, we can control our response.

Any time you get angry you lose some trust with people. People will not follow you long if your emotions are unpredictable. They won't open up to you and admit weaknesses if they're not sure you'll respond calmly.

This does not mean that leaders can't express emotions, but they must be controlled emotions. Some emotions expressed will draw people to you. Sorrow, grief, and joy properly expressed are very attractive in a leader.

How do we learn to control our emotions? Let the Holy Spirit take control! *"The fruit of the Spirit is.....self control."* (Galatians 5:22,23) The more in control the Holy Spirit is in your life the less out of control your emotions will be. Another thing that helps here, as it does in many other areas, is confession of sin to those you have offended. When you fail, fail forward! Even your genuine confession will draw people to you, because it is a sign of humility.

6. A SMILE

A smile is a powerfully attractive action that everyone enjoys. Universally, a smile conveys love and acceptance. A smile breaks down walls, disarms enemies, and changes the atmosphere of a room. When smiling, your voice is always positive. Difficult issues, said with a smile disarm the strongest man. Practice smiling. It doesn't cost anything and when you have given one away, you still have another one! It is the most inexpensive way to improve your looks. No one is too poor to afford a smile. Reflect on these verses:

"A cheerful look brings joy to the heart..." (Proverbs 15:30)
"A man that hath friends must show himself friendly" (Proverbs 18:24, KJV)
"A happy heart makes the face cheerful." (Proverbs 15:13)

154

Christians should be cheerful, pleasant people. Smile, laugh, enjoy life! Have a good sense of humor. People love to be around a smiling person. Take a break from reading and smile at someone just to see what happens. Then make it a habit.

7. ACTIVE LISTENING

We often associate leading with speaking, and leaders need to speak to communicate vision and passion. But leading also requires good listening skills and unfortunately many leaders have not worked at developing this skill. John Maxwell relates a story in which he learned that God "needs my listening ability, not my preaching ability."[44] Everyone wants to be heard and will gravitate towards people who will listen. It is no wonder that there are hundreds of references to listening in the scripture. Consider these verses:

"Everyone should be quick to listen and slow to speak." (James 1:19) We usually don't have a problem with being quick to speak, but listening demands patience and focus on the other person. Focusing on others is a key to making people a priority! I like the way *The Message* translates James 1:19: *"Lead with your ears, follow up with your tongue, and let anger straggle along in the rear."* What a powerful image for a leader, "Lead with your ears." I put this quote on my office wall to remind me to do more listening.

"He who answers before listening that is his folly and his shame." (Proverbs 18:13)

"Listen...and be wise." (Proverbs 23:19)

How can you improve your listening skills? Recognize that it is a skill that can be developed. Work at it and it will bring great results in places you never expected. Here are three specific actions that you can implement in your next conversation with anyone that will increase your listening ability.

---

[44] Maxwell, *Be All You Can Be*, 162.

155

Actions for effective listening:
• Make eye contact
• Don't interrupt
• Ask questions to make sure you've understood

8. A GOOD ATTITUDE

People are attracted to a winning attitude! No one likes a person who always sees the negative side of life and complains about everything. If your attitude stinks, be assured that people will keep their distance from you.

Paul tells us *"Your attitude should be the same as that of Christ Jesus:"* (Philippians 2:5) What a challenge for all of us, to have the attitude that Jesus did. It was Jesus' attitude that allowed Him to give up His titles, to serve on the earth, and to give up His life for us. Jesus never complained about the struggles of His life. He faced difficulty, but did not blame others. He continually saw the best in others, and overlooked repeated offenses and attacks on His character. His attitude was remarkable, and we are called to be like Him. This indicates that we have a choice about our attitude. It is not forced on us by circumstances; rather we choose what attitude we will have.

How can you evaluate your attitude? How you look at life? Is it generally positive or negative? Do you see the sun or the clouds? Do you see the potholes or the road? Do you see that the glass is half empty or half full? Do you see the good or the bad in people?

Different personalities will tend to have a more positive or negative attitude. This has been an area of real struggle for me since my natural tendency is to see the negative side of life. I recognize that this is not the way God wants me to be, and it certainly doesn't draw others to me. By God's grace, I have worked hard to change my attitude.

How can you improve your attitude? Recognize that you have chosen your attitude and you can also choose to change it. Meditating on positive scriptures, reading positive books, and purposefully relating to positive people has made a positive difference in my life. It will take time and effort but you can make a choice today to change your attitude.

CONCLUSION

We can choose to be magnets or porcupines. These eight keys are not magic formulas, but all of them can be developed if you are willing to pay the price. It may take you a year of continual effort, but you can become a person that people are attracted to by making an effort to practice these eight keys. I encourage you to study the book of Proverbs, as it is full of tips on relating well with other people. Take some time to go through the action assignment, evaluate yourself, and begin working on the areas that keep you from being effective in relationships. By God's grace, you can do it!

ACTION ASSIGNMENT

1. Rate yourself in each of the following people skills from 1-5 with 5 being excellent. Mark the number that applies to you. Review your notes as you do this exercise.

People Skill	1	2	3	4	5
1 A genuine love for people (shown in focusing on them and giving)					
2 Genuine humility (shown in admitting mistakes, being corrected, and serving others)					
3 Gracious speech (review points on the outline)					
4 A positive belief in people (shown in affirmation and encouragement)					
5 Control of emotions					
6 Smiling					
7 Listening					
8 A good attitude					

In which two areas are you the strongest?
1.

2.

In which two areas are you the weakest?
1.

2.

2. Choose one area in which you feel God wants you to change. Write it here. _____ Why do you need to change in this area and how will it help you as a leader?

3. What specific steps will you take to change in this area?

4. Are there people that you need to ask forgiveness in this area? Mark here when you have done this. _____

5. Find a scripture that relates to this area and memorize it. You may find one in the outline or look for one in Proverbs. Write the reference of the verse you memorized here. _____

6. Practice encouragement. Write a note of encouragement or affirmation to someone. Make sure it is all positive and will build them up. Mark here when you have delivered the note. _____

Chapter Eight
THE LEADER AND CHOOSING OTHER LEADERS

For a leader, nothing can match the joy of finding the right person for the right job. The match is perfect, the job gets done well, and everyone benefits. Sadly, every leader also knows the agony of choosing the wrong person. It is frustrating for the leader and the follower. Your success as a leader will be determined to a large degree by your success in calling and equipping the right people to work with you.

This chapter focuses on choosing the right leaders. How can you look at people and evaluate their potential to be effective leaders? All of us have had some success and some failure in this area. I have made some choices of leaders so good that I wanted to tell the whole world about them. But I have also chosen some that haven't worked out. Some have disappointed me deeply, and I want to learn from my mistakes. I have spent countless hours with our church council wrestling with issues of leadership selection.

In this chapter you will discover SEVEN things to look for when looking for a leader.

1. DETERMINE SPIRITUAL MATURITY

Before looking at other aspects of leadership ability, you need to examine a potential leader from a spiritual perspective. Is he or she spiritually qualified for the position? In some cases, such as elders and deacons, we have direct Biblical directives about the qualifications (See 1 Timothy 3:1-13; Titus 1:5-9). In other cases, you must simply judge the level of a person's spiritual maturity. There are several areas to examine:

Character

Think about the person's character. Character involves honesty, integrity, truthfulness, and consistency. Without a solid character, a leader will never develop, and will only bring grief to your church. No amount of skill or natural ability can replace character in a person's life. Character is developed in the furnace of life and unfortunately there are no shortcuts. You can teach character qualities to a prospective leader *if* they are teachable and willing to learn. But when you see glaring character deficiencies in someone's life, give God time to shape them more before calling them to leadership.

Look carefully at a person's life for clues about his character. Notice if the person takes responsibility for actions and mistakes, or blames other people. Look for unfulfilled promises. Does the person consistently do what he promises, or fail to honor his word? Does he have a spirit of humility and a willingness to be corrected? Does he tithe faithfully? Does he have a servant's heart? Look at his family life. The way that he leads at home will be the way that he leads in the church. If his wife is not happy, don't expect the church members to be happy with his leadership!

Growth

How has the person grown in his faith? Is he taking advantage of growth opportunities such as seminars, Bible studies, and discipleship courses? Is he praying? Learning

161

the Word? A leader should be eager and willing to grow by availing himself of any opportunity to grow. I remember one of my first contacts with a brother in our church who became an elder and then a pastor. I saw him at a two-week Bible school learning the Word at his own expense and time. He was committed to grow, and God was working in his life. LEADERS MUST BE GROWING. This does not imply a high academic level or a theological degree, but leaders must be moving forward in their spiritual growth.

Response to Authority

Look at the potential leader's response to authority. Is this person willing to be corrected? How does he speak about other leaders? Is he accountable to you? For example, when he is going to miss a service, does he tell you in advance? This is a good sign that he recognizes authority.

Ben Franklin said, "He who cannot obey cannot command." This simply means that those who do not respect and submit to authority cannot lead others well.

Spiritual Gift

What is the person's spiritual gift? It is crucial that before you put someone in a leadership position you have evaluated his spiritual gift(s). Putting a person in a position in which he is not gifted will only lead to frustration.

To say that leaders should be spiritually mature does not mean that they must be perfect. However, leaders must be ahead of their followers and be more spiritually mature than the others. The level of maturity required will depend on the position for which you are considering the person, as well as the maturity of those he will lead. It is obvious that an elder requires more spiritual maturity than an usher. Similarly, in a very young church, the level of leadership may not be as high, and the expectations are not the same as in a church that has been established for 20 years.

2. EVALUATE INFLUENCE

Apart from these spiritual characteristics, the most important thing that you need to look for in a potential leader is influence. Ask, "Is this person influencing others?" Of course this needs to be positive influence! Leaders are people that are going somewhere, and are able to persuade others to follow them. There should be something happening around this person, because leaders make things happen.

For example when choosing an elder, look for someone people are already going to for advice and counsel. Look for someone who is already visiting others and building them up. They are already influencing others.

Remember the "influence questions" from chapter one? "To whom would I go if I wanted to start something in the church? To stop something? To find out what is going on?" The names that come to mind indicate leaders in your church. You will want to observe them more closely.

Maxwell suggests that after asking these questions and identifying influencers, ask several more to learn more about their leadership qualities.

- Whom do they influence? (Who follows them?)
- Who influences them? (Whom do they follow?)
- Are they gaining or losing influence? (Do they have potential or is their influence past?)

3. CHECK PEOPLE SKILLS

As a church leader you are in the "people business." Church is all about people, and leaders who will work with you should have good people skills. They will never be perfect, but they must be able to work well with people. If you have a potential leader that no one likes to be around, forget about asking him to lead! He may be very spiritual and well gifted, but to be a good leader he must have people skills. Are people attracted to them? Do they know how to talk nicely to people? Can they correct others with a smile?

4. LOOK FOR PROBLEM-SOLVING ABILITY

Potential leaders should be able to solve problems, to think through an issue and come up with a solution. Ask  yourself, "What problems have I seen this person solve?" It may be family problems, church problems, or even work related problems.

Good leaders are people who think differently than many followers. While some followers may be grumbling about the problems, leaders are trying to fix them. These followers think, "I wish they would change." The leader thinks, "What can we do to solve this problem?"

Strong leaders should give ideas that help the organization to grow. When looking for people to serve on a church council, for example, don't look for "yes" people who agree with everything you want to say. Look for people who think, who contribute ideas, and who are not content with the way things are. Good leaders are always ready to improve things, or to try a different approach to get better results.

5. EXAMINE SELF-DISCIPLINE

Self-discipline could be examined as a part of character but it is helpful to look at it separately. Look at three "T's" of self-discipline in a potential leader.

Time

How does the person use his/her time? A growing leader will seize moments, and use them to grow and develop. Every person, from the president to the factory worker, has been given the same amount of time. The difference is in how we use it. Repeatedly in the church I have observed that the people with the least to do are often the least reliable! Many times the people that I can count on are the ones that are working all day, running a business on the side, keeping their family happy and still involved in the church! Why? They have learned how to manage their time.

I went to a leader's seminar one day, and arrived at the time it was to begin. Most of the leaders had not arrived, but one was there on time. Since the meeting had not started, he went to the library to listen to a tape while waiting! That's a leader who has learned to use time well.

Temper

Does the potential leader have control of his/her emotions, especially the emotion of anger? People who are quick tempered or who hold grudges won't make it in leadership. Leaders face many attacks and many discouragements. People will find it difficult to trust leaders who lack emotional stability.

Tongue

Does the potential leader have self-control in his speech? Does he speak the truth? Can he keep a secret? I recall many times while evaluating people for the church council recognizing that they were qualified in all other ways, but in this area they were not self-controlled, and we could not call them to leadership positions because of their tongue.

6. CHECK SELF-IMAGE

The person being considered for leadership should have a healthy self-image. He should not be proud, but he should feel good about himself. Being able to walk and talk with confidence is a characteristic of a leader. People will not follow someone who is not sure of himself.

Persons who are young or inexperienced may not initially have confidence that they can do what you are calling them to do. Some of that confidence will come as they develop their skills in leadership and ministry. You can help them grow and succeed, which builds a good self-image.

7. LOOK FOR A GOOD ATTITUDE

Leaders possess a good attitude. They don't grumble and complain. They are positive about life. They believe God is able to do great things. They see potential, where others see problems. They are fun to be around. They lift, while others pull down.

Check the attitude of the potential leader. Is his outlook positive or negative? How does he deal with difficulties? Attitude is contagious, and every person on your leadership team must have a positive attitude.

By now you might ask, "Can we ever find a leader who will pass all these tests?" Don't despair. Checking these areas does not mean we are expecting perfection in any potential leader. None of us is strong in all these areas. But the criteria help you identify those who will lead well, and avoid choosing persons unqualified for leadership. Use these seven tests to confirm or to "raise warning flags" about potential leaders. Seek God's wisdom as you are looking for leaders. In a young church you might not expect as much from leaders, but establish high standards from the beginning. In lower levels of leadership you might not demand as much as on higher levels. If you find a leader who is strong in most areas, but weaker in one or two, you can encourage and help him develop in those areas. It is crucial that you understand what a strong leader looks like, so you can develop yourself and others to lead effectively.

A final caution: take your time when appointing leaders. It is always easier to call a leader than to remove one who isn't doing the job well. If you have serious doubts about a person, wait. If you have reservations, appoint him for a limited time period, subject to review. If you make a mistake, don't despair. We all make some mistakes in choosing leaders. Learn from the mistakes, evaluate what went wrong, and you will continue growing. May God give you good leaders who will bring you joy as you grow together!

ACTION ASSIGNMENT

1. Think about the leaders in your church. Evaluate each of them in the seven areas. Plan to spend time developing them in areas that need improvement.

2. Look at the seven areas to evaluate a potential leader. Ask yourself the questions under "Evaluate Influence" to identify potential leaders. You will likely see some people that you had not recognized as leaders. List them below. Then use "The Potential Leader Checklist" to evaluate them. Prayerfully consider what God is calling them to do in the church.

POTENTIAL LEADER CHECKLIST

Ask the following questions to evaluate a potential leader. Give marks from 10 (excellent) to 1 (very low) to describe the person. This chart can be used for comparison among potential leaders. The higher the score, the stronger the person's leadership ability.

Category	Questions	Marks (1-10)
1. Spiritual Maturity A. Character	Is he/she spiritually qualified for the position? (1 Timothy 3:1-13; Titus 1:5-9) Character flaws to look for: -Failure to take responsibility for actions and mistakes -Unfulfilled promises -Failure to meet deadlines	
B. Growth	How has the person grown in his/her faith? Is he/she taking advantage of growth opportunities such as seminars, Bible studies, and discipleship courses? Is he/she praying? Learning the Word?	
C. Response to authority	Is this person willing to be corrected? How does he/she speak about leaders? Is he/she accountable to you?	
D. Spiritual Gifts	Is his/her spiritual gift obvious?	
2. Influence	Is this person influencing others?	
3. People skills	Are people attracted to him/her? Does he/she know how to talk nicely to people? Can he/she correct others with a smile?	
4. Problem-solving ability	What problems have I seen this person solve? Does this person give good ideas for positive change?	
5. Self-discipline Time Temper Tongue	How does the person use his/her time? Does the person have control of his/her emotions? How does the person talk?	
6. Self-image	Does he/she have self-confidence?	
7. Attitude	Does he/she have a good attitude?	
Total		

Chapter Nine
THE LEADER AND PERSONALITY

Each of our family members is unique. I love quietness and order, and hate change. If my desk is a mess, it means that I'm not doing very well. For me, a perfect evening is having the house to myself and a good book. Loice, my wife, is just the opposite. She loves being with people, and celebrations are her specialty. She loves to talk, laugh and have a good time with people.

Joshua, our oldest son, is well-organized and self-disciplined. We rarely need to remind him to study for school; he just does it. His room is usually quite orderly, even as a teenager. Joseph loves life and relationships, and has fun telling jokes and stories. The condition of his room has been the topic of many conversations between us. On one occasion, after he grew weary of my requests to inspect his room for cleanliness, he posted a sign on the closed door which said, "Blessed are those who have not seen and yet believe!" We still get laughs from that sign. Elizabeth, our daughter, is a determined girl and doesn't need much help to set goals or create "to do" lists. When she was around 5 years old we were having our family devotions and as usual, I was leading. She looked up and

170

asked boldly, "Dad, can I lead?" Ever since, I've been trying hard to keep up with her ambition to lead!

My guess is that your family is just as diverse as mine. How would you describe yourself to someone who has never met you? Would you say you are quiet or talkative? Are you shy or outgoing? Do you focus more on tasks or people? Are you a perfectionist or generally disorganized? Do you tend to see the bright side of life or the problems? The way you answer these questions says a lot about your personality or temperament.

What is personality? In chapter two we noted Tim Lahaye's definition, "The combination of inborn traits that sub-consciously affect man's behavior."[45] This definition provides several concepts that enable us to understand better the meaning of personalities. First, these traits are inborn. Some children come into the world like lambs, others come in like lions! Parents observe these distinct differences in children at a very young age. Second, these traits impact each of us at a sub-conscious level and shape the way we see the world and respond to everyone around us. Our personality impacts the way we talk, study, drive and eat! Unless we deliberately study this subject, we are not normally aware of how deeply we are shaped by our personalities. Finally, our personalities are a combination of traits. Although we will look at general categories that help us identify ourselves and others, each person is a unique combination of many traits. There is no one quite like you! Your personality is God's gift to you and to the world, and a fascinating part of our lives together.

WHY STUDY PERSONALITIES?

Learning about personalities can help us in several ways:

1. UNDERSTANDING OURSELVES

Understanding our personalities helps us learn why we act the way we do, and identifies our natural inclinations.

---

[45] LaHaye. *Why You Act the Way You Do*, 23.

Knowing our personality helps us identify our strengths and weaknesses. This insight has many implications for recognizing areas in which we will thrive in relationships and vocations. Recognizing our personality provides a strong foundation for developing our unique potential in Christ. As we identify potential weaknesses, we will be able to identify areas of our lives that need improvement and make necessary corrections. At the same time, we will freely accept our uniqueness as a gift to be cherished and developed, instead of wishing we were different.

2. UNDERSTANDING OTHERS

As we better understand ourselves, we also learn more about others. People are different, and the better we understand people, the more likely it is that we will relate well with them. Since leaders are in the "people" business, the better we understand people, the more effective we will be in leadership. Relationships with our spouses, our children and those we lead will improve dramatically when we understand personalities.

3. UNDERSTANDING THE VALUE OF TEAMWORK

As we learn about ourselves and others we begin to recognize in a greater way the value of teamwork. In recognizing my strengths and weaknesses, I realize that I need others around me to complement me. I learn to value the perspectives of others and the need to work together with them to lead more effectively. The Body of Christ is a great example of this. Paul says, *Just as each of us has one body with many members, and these members do not all have the same function, so in Christ we who are many form one body, and each member belongs to all the others. (Romans 12:4-5)* A body needs many different parts to function effectively, and leaders recognize that each part has a unique contribution to the team. We will look more closely at this in the next chapter.

Before we look at the different personalities, take a few minutes to think about yourself. Read through the four lists of characteristics in the personality quiz below. For each characteristic put the number in the blank that best describes how that characteristic relates to you with the following scale:

5 -Usually describes me
4 -Often describes me
3 -Sometimes describes me
2 -Seldom describes me
1 -Never describes me

Personality Quiz
1._____

Outgoing	____
Optimistic	____
Difficulty with appointments	____
Impulsive	____
Egotistical (self-centered)	____
Lives in the present	____
Difficulty concentrating	____
Restless	____
Friendly	____
Enjoyable	____
Talkative	____
Weak-willed	____
Difficulty keeping resolutions	____
Undisciplined	____
Easily discouraged	____
Impractical	____
Compassionate	____
Emotional	____
Total	____

2._____

Optimistic	_____
Goal-oriented	_____
Self-confident	_____
Self-sufficient	_____
Activist (makes things happen)	_____
Domineering	_____
Aggressive	_____
Leadership ability	_____
Persistence	_____
Strong-willed	_____
Hot tempered	_____
Insensitive	_____
Unsympathetic	_____
Determined	_____
Decisive	_____
Sarcastic	_____
Practical	_____
Outgoing	_____
Total	_____

3._____

Very quiet	_____
Pessimistic	_____
Introvert	_____
Not aggressive	_____
Spectator in life	_____
Indecisive	_____
Slow & lazy	_____
Easy-going	_____
Calm & cool	_____
Efficient	_____
Dependable	_____
Witty, dry humor	_____

Teasing _____

Selfish _____

Orderly habits _____

Stingy _____

Stubborn _____

Works well under pressure _____

Total _____

4._____

Introvert _____

Organized _____

Pessimistic _____

Indecisive _____

Critical _____

Moody _____

Creative _____

Harbors resentment _____

Perfectionist _____

Introspective _____

Suspicious _____

Enjoy working out of public view _____

Faithful friend _____

Self-sacrificing _____

Easily offended _____

Self-centered _____

Sensitive _____

Deep Feeling _____

Total _____

At the end of each of the four sections, add the total of your numbers for that section and put it in on the 'total' line. So what does it mean? We'll find out as we begin to look at the different personalities.

THE FOUR BASIC PERSONALITIES

The concept of temperaments or personality types goes back at least to the Greek doctor Hippocrates (460-370 BC), who believed certain human behaviors were caused by body fluids. Others added to his work and around 190 AD Galen, a Greek physician, came up with four names for the temperaments that we still use today, the choleric, sanguine, phlegmatic, and melancholy.[46] Each of the temperaments has its own strengths, potential weaknesses and fears. We will also look at a Biblical example of each temperament.

POWERFUL CHOLERIC

The choleric is a take-charge, goal oriented person, and able to get the job done. The choleric is decisive, opinionated, and focuses on action. The powerful choleric is able to be involved in several projects at once, often dreaming of  new ventures before the old ones are even off the ground. Cholerics are perhaps the most strong-willed of the personalities and while they accomplish a lot, they often seem cold and unemotional in interpersonal relationships. They tend to focus on the task at hand, seeing others as a means to accomplish the goal. They don't have a lot of patience if a team member fails to perform and may quickly step on people as they climb to the top. Although natural risk-takers who see possibilities in every venture, they often find it hard to anticipate problems and can be surprised when things don't go as planned. The natural inclination to take charge often propels the choleric into leadership positions. Many leaders of companies, founders of organizations, and business entrepreneurs are cholerics. As a group, they comprise some 3% of the population.

---

[46] Blanchard, *The Heart of a Leader*, 14.

A great fear of a choleric is that others will take advantage of him. He wants to get the job done and will involve others to make it happen, but his independent nature often wants to take the credit alone and to protect himself from anyone who would take away his control.

A Biblical example of this personality is the apostle Paul. He was a pioneer, a visionary who was constantly on the go to make things happen. The list of his accomplishments is impressive: church planting, writing, enduring persecution and many miles of travel. He built a team around him and enjoyed the company of Mark until the young man turned back. Then Paul had no patience to give him a second chance. To his credit, later in his life he realized the value of this team member and worked with him again.

POPULAR SANGUINE

The sanguine is a popular, fun-loving person, extremely outgoing and full of life. Talking and telling stories come naturally to the sanguine, who loves to be the center of attention. Everyone knows when the sanguine walks into the room and often his presence is heard even before he enters! Sanguine personalities are usually positive and upbeat, although they are very emotional with extreme highs and lows that are very apparent. Their carefree nature makes concentration and attention to detail a real problem, and they are often unproductive workers. Their knack for telling stories and talking often leads to exaggeration or worse sins of the tongue and they can easily be self-centered. Sanguines tend to be disorganized and often are looking for things that are lost. Their ability to connect with others allows them to gather a group around them to help enjoy the hunt! Their bubbly personality adds much life to our world.

Because of their love for interaction with people their greatest fear is rejection and loss of approval. Being loved

177

and accepted by others deeply motivates their actions and they comprise about 11% of the population.

A Biblical example of this personality is the apostle Peter. He was always the first to speak and talked more than all the others put together! He was quick to promise his loyalty to Jesus and wept bitterly when he failed. Yet God used him as a key leader in the early church.

Both the sanguine and choleric are extroverted personalities, finding lots of energy from being with people. On the quieter (introverted) side of life are the next two personalities, phlegmatic and melancholy.

PEACEFUL PHLEGMATIC

The phlegmatic is the most peaceful and quiet personality. He often possesses a dry sense of humor and does not usually get noticeably angry. He is an easy-to-please person. If you  ask what kind of drink he wants, he will likely respond "Oh, whatever is available." If you ask, "What would you like to do tonight?" you'll hear something like, "Whatever you want to do." The phlegmatic tends to be a spectator in life, and can easily spend most of his time on the sofa, in front of the TV or at the computer. The phlegmatic person tends to be unmotivated and excels at procrastination. Because of his peaceful nature he doesn't cause many problems while doing nothing! However, he is dependable and can be an effective leader when motivated. With a diplomatic and objective nature, he is a natural peacemaker. He can be indecisive and fearful of taking risks and this can easily dampen the enthusiasm of the extrovert personalities. An efficient and organized person, he does not enjoy changes in the routine. This personality represents the vast majority of the population as some 69% of people are phlegmatics.

Loss of security and confrontation are two great fears for the phlegmatic since routine and peace are highly valued. The person with this personality will go to great lengths to keep things around them the same, including relationships.

A Biblical example of a phlegmatic is young Timothy. He seems to have been a timid, shy person. Paul exhorted him to fan his gift into flame and not to neglect it. He further challenged Timothy not to have the spirit of fear but of power. Paul recognized Timothy's potential but realized that he needed much encouragement to develop his gift and calling.

PERFECT MELANCHOLIC

The melancholic is a gifted personality, often a perfectionist. Many doctors, musicians, artists and highly skilled persons are melancholics. They are loyal but do not make friends easily and are often uncomfortable in group settings. They possess a very analytical mind, enabling them to see potential problems with any project and can lead to a critical attitude.  The melancholic is well organized and loves neat stacks of materials and nice file drawers. He is highly self-disciplined and works well without close supervision. While his personality excels at working with details, his perfectionism can get him bogged down in the fine points. His nature tends to view the negative side of life which can lead to extreme moodiness and a sense that everyone is against him. Melancholics comprise about 17 % of the population.

The great fears for the melancholic are being criticized, imperfection in himself or others and changes in circumstances. Like the phlegmatic he prefers for things to remain the same.

A Biblical character who was a melancholic is Luke. He was a gifted doctor who delighted in doing thorough research as he wrote his two books. His records were meticulous, showing his analytical mind.

These are the four major personalities. Admittedly, many of the statements are generalizations, but it is intriguing to look at the contrasts in people. It is important to note that everyone is a unique blend of these personalities. No one is 100% choleric or phlegmatic. For example, an individual might be 70% choleric, 20% sanguine and 10% melanchic. Tim Lahaye lists 12 different combinations or blends with unlimited variations. The more dominant one personality type is the more the person will reflect the characteristics we described. See the chart at the end of this chapter for a summary of the four personalities.

APPLYING WHAT WE HAVE LEARNED ABOUT PERSONALITIES

With this foundation, there are several ways to apply what we have learned about personalities.

IDENTIFY YOUR OWN PERSONALITY

It's time to take a good look at yourself! Perhaps you've been told that it is prideful to think about yourself. But Paul exhorts us in *Romans 12:3, "For by the grace given me I say to every one of you: Do not think of yourself more highly than you ought, but rather think of yourself with sober judgment, in accordance with the measure of faith God has given you."* It is proper to think of ourselves with 'sober judgment' or in a balanced way.

Quite likely as we went through the descriptions, you saw yourself in one or more of the categories. Now go back to the test you took at the beginning of this chapter. Put the following personality types next to the appropriate number:

1. Sanguine   3. Phlegmatic
2. Choleric   4. Melancholic

180

Look at your scores in each category. What personality is your highest score? What is your second highest? Is that what you thought it would be? This test, though not comprehensive, is useful to quickly identify your primary and perhaps a secondary personality trait.[48] Visit our website to find a printable version of this test which you can use to have someone else evaluate you.

Recognize Different Personalities in Life Situations

It can be humorous to reflect on how different personalities respond differently to the same situations. Let's look at several common activities and how each personality emerges.

Eating

Personality affects the way we eat our meals. The **choleric** tackles his food with vigor, seldom changes menus, talks while gulping down his food and eats while preparing to move on to the next project. The **sanguine** eats anything in sight, talks until the waitress comes with the menu, and enjoys trying new types of food. The relationships around the table are more important than the food. The **phlegmatic** rarely tries new foods, preferring the familiar menu. He eats quietly and is often the last one to finish. The **melancholic** takes "forever" to decide what to eat. He arranges his food very nicely on the plate and eats systematically, either completing one item before starting another one or eating one bite of everything and then repeating the process.

Shopping

If you take the four personalities shopping, get ready for some interesting differences. The **choleric** shops fast, can be

---

[48] As quoted by George Barna, The Power of Team Leadership (Colorado Spring, CO: WaterBrook Press), 76.

an impulsive buyer with quick decisions, always looks for the shortest line to check out. Shopping is a task to check off of his 'to-do' list, and the faster it is done, the faster he can  move on to greater things. The **sanguine** always wants to take a friend along so they can talk as they shop. If that isn't possible, the sanguine finds some new friends in the store! He wanders all over the store looking for items, often gets several things that catch his eye, and usually forgets at least one thing that he really needed. The **phlegmatic** would rather shop alone, and likes to go back to the same places to shop. He carries his list of items along and rarely makes impulsive choices. The **melancholic** plans every detail as if shopping were a major military campaign. He plans the best route to the store, and moves methodically through the store, picking up all the items on his list in order. His calculator comes in handy for adding up the totals, and he watches the cashier carefully to confirm every price. Price saving coupons are kept neatly in the same pocket for maximum savings.

Driving

Put each personality behind the wheel of the vehicle and your driving experience will be very different. The **choler-ic** drives fast, rushing to get to his appointment on time and trying to accomplish several things while driving to finish his 'to do' list. He gets lots of speeding tickets, but counts that as a small price for changing the world. **Sanguines** drive erratically, sometimes fast  and sometimes slow, and are quickly distracted by talking to someone in the car or by telephone. The sanguine has no idea when the car needs to be serviced and doesn't pay attention to the car until something breaks down. His reverse gear is used often to find the way back to the right road. The **phlegmatic** drives steadily, is in no rush to get anywhere and has no need to change lanes to save time. He rarely breaks any laws so seldom gets tickets. The **melancholic** also follows the laws and rarely goes too fast. He keeps a detailed record of all the times the car is serviced and can quickly identify when the next date will be. He plans his route, so rarely gets lost.

In a Lift/Elevator

When it is time to go to the top of a skyscraper, our four personalities each have a different experience. The **choleric** waits impatiently for the elevator to arrive, pushing the buttons as he mutters under his breath about how slow elevators  have become. He stands next to the door if possible so that he can get off quickly. The **sanguine** loves elevators, and can't wait to see who will be on the next ride. The **phlegmatic** waits patiently in line, and if the elevator appears too slow may take the stairs without complaining. The **melancholic** enters the elevator and stands next to the sign giving the maximum allowable weight. He silently calculates the approximate weight of each passenger to assure himself that they are within the stated limit.

Isn't God creative? It's wonderful that we are all created differently and respond so uniquely to various situations. Life would be so boring if we were all alike!

ALLOW GOD TO TRANSFORM YOUR PERSONALITY

God has given you a unique personality that has wonderful strengths. However, sin has corrupted each personality and magnified the potential weaknesses. As Christians we

183

have the great opportunity to ask God to shape our personality so that we more fully reflect His beautiful character.

The fruit of the Spirit described in Galatians 5:22-23 is for every believer and every temperament. *"But the fruit of the Spirit is love, joy, peace, patience, kindness, goodness, faithfulness, gentleness and self-control. Against such things there is no law."* Some temperaments need more of one fruit than another. For example, the choleric may need more love for people than the sanguine. The phlegmatic may need more self-control than the choleric while the melancholic may need extra measures of joy to offset his pessimistic nature. Tim Lahaye proposes that there are two major emotions that affect every human being: Anger and Fear. These have been present in human experience since the fall. These two root emotions may lead to many wrong behaviors and sin.

Anger may lead to bitterness, malice, clamor, envy, resentment, intolerance, criticism, revenge, wrath, hatred, seditions, jealousy, attack, gossip, sarcasm, and unforgiveness.

Fear may lead to worry, anxiety, timidity, indecision, superstition, withdrawal, loneliness, over-aggression, doubts, inferiority, cowardice, suspicion, depression, hesitancy, haughtiness, and shyness.

As it relates to the temperaments, sanguines and cholerics struggle more with anger, while phlegmatics and melancholies are more prone to fear. It takes the Spirit of Jesus to help us overcome these emotional weaknesses. God can transform our temperaments so that we are daily walking in the strength of the Spirit and under His control. We must do our part by repenting and allowing the Spirit to change us. Our goal should be to minimize the weaknesses that come with our personalities, and allow the strengths to shine even brighter. The more the Spirit controls us and produces His fruit in us, the more beautiful we become. Although we cannot change our basic personality, as we allow the Spirit to shape us for many years, it will become harder to clearly identify our personality on a test like the one in this chapter.

LEAD DIFFERENT PERSONALITIES

Since people are so different in their personalities, our leadership style must reflect this reality. It does not work to lead everyone the same. Think about your own personality and what types of people it is easy for you to connect with. Connecting with those who are different may be difficult, but not impossible. To be more effective in leadership you will need to learn to reach out to those who are different. Here are some tips for leading different personalities, and thoughts about how your leadership is impacted by your personality.

Choleric

If you are a choleric leader, you have great potential to accomplish much through others by deliberately affirming and connecting with those around you. Recognize that your communication style may be interpreted more harshly than you intended, so consciously use more gentle words. Write notes of affirmation to build up those that are working with you.

If you are leading a choleric, good luck! Humor aside, this is a difficult combination, but it can be done. Learn to communicate to the choleric that you appreciate him and his work. Recognize that he is motivated by achievement and finds satisfaction in tackling huge tasks. With the choleric, use very direct communication. If necessary, increase the volume a bit to get his attention.

Sanguine

If you are a sanguine leader, your strength will be in developing relationships with others. You will excel in building networks, drawing people to your side, and being an encourager. Learn to listen to others and focus on their

185

needs instead of your own. You will also need to develop enough self-discipline to accomplish the mundane tasks of leadership.

If you are leading a sanguine, give him lots of attention and approval. Take time to listen to him. Plan to spend a few extra minutes each time you meet. If you're a phlegmatic try hard to get excited with him! Remember his stories and ask for an update the next time you see them. Find assignments that will maximize their strengths with people and require as little detail work as possible!

Phlegmatic

If you are a phlegmatic leader, you have potential for great influence. Your ability to get along with all types of people serves you well in leadership. A strong passion for following Jesus will help you overcome your natural lack of motivation, so you will accomplish significant things. Work hard on maintaining a positive attitude, and deal with your reluctance to change by trying something new.

If you are leading a phlegmatic don't expect him to change quickly. Give him advance notice of impending changes and help him see the benefit of the change. Work with him to set attainable goals. Use his stability to smooth the rough edges of other team members.

Melancholic

If you are a melancholic leader you have many strengths that can help you be effective. You can use the power of your mind to remember names and details about those you are leading. Your gift of organization will enable you to run an efficient, productive organization. Work hard on developing your social skills to be comfortable around others. Develop a more positive outlook on life, and be willing to take risks.

If you are leading a melancholic, recognize his need for order and stability. Give him work in advance and allow him to decide how he will get it done on time. Value his cautions without allowing his negativity to influence the others.

BUILD A TEAM AROUND PERSONALITIES

The beauty of personalities is that each can contribute powerfully to a strong team. In fact, it is impossible to have a team functioning at maximum potential without all types of people. As a leader you might be any combination of the four personality types. Your leadership effectiveness will be significantly determined by your ability to build a team that reflects the strengths of each personality. Recognize that each personality has something significant to contribute to your team and work to bring all of them together. Reflect on the section above with the tips for leading each of the personalities. Where have you been strongest in the past? Where do you need to improve?

Teach your team about personalities, so that there is understanding about the value of each one. Talk about how you can relate to each other in building the team. The next chapter will focus more on the crucial aspect of team building.

CONCLUSION

Learn all you can about yourself and why you act the way you do. Work on significant areas that keep you from functioning well, but focus on your strengths. Learn to recognize, appreciate, and respect the personality of others, and your leadership ability will rise several notches higher!

THE FOUR BASIC PERSONALITIES

Personality	CHOLERIC (3%)	SANGUINE (11%)	PHLEGMATIC (69%)	MELANCHOLIC (17%)
Description	The Choleric is an extrovert, but not as much as the Sanguine. He is action oriented, able to get the job done. He is always on the move. He is opinionated and decisive, making him a natural leader.	The Sanguine is a warm friendly, extremely out-going person, full of life and fun. He loves to talk, tell stories and entertain others. He's the "life of the party." He shows great emotion, has extreme highs and lows.	The Phlegmatic is a calm, easy-going person with a pleasant disposition. He enjoys a dry sense of humor, seldom gets noticeably angry. He tends to be a spectator in life, but can be a capable leader. He is a natural peacemaker.	The melancholic is a very gifted and sensitive person. He is introverted and although loyal, does not make friends easily. He is thorough and persistent, often a perfectionist. He enjoys the fine arts (music, art, etc.). He is analytical and can see potential problems in a project.
Strengths	1. Strong-willed 2. Independent 3. Visionary 4. Practical 5. Productive 6. Decisive 7. Leader 8. Risk taker	1. Outgoing 2. Responsive 3. Friendly 4. Warm 5. Talkative 6. Enthusiastic 7. Compassionate 8. Encouraging	1. Calm 2. Quiet 3. Easygoing 4. Dependable 5. Objective 6. Diplomatic 7. Efficient/Organized 8. Practical 9. Humorous	1. Gifted 2. Analytical 3. Creative 4. Self-sacrificing 5. Industrious 6. Self-disciplined 7. Orderly/organized
Potential Weaknesses	1. Cold 2. Unemotional 3. Self-sufficient 4. Impatient 5. Domineering/ bossy 6. Unforgiving 7. Sarcastic 8. Angry 9. Cruel 10. Rarely anticipates problems	1. Undisciplined 2. Exaggerates 3. Emotionally unstable 4. Unproductive 5. Egocentric 6. Inattentive to detail	1. Unmotivated 2. Procrastinator 3. Selfish 4. Stingy 5. Self-protective 6. Indecisive 7. Fearful 8. Worrier 9. Dampens enthusiasm 10. Resists change	1. Moody 2. Self-centered 3. Persecution-prone 4. Revengeful 5. Touchy 6. Theoretical 7. Unsociable 8. Critical 9. Negative 10. Gets bogged down in details
Greatest Fear	Being taken advantage of	Rejection; loss of approval	Loss of security; confrontation	Criticism; change in circumstances; imperfection
Example	Paul	Peter	Timothy	Luke

188

ACTION ASSIGNMENT

Reflect on your personality assessment. What have you learned about yourself from this lesson?

What areas of your personality keep you from developing your full potential, and what can you do to change?

Think about your immediate family members. List their names below and indicate their personality.

What can you do to relate better with them now that you recognize your personality and theirs?

Think about the group you lead. List the names of 5-8 key persons and indicate their personalities. Then indicate what you can do to lead them more effectively based on their personalities.

Name	Personality	Action Step

a.

b.

c.

d.

e.

f.

g.

h.

Chapter Ten
THE LEADER AND TEAMWORK

Fifteen seconds remained. The crowd was on their feet for the grand climax of the hard fought championship soccer match. With the score tied, the home team players deftly worked the ball down the field, finally passing it to their best striker on the far right side of the goal. With a final burst of energy he dribbled towards the goal, almost tripping over a defender. He recovered with just enough time for one shot at the goal. The ball soared over the outstretched arm of the leaping goalie and curved into the net just under the bar, a perfect kick. The stadium erupted with applause and the team mobbed the striker as they celebrated achieving their year-long dream.

Who scored the winning goal? Was it the striker? Although he received most of the attention, the whole team scored the goal. Without the hard work of teammates who passed the ball to him, he could not have scored the decisive shot to fulfill the dream of the entire season. It was a team effort.

On the sideline stood the coach, the person who had shaped the group into a championship level team. It was his work that found the right position for each player, encouraged them to develop their skills, maximized their individual strengths, and minimized their weaknesses. As a leader, he helped them become a winning team.

How do you reach the vision that God has given you? How do you make the dream work? If your vision is from God, it is bigger than you can achieve on your own. It will take a team to make it happen. In fact, the bigger the dream, the more crucial the team that is required. If you want to hike up a hill you don't need a strong team; if you want to climb Mount Everest, you must have the right team!

God's plan for you and the group you lead is a Mount Everest-sized vision which requires a great team. You are the leader-coach, and your ability to bring out the best in your players will help you reach the top.

Paul worked with a team, which allowed him to accomplish much more than he could have alone while building leaders for the future. He often refers to a member of his team as a fellow worker, partner or fellow servant as in the following verses:

We sent Timothy, who is our brother and God's fellow worker in spreading the gospel of Christ, to strengthen and encourage you in your faith, (1Thessalonians 3:2)

As for Titus, he is my partner and fellow worker among you; as for our brothers, they are representatives of the churches and an honor to Christ. (2 Corinthians 8:23)

In this chapter we will look at five principles of building teams that will help us function more effectively as leaders.

THE POWER OF A TEAM

Effective teams are powerful groups of people. They have potential to produce in two areas:

TEAMS CAN PRODUCE MORE QUANTITY

This acronym for a TEAM is informative:

T – Together
E – Everyone
A – Accomplishes
M – More

The power of teamwork is that teams produce more than the sum of the individuals. Helen Keller observed, "Alone we can do so little; together we can do so much." Teams multiply energy. Horses pulling in a team can pull more than the total of their individual strength. If a team of horses is joined together and one is able to pull 5,000 pounds and the other is capable of pulling 4,000 pounds we would expect the team to pull 9,000 pounds. But in fact, they will be able to pull 12,000 pounds together! This power of teams to produce more quantity works in the human realm as well as in the world of horses!

This concept is strongly supported in Scripture. Consider the following verses:

How could one man chase a thousand, or two put ten thousand to flight, unless their Rock had sold them, unless the LORD had given them up? (Deuteronomy 32:30)

Though one may be overpowered, two can defend themselves. A cord of three strands is not quickly broken. (Ecclesiastes 4:12)

Two are better than one, because they have a good return for their work. (Ecclesiastes 4:9)

Clearly, more happens when people work together to accomplish a goal.

TEAMS CAN PRODUCE MORE QUALITY

Not only can teams accomplish more, but the *quality* is improved when people work together. How can this happen?

Teams multiply ideas

Teamwork produces better ideas, because two heads are better than one! Any person can sit down with a blank piece of paper and come up with a few ideas. But getting together with others produces a synergy that multiplies ideas and strengthens existing ones. One person says, "I think we could...." This sparks another idea and someone else says, "What about this...?" This triggers more ideas. From many ideas a few excellent ideas can emerge. As author Ken Blanchard writes, "None of us is as smart as all of us."[49]

Teams maximize strengths

If I work alone, there is no way to move past my areas of weakness. But when I work on a team, the strengths of the other allow me to focus on my strengths. The person who is skilled with words can help the person who loves to work with his hands. The visionary dreamer is assisted by the developer. The sanguine can make the sale and the melancholic can keep the accounts. One person is good at raising money; another at spending it...together they make a team! Management leader and author Peter Drucker sagely observed, "The purpose of a team is to make the strengths of each person effective and his or her weaknesses irrelevant."[50]

Here's another way to look at it. If I am working alone and am strong at 50% of what needs doing, 50% will be done well but 50% will be done poorly. I will work half of the time in my strengths and half of the time in my weaknesses. Suppose you are in the same situation, but with opposite strengths and weaknesses. What happens if we join together and each focus on our strengths? We can both work at what we do well and complement each other's weaknesses. We will get more done and it will be done better. If we use numbers to represent our output, here's how it looks:

---

[49] Blanchard, *The Heart of a Leader*, 14.

[50] As quoted by George Barna, *The Power of Team Leadership* (Colorado Spring, CO: WaterBrook Press), 76.

Working alone	Working together
Person one: 100+50=150	Person one: 100+100=200
Person two: 50+100=<u>150</u>	Person two: 100+100=<u>200</u>
Total output: 300	Total output: 400

When I work alone, half of my work will be poor, but when I work with you and focus only on my strengths, all my work is effective. By working together we are able to maximize our strengths. Quality and quantity have both improved.

Philanthropist Andrew Carnegie declared, "It marks a big step in your development when you come to realize that other people can help you do a better job than you can do alone."

Biblically, the concept of spiritual gifts works on the premise that we each need one another to be complete. Each part has to do its part for the whole to function well. Paul says, *From him the whole body, joined and held together by every supporting ligament, grows and builds itself up in love, as each part does its work.* (Ephesians 4:16) In First Corinthians he uses the analogy of the body to illustrate how each part has a role to play.

Now the body is not made up of one part but of many. If the foot should say, "Because I am not a hand, I do not belong to the body," it would not for that reason cease to be part of the body. And if the ear should say, "Because I am not an eye, I do not belong to the body," it would not for that reason cease to be part of the body. If the whole body were an eye, where would the sense of hearing be? If the whole body were an ear, where would the sense of smell be? But in fact God has arranged the parts in the body, every one of them, just as he wanted them to be. (1Corinthians 12:14-18)

THE PURPOSE OF A TEAM

Why do we have a team? The practical reasons above make a strong case for teams instead of individual efforts.

195

However there is one fundamental reason for the existence of the team.

THE PURPOSE OF THE TEAM IS TO ACCOMPLISH THE VISION

The team exists only to accomplish the vision. This seems obvious, but in practice many teams lose sight of their objective. After functioning for some time, the team may come to believe that they exist to serve themselves instead of the vision. The vision should be kept clearly in front of the team and repeated often enough to remind the team members why they are working together.

Think about the vision you have for your church or organization. Does the team know what it is? Have you reminded them why they are doing what they are doing? How will you know when you are making good progress towards the vision?

One of the things that makes sporting events so attractive is that there is immediate feedback and the score is obvious to everyone. A winner is determined in every game. In organizations, leaders are responsible to ensure that every player understands the goal and what scoring looks like. This is harder for churches, since we often make the vision so spiritual that we never know when we 'win' and often fail to celebrate our victories.

Churches score when...
- A new person visits
- A person comes to Christ
- A person is released into ministry
- A person is sent out
- A leader is raised up!

Think about other 'scores' you can add to this list for the group you lead.

This purpose implies that **the purpose of the team is greater than the individual.** The team is not really about me, it is not about you, it's about what we are called together to do. We have a human tendency to say, "What's in it for me?" But this is not the real issue. We are not on a team for ourselves.

Our natural tendency as an organization grows is to begin to think that the organization exists for the welfare of its staff. If we lose sight of the vision, we begin to focus on our own needs and to lose the power of the team. Any time that I put my interest above the team purpose, I have made a serious mistake. Team members have to think first of the team, not themselves, if the team will reach its potential. Consider your team and your role. Do you think about the purpose of the team first, or your own needs and desires?

THE PASTE (GLUE) OF A TEAM

What holds a team together? What will keep us moving in the same direction as a team? We have different gifts, strengths, perspectives, and many other differences that can send us in diverse directions. To stay together as a team, we need to hold at least three things in common:

COMMON VISION

To function effectively as a team, we must have a common vision. This is not only the purpose of a team, but also a critical component of keeping us together. As we recognize the overall vision of the team, we should have a clear picture of how our part fits into the overall vision. Our role may be an out front role of leadership or it may be a supportive role, but each member of the team must understand how he or she helps the team to accomplish the common vision.

Think about your team and evaluate where you rate in this area.

Rating: How are we doing in the area of common vision? (1-10, with 10 being perfect.) _____

197

COMMON VALUES

We may be all moving together towards the same vision but have very different ideas about how to get there. One person may value the intimacy of a small group, while another thinks that growing bigger is the way to go. We can't work together as a team unless we share common values. Values need to be identified and talked about to ensure that they are held in common. You may begin to identify what you value by what is rewarded in your organization. You may lead your group through a process of discovering what values you hold in common and then work at reinforcing these values.

Rating: How are we doing in the area of sharing common values? (1-10, with 10 being perfect.) _____

COMMON EXPERIENCES

Sharing experiences builds a team. This can be informal experiences of chatting over lunch, sharing about our families and other significant issues, praying together, or more formal ways like retreats or time away from the working environment. Shared experiences build understanding and trust which are essential for teams to function.

If you are leading a business or non-profit organization, ask yourself what you do to promote common experiences. Do you encourage chatting around the water cooler or during breaks? Are there times that you take your team away for a time of sharing vision and building trust?

If you lead a church group, think about how to build common experiences for your team. This may include meals together in the church environment or in homes, church retreats, common ministry experiences, work projects, times for relaxation and fun together, etc. Use your imagination to think of others.

Rating: How are we doing in the area of common experiences? (1-10, with 10 being perfect.) _____

THE PROBLEMS OF A TEAM

Teamwork makes the dream work, but it is not automatic or easy. There are common obstacles that keep teams from functioning well together. That's why a leader is needed to build a team. Brian Molitor, in his book *The Power of Agreement* writes, "People must be convinced that it is to their advantage to co-operate with peers. We should make no mistake that, for many people, cooperation with others is not natural. It is a foreign act that must be taught and reinforced continually after the training has been completed."[51]

Let's consider three giants that can kill teamwork:

LACK OF TRUST

Trust is essential if we are going to work together. I must trust you in order to be vulnerable enough to allow you to cover some of my weaknesses. I need to trust that you are moving towards the same goal and share my values.

Patrick Lencioni in *The Five Dysfunctions of a Team* says that trust is foundational to a team and is created by a willingness to be vulnerable. He encourages teams to build trust simply by getting to know each other as people, and learning to acknowledge individual strengths and weaknesses. Without trust, the team will waste time skirting around the issues and not be willing to disagree.

If we can't disagree openly, we will not make progress on issues and not really be able to bring all our ideas to the table and commit ourselves to the action agreed upon by the team.

Building trust is a priority for a team leader. Consider first of all if you are a trustworthy person. Trust is built over time, and there are no shortcuts. In *The Seven Habits of Highly Effective People* Stephen R. Covey writes, "By making and keeping promises to ourselves and others, little by

---

[51] Brian D. Molitor, The Power of Agreement (Nashville, TN: Broadman & Holman Publishers, 1999), 220.

little, our honor becomes greater than our moods."[52] As this happens we build trust with others. Then we can focus on building trust with our team using some of the suggestions above to get started.

Evaluation: How do we do in this area of trust on a scale of 1-10? _____

LACK OF COMMUNICATION

Many issues arise on teams because of miscommunication, either a lack of communication or bad communication. It is not difficult for someone's feelings to be hurt, or for someone to feel that he/she has not been heard or just left out of the information flow. Clear communication builds teams.

When miscommunication has occurred, practice the 24 Hour Rule. Never let an issue be unresolved for more than 24 hours. Talk about it. Get it out on the table and deal with it. This is especially critical for personal issues that can affect our teamwork.

In today's world we use electronic communication frequently. Email is a great tool for helping us work together but it is severely limited for communicating feelings, thoughts, and ideas and it is not a strong tool for building relationships. If conflict or miscommunication is occurring, use face to face communication if at all possible. Use email for communicating information or issues that have less room for misunderstanding.

Evaluation: How do we do in this area of communication on a scale of 1-10? _____

LACK OF GROWTH

Individual growth has been discussed in previous chapters, but it is a huge area that affects the development of a team, not just the individual. Just as a chain is only as strong as its weakest link the team is only as strong as its weakest player.

---

[52] Covey, *The Seven Habits of Highly Effective People*, 92.

Individuals on a team must be passionate about their own growth, but the team should also be collectively engaged in growing together. Teams must recognize that if they do not grow, the organization will also stop growing. The team can learn to work together more effectively, to manage time better, to trust more, to focus on strengths of the others, etc. This will only happen as the team grows and develops. Don't expect growth in the organization to happen if the team remains at the same level. I love Maxwell's quip, "If you always do what you've always done, you'll always get what you've always got!" Growth in the organization will come through growing individuals in the organization or replacing them with new people! I suggest that it is smarter to help your team grow.

Is your team growing? Are you stretching to become all that God created you to be? Are you willing to change ways of doing things in order to grow? Do you take time to grow? Have you developed a culture of growth in your organization?

Evaluation: How do we do in this area of growth on a scale of 1-10? _____

THE PRACTICES OF A TEAM

Let's apply the principles we've learned in this chapter as we look at what each team member can do to strengthen the team.

RECOGNIZE YOUR ROLE

Be absolutely clear about how your part fits into the big picture of the team. Don't undervalue or overvalue your role. Put the team above personal ambitions but acknowledge the value of your contribution. Realize that your role is not to be the entire team; you play a part and need the others to play their parts. Take a moment to write down, as con-

201

cisely as you can, the role that you play on the team and how that helps the team.

_____

_____

_____

_____

_____

_____

_____

_____

_____

_____

STRENGTHEN YOUR ROLE

Develop yourself so that you excel at what you do. When you do your job with excellence, the entire team benefits. Conversely, if you are weak, it hurts the whole team. A dirty floor may cause a visitor not to return; a rude remark may turn away a potential member or customer. If the finances are not kept well, the leaders can't make right decisions. If papers are not put together properly, the meeting looks unorganized. Your role needs to be performed as though it is critical for the mission, and indeed it is! This may call for developing greater skills or capacity. In his email newsletter *Leadership Wired,* (May 2002) John Maxwell issues a challenge to develop:

"You cannot give what you do not have, so self-improvement precedes team improvement. The first step toward improving the team is to improve yourself....The greatest way that I can add value to my team is to make myself more valuable. If I can become a better player, if I can continually increase my skills, if I can continually become enlarged within myself, then I have the capacity to enlarge others. Too many people are still trying to give what they learned fifteen years ago, and they're in trouble."

What steps do you need to take to strengthen your role?

- _____
- _____
- _____
- _____
- _____
- _____

APPRECIATE THE OTHER'S ROLE

Recognize that each person is needed on your team, and learn to appreciate what they offer. Their differences become strengths for the team. Make a conscious effort to understand and appreciate the unique contribution that each one makes on your team. Be generous in thanking other members of the team for what they do. Take a moment now to thank someone on your team for his/her role. Use email, a note, or a phone call to express your thanks.

PASS THE BALL

Remember our soccer story? The striker scored because someone passed the ball to him. He was the right person to have the ball at that moment because he was the best striker on the team. Others may have wanted to make the score, but it would have been selfish for a less skilled player to take the shot and lose the game.

What can we learn from this? There are times that we need to pass the ball to others on the team. Give another team member a chance to succeed. When he scores, you also score! We don't need superstars, but players that will benefit the whole team.

We may love to do a certain job, but if someone can do it better, or if there are things that we could do to help the team more, we should pass the ball. This is not dumping work on others, but allowing them to shine in areas that they are strong, while also strengthening the team.

For reflection: Are there things that I am doing that I should pass on to others on my team?

CELEBRATE SUCCESS

One of the reasons that sports events are so popular is that they provide an opportunity to celebrate wins. Everyone loves a celebration and teams find ways to celebrate together. The work of a leader is to lead the team to victory and then celebrate what they have done. When you've done well, stop for a moment and celebrate! Look for opportunities to acknowledge victories. Find ways to honor individual accomplishments as well for team members, like birthdays, anniversaries, graduations, etc. Celebrations reward good effort and build momentum for the future.

How can you celebrate a recent success with your team?

Self-Evaluation: Of the five actions listed above, in which area am I strongest?

Weakest?

What do I need to do to change?

CONCLUSION

Effective leaders work deliberately to build strong teams. Recognize that you will not rise above the team around you. Choose them well, equip them to work effectively together and you will reach the dream God has given to you. Complete the action assignment to reflect on what you have learned and to develop an action plan for your team.

ACTION ASSIGNMENT

Identify your team: Who do I consider my "team?" (This can be a committee, board, task force, work group, informal group, etc.)

RATE YOUR TEAM

1. Work through the ratings in the chapter and evaluate your team for each of the questions.

2. Choose one of the ratings that you felt was the highest for your team. Write it below and give an example of why you feel your team is strong in this area.

3. Choose one of the ratings which was low for your team. Write it below and explain why it is low.

What can be done to strengthen this area of team effort?

RATE YOURSELF
  1. How much do I value my team?
     In what ways do I show it?

  2. Do I see myself as a team player or an individual player?

  3. What is my unique contribution to the team?

  4. What can I do to strengthen my performance and thereby enhance the entire team?

  5. What other steps is God calling me to take to strengthen our team? (Be as specific as possible and include how and when you will take these steps.)

Chapter Eleven
THE LEADER
AND SPIRITUAL GIFTS

It was 6:30 Sunday morning, 30 minutes before our first service was scheduled to begin as I entered the church property. Two members were at the entrance installing a special banner to welcome visitors. The head usher was busy preparing the bulletins and getting the offering baskets ready for the service. Another member was doing a sound check on the equipment, to see that the sound system was working properly, while the musicians tuned their instruments. Several people were wiping the seats to remove the last bit of dust. Intercessors were in the basement praying for the service. Members of the hospitality ministry were preparing the room where they would welcome visitors. All of this was happening without my direct involvement!

Your church has the same potential as mine! Inside your followers lies potential that when tapped will result in new life and energy in the church, expansion of ministry, and reduced stress for you! The secret lies in unleashing the power of the spiritual gifts in your church. Your task as a leader is to: 1) understand God's plan for the spiritual gifts and, 2) use them in your church.

A key passage for understanding God's plan is Ephesians 4:11-16.

"It was he who gave some to be apostles, some to be prophets, some to be evangelists, and some to be pastors and teachers, to prepare God's people for works of service, so that the body of Christ may be built up until we all reach unity in the faith and in the knowledge of the Son of God and become mature, attaining to the whole measure of the fullness of Christ. Then we will no longer be infants, tossed back and forth by the waves, and blown here and there by every wind of teaching and by the cunning and craftiness of men in their deceitful scheming. Instead, speaking the truth in love, we will in all things grow up into him who is the Head, that is, Christ. From him the whole body, joined and held together by every supporting ligament, grows and builds itself up in love, as each part does its work."

There are several key teachings in this passage that will help you understand God's plan for the spiritual gifts.

GIFTS ARE GIVEN TO EVERY BELIEVER

In this and other passages (Ephesians 4:7; 1 Corinthians 12:7), God makes it clear that He has given a spiritual gift to every believer. That includes you and every Christian in your church. I've talked to many believers who didn't believe they had a gift until I showed them what the Bible teaches. Once they believe God has given them a gift, they want to discover it and begin to use it in the church.

GOD'S PLAN IS FOR THE LEADERS TO EQUIP THE MEMBERS

Paul identifies these gifts of leadership, sometimes called the five-fold ministry: apostles, prophets, evangelists, and pastors/teachers. What is your job as a leader? Is it to do the ministry? NO! A THOUSAND TIMES NO! Your job is to equip the people for the work!

Many pastors and church leaders think that God will judge them on how much work they did: how many they brought to the Kingdom and how many sick people they visited. But God's standard is completely different. The job He has given to leaders is to *equip people for ministry.* Anything less than this fails to measure up. What a revolution this would bring in our churches if leaders would understand and embrace this concept.

GOD'S PLAN IS FOR EVERY BELIEVER TO USE HIS OR HER GIFT

God's people must be equipped for "works of service" and will grow when "each part does its work." God has a job for everyone in His army; no one is enlisted to sit! When believers are using their gifts, they will be growing. Paul makes it clear that if Christians are not using their gifts, they will remain immature in their faith. But when spiritual gifts are used, believers will grow spiritually and also enable the church to grow in numbers. This happens because many people become involved in the work, and the load is shared. This creates an atmosphere in which people are highly motivated to participate. We don't need more spectators in the church; we need more participators!

Can you see it? Just visualize the results of exciting growth that will be unleashed when you begin emphasizing the spiritual gifts. Meditate on Paul's message and let it settle deep in your heart. You don't have to do all the work; in fact, you should not do it all! Your work is to equip others to do the work. Anything short of that will cause you to miss God's best in your life and ministry.

What can be done by a leader to use the gifts God has placed in the church? There are at least two things you can do.

First, <u>know your own gift</u>. It will be difficult for you to train others in their gifts if you don't know your own. When you know your own gift you will be able to work on making it more effective. Paul told Timothy in 2 Timothy 1:6, *"For this reason I remind you to fan into flame the gift of God, which is in you through the laying on of my hands."* To "fan into flame" means to work on it, develop it, and make it more powerful in ministry. Our gifts are given to us supernaturally, but God expects us to develop them. Don't look at someone who is highly developed in a certain gift and think, "God poured out His Spirit on that brother." No, God gave him the gift, but the brother developed it. He made mistakes, learned and grew until he ministered powerfully in that area.

> Your work as a leader is to equip others to do the work. Anything short of that will miss God's best in your life and ministry.

When you know and use your gift, you will also be released from guilt. My gift is teaching, and God changes people's lives when I use that gift. However, I don't see multitudes of people saved in my ministry, since I don't have the gift of evangelism. I shouldn't feel guilty, since that's not my gift. I can focus on teaching and encourage the person with the gift in evangelism to excel in that area.

If you don't know your spiritual gift, I recommend that you read my book, *Use That Gift,* or another book on spiritual gifts.

Secondly, <u>equip others to use their gifts</u>. We have identified God's plan for leaders to equip others in the church for ministry. If we apply this truth in our lives, what a difference it will make in our ministry. This is discipleship, equipping, leadership training all rolled up together!

How can we develop the gifts of others? Let's take the word EQUIP and see what each letter stands for....

EVALUATE

The first step in equipping is to evaluate the people you are working with, looking for their spiritual gift. A leader should understand his people, especially those who are close to him. A pastor should think about his elders, deacons, church board and ask himself, "Do I know the gifts of each individual?" Here are three things to look for in evaluating a person.

A. EXAMINE THEIR PERFORMANCE

Look at what a person does well. Where does he/she perform the best? Look for fruit in a particular area of their lives in which God really uses them. Where is the fruit? Where do they shine?

B. EXAMINE THEIR PASSION

What really excites them? When can you see the fire in their eyes? It may be evangelism, or serving, or administration. The area in which God has gifted them will produce passion in them. Think about this when you are placing people on committees.

C. EXAMINE THEIR PRIORITIES

Ask the question, "What is the most important thing for the church to do?" You will get different responses, based on the individual's priorities. Their priorities usually relate to their gifts.

When you find areas in which a person is performing well, has a passion for and sees as a key priority in the church, you have likely identified their area of giftedness.

QUALIFY

Once you identify a person's spiritual gifts, you need to qualify or train them for ministry. This requires concentrated time and energy. How can you train people?

First, **teach them**. Teaching people about their spiritual gifts is foundational for new believers after they have been grounded in the faith. Take several Sunday sermons to teach about spiritual gifts. Then get groups of people together according to their gifts and teach them more specifically!

Second, **train them**. Too often we assume that because people have a gift, they know how to use it. However, we need to train them. If it is prophesying, they must learn how to do it well. If they are gifted in serving and are asked to be an usher, we must teach them what it means to be an usher. If it is leading worship, someone needs to tell them how it should be done! Your primary work as a leader is to equip others, to train them for the ministry. If you don't know how to do it yourself, it is your responsibility to find someone to train your members.

This will take time, commitment, money, and patience! Be prepared to invest heavily in the lives of people. To train people plan seminars, informal teaching, and individual counseling. Be aware that initially, training others will cost you more time than doing it yourself! But in the end it is a wise investment which will bring powerful results.

UNITE THEM WITH OTHERS WITH THE SAME GIFT

Get people with the same gifts together. You may need to call a meeting for those who have a gift of healing. In such a meeting training can take place. Mentoring may also develop in this context, with the more experienced guiding the younger ones. Sharing insights, successes, and failures will help everyone to grow stronger. It can also provide a lot of encouragement to know others who have the same gift.

INSPIRE

People need inspiration, to know their work is significant. This is most encouraging when it comes from the leader. The person who cleans the floor needs to be encouraged that his/her work is vital. The choir responds to reminders that their anointed singing is vital to worship. Every one must see his/her work as crucial to the overall goals of the church. Be careful not to say, "Your work is the *most* important," But make sure they know the importance of their role.

How can you inspire people to use their gifts? Here are four practical ways to inspire people.

1. Verbal affirmation and encouragement. Talk to people. Encourage them. Tell the usher he/she looks nice! Thank the worship team for the time and effort they took to practice so they could sing well.

2. A written note. Take three minutes to write a note that someone might keep in his or her Bible for years. Thank them for serving the Lord with you. A brief personal note does wonders! Have a goal to write at least one every week.

3. Public recognition. Recognize people who are using their gifts. Commend noteworthy service without offending others. Give a monthly service award or highlight a special ministry in your bulletin. Have the ushers stand while everyone claps for them. What a motivation! The pastor cares about what I'm doing!

4. Continued training. Provide growth opportunities for the gifts. This shows that you value what they are doing. Arrange seminars for teachers, youth leaders, and other workers. Have retreats for your key leaders. Pass along an article or book you found that will help them grow.

PROMOTE

The final step in equipping is to promote each person through public recognition and affirmation. By promoting people, you show them what you value, and create a climate where spiritual gifts will flourish.

Promotion includes giving people a higher responsibility, when merited. If they have served well in an area, they are ready for more responsibility. <u>Be careful, however, that you do not promote them outside of their gift!</u> Just because they have done well as an usher doesn't mean they will do well on the missions committee. But give them opportunities for their gift to be promoted. If they have taught well, give them a bigger assignment. If they have taught the Sunday school well, consider having them train other teachers (as long as they are gifted in this area as well.)

CONCLUSION

As a leader, give high priority to developing gifts among your people. Begin to recognize and develop the gifts of others around you. In a small group, look for gifts and fan them into flame. In your youth ministry identify different gifts and put them to work. Release the gifts and watch your people and your church grow!

ACTION ASSIGNMENT

1. Carefully evaluate your own gift. (Use the lists of gifts given in the following passages: 1 Corinthians 12:8-31; Rom. 12:1-8; Ephesians 4:11 to assist you.) What is your primary spiritual gift?

What other gifts do you feel God has given you?

2. Go to a close friend, (spouse if you are married) and ask them what gift(s) they see in you. What gifts did your friend identify?

3. What are you doing to develop your gift?

4. List below the names of at least 5 persons that you lead. (If you are a pastor this should be your elders or council members.) Beside each one list the gift(s) that you feel that person has.

	Name	Spiritual Gift
A.		
B.		
C.		
D.		
E.		

What can you do to EQUIP these people? Be specific and give a date when you will do this. Your plan may be for only one person or the entire group of people listed above.

1.

2.

3.

Chapter Twelve
THE LEADER
AND CHURCH DISCIPLINE

James walked slowly towards home, tired after a long day of work. As he turned to enter the gate he saw his neighbor, Janet, approaching from the other direction. Janet was a single sister from his church and a member of the choir. This evening there was a young man with her, and James wondered who it could be. As they walked past they were deep in conversation and didn't even acknowledge James' presence. As he watched them enter her house, he prayed for God to keep Janet from sin. All evening James was troubled as he reflected about sister Janet, and wondered if the young man was still at her place. *What could have happened to her relationship with God?*

At daybreak James left for work. To his surprise, he saw Janet leaving hurriedly with the same young man. Now James was sure that something was wrong. He spent the day wondering what to do. He wondered if he should report it to the pastor. Maybe he should talk with Janet's sister, and ask her to talk to Janet about what he had seen. Perhaps he should keep quiet and pray about it. Or should he inform the small group that would meet tonight, and ask them to pray for Janet?

At last he decided to seek advice, so he visited you and told you the story. What would you advise James to do? (Decide before you read further!)

This chapter will help you understand the Biblical process of dealing with discipline in the church. Conflicts, sin, and broken relationships are a real part of church life that the leader must deal with. Church discipline is one of the most unpleasant tasks of leadership, but it cannot be ignored.

It would be nice if we didn't even have to deal with this topic, but it is a sad fact of Christian life that not all who begin the race will complete it. Along the way some will backslide. What do we do then? Offenses will occur. How will we deal with them? What is the responsibility of the church, and how can it be done in a Christ like manner? How do we as leaders guide the church in the area of discipline? These are some of the questions we will answer in this chapter.

THE PURPOSE OF DISCIPLINE

What is the primary purpose for Church discipline? Is it to punish the wrongdoer? Is it to keep the Church pure? Is it to demonstrate our authority? Is it to keep a clear witness in the community? Scripture provides two reasons for discipline in the church.

The first purpose is **to express love.** This might come as a surprise, but I believe it is the primary motive of all discipline. Why does God discipline us? Hebrews 12:6, 10 gives the answer: *"The Lord disciplines those he loves... God disciplines us for our good, that we may share in his holiness."* God loves us, and His love compels Him to at times take a painful action so that we might become more like Him. But the motive is His love. Paul echoes this thought when he tells Timothy to silence false teachers, *"The goal of this command is love, which comes from a pure heart and a good conscience and a sincere faith."* (1 Timothy 1:5)

It may seem contradictory to think of discipline as an expression of love. Yet, love must always do what is best for the person, and at times that means discipline. If I say that I love my children, but don't discipline them, what kind of love is that? My love for them demands that I discipline them when they are wrong, to correct and train them properly. Love and discipline go together, and should never exist without each other. If we do not discipline with genuine love, we are not disciplining like God does.

A second purpose of discipline in the church is **to save.** Our goal in discipline should be to save the person. Paul said that the church in Corinth should put a man out of the fellowship *"So that the sinful nature should be destroyed and his spirit saved on the day of the Lord."* (1 Corinthians 5:5)

Discipline in the church should only be done to save the person involved. The erring one may be removed from the church only as a last resort, and only for the purpose of saving that person. The church is saying in essence, "The only way that we believe you can now be saved from eternal destruction is to remove you from the church, so that you will experience the pain needed to bring repentance."

All that we do in the church should be to save people. Our goal should not be to destroy anyone; we are here to save and to bring people into the eternal Kingdom. DISCIPLINE IS TO SAVE. It is to purify the person and bring them to repentance, not to punish them for their sin. Sometimes leaders are tempted to think that they have been given authority to punish people for their

> # DISCIPLINE IS TO SAVE

sin. I don't find any scriptural support for this idea. In 2 Corinthians 13:10, Paul says about his authority, *"...the authority the Lord gave me for building you up, not for tearing you down."* We must be very careful how we use the authority God has given to us.

"But," you might ask, "what about the purity of the church?" Don't we discipline to keep the church pure? I looked for a scripture that would support this and couldn't find any! (Possibly "Get rid of the old yeast" in 1 Corinthians 5:6,7 could be used for this reason. However, the context of this verse makes it clear that the excommunication was to be done "so that the sinful nature may be destroyed and his spirit saved on the day of the Lord.")

When I didn't find strong evidence that we should discipline to keep the church pure, it caused me to think. Why doesn't scripture give this as a reason for discipline? I believe that when discipline is done for the purity of the church, it indicates that we are not motivated by love for the person. What am I saying? If there is a member that has sinned and discipline is needed, I might be tempted to think that because of the purity of the church this person must be excommunicated. In this I show that I love the church more than the person. I am more concerned about my reputation as a leader, or our reputation as a church, than I am about the person involved. Discipline for the sake of purity focuses on the organization instead of the person. If we truly love the person, we will discipline and the church will remain pure. But if we focus on purity of the church, we will discipline without love and contaminate what we are trying to preserve!

What happens when discipline is done with the motive of keeping the church pure? The person being disciplined may sense this motive and react to it, rather than being humbled. It will also be difficult for us to receive the person back, because we have been motivated by a concern for the church rather than the person. Yes, Jesus wants His church to be pure and we need to be careful about the church's reputation, but this should not be the purpose of our discipline.

Think about the way we discipline in our families. Perhaps I take my children to visit at someone's house and they make an embarrassing remark like, "Daddy, this seat has a hole in it!" I feel humiliated and embarrassed. I will be tempted to discipline my son out of anger that he has caused me to look bad or because he has ruined the "family name." But this is a selfish motive, more concerned about "me" than about my son's growth. Instead I should discipline him because of my love for him and my desire to see him mature. Discipline of children and discipline within the church are closely related. (Maybe this is part of the reason Paul requires that leaders have well-disciplined homes!) When someone sins in the church, and we are ashamed of what is being said about it by the non-Christians, we may react and kick someone out of the church because he has embarrassed us. Our motive is now selfish rather than loving discipline.

Keep this clearly in mind when you are faced with the issue of church discipline. Why are you disciplining? Is it based on love and a desire to see the person repent, or is it based on a desire for our own reputation?

THE PROCESS OF DISCIPLINE

We have established the purpose of discipline; now let's move to how we actually do it. We will first examine the actions involved, and then the attitudes.

THE ACTIONS

The primary text for how we are to carry out discipline in the church is found **in Matthew 18:15-20.**

"If your brother sins against you, go and show him his fault, just between the two of you. If he listens to you, you

have won your brother over. But if he will not listen, take one or two others along, so that 'every matter may be established by the testimony of two or three witnesses.' If he refuses to listen to them, tell it to the church; and if he refuses to listen even to the church, treat him as you would a pagan or a tax collector. "I tell you the truth, whatever you bind on earth will be bound in heaven, and whatever you loose on earth will be loosed in heaven. "Again, I tell you that if two of you on earth agree about anything you ask for, it will be done for you by my Father in heaven. For where two or three come together in my name, there am I with them."

This passage outlines several steps that are to be taken when someone sins.

Step One: One to One

Jesus says that the first step is to *"go and show him his fault, just between the two of you."* This is personal and private.

• This step is Personal

Notice that the action is to be done by the person who recognizes the fault. The one who sees the sin is responsible, not the prayer cell leader, not the pastor, or anyone else. It is not an issue to discuss with a best friend, or to share as a prayer request!

This step takes a deliberate action by the one who is aware of the problem. Jesus says, "Go and show him his fault." This step cannot be accomplished by prayer alone! Of course it is necessary to pray about the situation, but prayer must be accompanied by action.

• This step is Private

How many people should be involved at this point? ONLY TWO! Only two persons are to be involved in or even be aware of the issue.

222

Why does Jesus say to go privately? None of us likes to be told that we have failed or wronged someone. Privacy makes it a little easier to accept. It protects the person's reputation and demonstrates true love.

Jesus also understood the problems that would arise when this instruction is not carried out. In the case of James and Janet, suppose James takes the report to the pastor. The pastor then goes to see Janet. After exchanging greetings, the pastor says, "I have been told that you were seen with a young man." What will Janet's response be? She'll say immediately, "Who told you?" Now instead of dealing with the issue involved, the discussion will center on the procedure. Janet instinctively realizes that those who are talking about her sin to the pastor have also wronged her.

What will happen if Jesus' instructions are followed in Janet's case and James goes to visit her? There are several possibilities. First, she might admit her sin and repent. Jesus says, "You have won your brother over." The issue can be resolved, and Janet can be restored to a right relationship with God. (Perhaps she will need further counseling to gain victory over her sin, but that is an issue of helping her to grow stronger, not disciplining her.)

Second, when James goes to see Janet he might find that he has completely misunderstood her actions. She might tell him, "Oh, James. I'm so glad that you came. Let me tell you what happened. That young man is my cousin, and we met in town that day. He told me that my grandmother had died and the funeral was to be the following day. Since it was too late to travel that evening, I invited him to spend the night at my place, and we would travel together the next day. I was so disturbed when we passed you that I failed to greet you. He slept at my place, I slept with another neighbor, and then we traveled home the next day."

Yes, I realize that not every suspicious visit can be connected to a death in the family, but this illustrates how easily we "jump to conclusions" when no sin has occurred! Imagine the damage caused if James had gone to the home group, reported the incident, and asked for "prayer." The next time anyone in the group saw Janet, they might not even greet her, and she wouldn't know the reason!

A third possibility is that Janet would refuse to talk or completely deny the whole issue. If so, then Jesus' next step should be taken.

Before going to that step, I want to emphasize this first step because it is usually ignored or twisted. Yet, when applied properly, I believe it would solve 90% of the conflicts in the church. Yes, 90%, assuming that it is done in the right way and with the right attitude. Almost all issues would be resolved at this level if the practice were followed.

This step is so simple. It may be difficult to put into practice, but it is very clear what Jesus meant. People will give many excuses why they should not go directly to the person involved, but this is a clear command of Jesus and ANY ACTION OTHER THAN THIS IS SIN!

- Gossiping is surely sin, as well as listening to gossip!
- Simply praying about it without any action is also direct disobedience to the Word of God!
- Taking it to the pastor is also sin!
- Asking another person to pray about it is sin;
- Keeping quiet is sin.

Sin is costly. It will damage our relationship with God, and will harm relationships within the church. We have all been in such situations, and we know the pain involved. Jesus' instructions are actually meant to save us pain.

A final caution to you as a leader. At this level, the issue does not involve the church leadership. Don't be trapped as a leader to involve yourself in a case at this level. People's natural tendency when they see a problem is to run to the pastor.

"Oh, pastor, did you know what brother so and so did?" How do you respond to that? You will be tempted to quickly get involved, but according to the instruction of Jesus here, you should ask the person who has come to you, "Have you talked with that person about this?" If they haven't, read Matthew 18 to them and send them away to obey! Jesus knows what He is talking about! You do not have time to get involved in every little issue that will come up as a normal part of church life. You must teach people to take their responsibility as part of the body of Christ. You will be tempted to get involved because you want to feel important, or because you see yourself as the spiritual "police" in the church, or because you want to "know" everything going on in the church. Don't fall into that trap. Determine that you will never again disobey Christ's clear instructions.

Our goal in this step is reconciliation. However when this does not happen, Jesus has instructed another step.

Step Two: Go to the person along with one or two others

Jesus says that if things are not resolved with the first step, *"Go to the person along with one or two others."* Again, this instruction is not complicated. He says we should go with one or two others. Not three or four, not the whole church board, but one or two others. How many should now be involved? Only three or four, the original two plus one or two others.

The purpose of taking the others is to establish the issue properly with witnesses. It is crucial that we carefully choose who will go with us at this point. The person(s) chosen should be:
- **Respected by the member with the problem**
- **Known for sound judgment**

Look for someone the member will respect. If you bring someone who will likely take your side, the member will become defensive immediately.

Also look for a person with sound judgment. It takes a wise person to help resolve issues between two persons. Don't take someone who has a loose tongue or who is quick tempered. Find a person who can be objective, and can help work through the issue. I recommend that you don't tell them the details, but simply ask them to accompany you to resolve an issue. Then when you arrive at Janet's house, you will be able to say, "Janet, we met yesterday to talk about an issue I raised with you, and we didn't resolve it. Today I brought Mary with me. I haven't even told her what we talked about, because I wanted to say it in your presence." This approach makes every effort to bring reconciliation.

Again, if properly handled, the result of this meeting will often be positive, the person will see the seriousness of the situation, and be willing to repent. He or she should also sense the sincerity of the love from those who are visiting. Alternatively, the one(s) who have accompanied you may see that you don't really have grounds to accuse the member, and the issue can still be resolved with an apology.

Notice that this is still not a church issue, although a leader may well be involved at this point. It is a second attempt to bring repentance or understanding, and resolve the matter. It is somewhat more public but still not known by everyone. It is still not time to solicit prayer support or to share information about someone else. Only when these two steps are followed and do not produce results is the third step to be taken.

Step Three: Take the matter to the church

Jesus says, *"If he refuses to listen to them, tell it to the church."* Now the issue is placed into the hands of the leadership and it is now time for them to deal with it.

Notice that "tell it to the church" does not assume that the person is to be kicked out of the church! It is time for the church to confront the member who has sinned. The goal is for him to "listen to the church." The leaders at this point should make sure that they have all the relevant information about the issue, and not jump to conclusions. It is premature to make an announcement to the congregation. The leaders should arrange a meeting together with the persons involved, listening carefully to all sides. The goal is to continue showing the love of Christ, seeking a way for the person to be restored to a right relationship with God and the church.

Only when the person refuses to listen to the church should the next step be taken.

Step Four: Excommunication

Jesus says that if the person refuses to listen to the church, *"Treat him as you would a pagan or a tax collector."* This is now the point at which the person is removed from the church, or excommunicated. In other words the person is now no longer considered a brother or sister in Christ, he or she is to be regarded just like a person in the world, a pagan or tax collector.

> Often a person who has been excommunicated is treated worse than an unbeliever!

Paul uses the words *"hand this man over to Satan"* to describe this step. (1 Corinthians 5:5) Persons removed from the church for refusing to repent are no longer under the protection that the church provides, and are literally being returned to the kingdom of Satan. There they will be exposed to the full influence of Satan as a discipline from God. Obviously, this is not a step to be taken lightly.

Jesus says that the church should now treat this person as "a pagan or a tax collector." How do we treat unbelievers? We pray for them, witness to them and even eat with them like Jesus did (Matthew 15: 21-28), but we no longer have intimate fellowship with them. Paul warns of the danger of having close fellowship (eating) with someone who calls himself a brother but is living in sin. (1 Corinthians 5:11)

Unfortunately, often a person who has been excommunicated is treated *worse* than an unbeliever! Church members often totally ignore the person and don't even try to win him back to Christ. This is also disobedience to Jesus' instructions, and shows that our motive was not actually love for the individual involved.

The steps that Jesus gives are very clear, and it is crucial that they be followed precisely. When we fail to go by the "Book" we open ourselves up to all kinds of problems that we will soon see. Before that, let's examine a final step.

Step Five: Reconciliation

Reconciliation can occur at any point in the process of church discipline. Jesus alludes to this step when again He says, *"If he listens to you, you have won your brother over."* If at any point the person repents, we should receive him back into the fellowship. Paul says that when the person has repented we should *"forgive and comfort"* him. (2 Corinthians 2:6-11) We must remember that this is our primary purpose in discipline, and it is never too late for the person to repent and return to the fellowship. This may occur *before or after* excommunication.

This raises a crucial question. How can we know if a person has truly repented? Perhaps after Janet is removed from the church, she comes to you crying and asking to be forgiven. How can you know if she is sincere?

Paul gives some guidelines on that issue in 2 Corinthians 7:9-11 where he talks about *"godly sorrow"* and *"worldly sorrow."* He describes characteristics of godly sorrow, or genuine repentance, as producing "earnestness...eagerness to clear yourselves...indignation...alarm...longing... concern... readiness to see justice done."

One of the key indicators to look for in a person is a willingness to do whatever is necessary to make things right.

Paul calls this a *"readiness to see justice done."* If someone is truly repentant, he won't resist a public confession, or fight about losing his position of leadership. But when he comes with terms and conditions, the repentance is usually not genuine. If he says, "I want to be restored, but don't…" it raises a serious question about his sincerity. There should be a teachable spirit in the repentant person, and a willingness to receive counsel from the pastor or church leaders.

Before we finish talking about procedures, there is a special instruction given in 1 Timothy 5:20 for leaders. It says, *"Those who sin are to be rebuked publicly, so that the others may take warning."* It is a serious matter to discipline a church leader, and it requires a public rebuke. Paul gave Peter a public rebuke (Galatians 2:14) when he was in the wrong. Much is expected of a leader and the consequences of his sin are greater. James says, *"Not many of you should presume to be teachers, my brothers, because you know that we who teach will be judged more strictly."* (James 3:1) This is a cost of leadership. Leaders have influence over people, and their actions can affect others as well as their followers. For this reason when a leader sins he is often asked to step down from his position at least for some time. The reason is that although he has been forgiven of his sin, he has lost trust with people, and that trust must be restored before he can be effective as a leader. This also allows time for God to deal thoroughly with the issue that caused the sin.

THE ATTITUDES

It is crucial not only that we take the right actions when dealing with discipline in the church, but also that we have the right attitudes. There are three key attitudes the Bible commands us to have as we discipline others.

GENTLENESS

Galatians 6:1 says, *"Brothers, if someone is caught in a sin you who are spiritual should restore him gently. But watch yourself or you also may be tempted."* It is hard to discipline gently. We want to be rough; to make sure that the person gets what they deserve. This is especially hard, I believe, for those who have the gift of evangelism or prophecy, or the temperament of a choleric. It is very natural to feel, "You sinned, and now you will suffer." But the verse says "gently!"

HUMILITY

After instructing us to deal with the person gently, the same verse says, *"but watch yourself or you also may be tempted."* When we discipline others we must be aware of our own weaknesses. We are also able to fall. It is so easy to think *I could never do that sin!* But remember, *"Pride goes before a fall."* (Proverbs 16:18 KJV) Don't think that because it is someone else who has sinned, you are better. Satan would love to have you fall into this trap. If you recognize this, you will discipline with the attitude of humility.

Paul was also warning us that we may be tempted at the time of disciplining another with the wrong attitudes or actions. We can be so angry at the person who has sinned, that we fail to see our own hypocrisy. We need to ask God to search our hearts as we discipline others.

GRIEF

In 1 Corinthians 5:2, Paul tells the Corinthian Church that the proper attitude towards the sinning brother should be grief. Grief is a strong word describing intense sorrow. It should grieve us that the person has not been willing to repent. It should grieve us to be putting the person out of the church. We are losing a brother or sister. The devil is winning and unless the person repents, he will spend eternity in hell! That should cause grief.

It is easy to feel good about it, instead of having genuine pain for the person involved. Sometimes in the church, when an excommunication is announced, people respond with joy as they think, *Finally, the pastor has taken a step and now the church is pure again!* A lack of grief always reflects a lack of love for the person involved and a lack of awareness of our own weaknesses.

Our attitude is extremely important and we must watch it very carefully. It is not only important what we do, but how we do it. Many problems of discipline come from improper attitudes.

THE PROBLEMS IN DISCIPLINE

In the process of church discipline several problems can arise. We have already observed several of them, but it will be helpful to focus on what happens when we have the wrong process or wrong attitudes.

WRONG PROCESS

When the process outlined by Jesus is not carefully followed several problems will result.

1. The pastor can become involved too quickly

One of the most common mistakes in church discipline is when the pastor becomes involved too quickly. This may result in the person's being defensive because he has not been properly admonished in secret. It breeds resentment and leads to many explanations that don't really focus on the wrong action but on the process. It also makes the pastor spend too much of his time being a "spiritual policeman."

2. The wrong person(s) are chosen to accompany for step two

The person(s) chosen should be respected by the member with the problem, and should be of sound judgment. It is not wise to find persons who will just be sympathetic to your position. Find a neutral person who can be objective. If you take biased persons along, the member will become defensive and the chances of reconciliation are slim.

3. The church can be left out of the process

Sometimes cases of discipline are handled only by one leader, usually the pastor. This opens the door for many misunderstandings, which will generally leave some persons sympathetic with the individual involved. There may be a lack of communication, and misinformation will result. When not dealt with publicly, the situation will be open to gossip and misinterpretations. 2 Corinthians 2:6 reminds us that the *"majority"* imposed the discipline. Church discipline should not be a one-person issue. It is too easy for one person to be biased or to come to wrong conclusions. At least the leadership of the church should be involved in the process, sitting with the parties concerned. The elders should do some investigations and ask tough questions to all sides. This will help protect the pastor from personal offense.

4. The punishment might be too harsh or last too long

This happened in the Corinthian church. (2 Corinthians 2:7-8) The result was *"excessive sorrow"* on the part of the one who was excommunicated. It takes wisdom to know when enough is enough. Paul urged the church to receive the person back into the fellowship.

5. The issue is a questionable issue

Make sure that the "sin" in question is a clear violation of scripture and not just a difference of opinion. Paul makes it clear in Romans 14:1 that there are some *"disputable matters."* We need to be careful that we don't excommunicate someone over an issue that is not clearly wrong.

232

6. Improper investigations

Many times issues of sin and discipline are hampered by improper investigations. No one likes to investigate cases of sin, but when it needs to be done, it must be done right.

Here are key things to observe when conducting an investigation:

- **Talk with the sources**
  Confirm accounts firsthand. Don't rely on second hand reports, "So and so said..." It takes time and energy, but love compels us to make sure that we are getting the full story. Tell people when you meet with them, "If you mention someone else, I ask them to confirm the story."

- **Don't reveal any more than necessary**
  Other people don't need to know everything. Keep your observations to yourself. For example, if you are trying to verify the reports about Janet, and James has told you that Lucy also saw them, you will need to talk with Lucy. However, when you meet Lucy don't say, "I have received reports that Janet was sleeping with a young man." Simply ask, "What is your observation about Janet? Have you seen anything that compromises her testimony?"

- **Don't jump to conclusions**
  Always give the person the benefit of the doubt. Don't assume that they are guilty until proven otherwise. Somehow, we naturally assume the worst about people instead of the best! Remember, *"Love does not delight in evil but rejoices with the truth. It always protects, always trusts, always hopes, always perseveres."* (1 Corinthians 13:6,7) If you are not able to judge impartially, the whole issue will be contaminated with your sin.

WRONG ATTITUDES

1. Pride

A sin of pride can devastate the intended discipline. If the person who is receiving discipline senses a spirit of pride he/she will react against it. We must constantly guard against this attitude. Any time of discipline should be a time of examining ourselves and asking God to cleanse us of any sin. Ask yourself, "Do I truly love the person I am disciplining, or am I reacting in pride?"

2. Lack of Forgiveness

A church that is serious about maintaining a standard of holiness can easily develop an unwillingness to forgive. Interestingly, right after Jesus taught about discipline in Matthew 18, Peter asked about forgiveness. Jesus answered with the story of the unmerciful servant (Matthew 18:21-35). We who have been forgiven so much should also be able to forgive that brother or sister who has committed fornication or has stolen. Are we able to forgive? Think about someone you know who has been excommunicated. Have you forgiven them and welcomed them back? If this is difficult, it's probably because of pride, or a lack of genuine love for the person. 2 Corinthians 2:5-11 urges the church to forgive the person who has repented. I've heard of cases in which people were told, "Even if you do repent, don't come back to this church!" Instead, we should have a time of rejoicing when someone comes back to the church.

The task of church discipline is not pleasant, but it will inevitably need to be done. When properly handled, it has the potential to be a growing process for everyone involved. Your role as a leader is crucial. You have three primary responsibilities relative to church discipline:

• **Understand the Biblical purpose and process of discipline.** This chapter has enabled you to think deeply about the issues. You should continue your study on the subject, especially of the key Biblical passages.

• **Teach the people the same.** Many leaders have never taught their people the process of church discipline as given by Jesus in Matthew 18. Set a date to teach your people what you have learned.

• **Make sure that God's pattern is carried out in the church.** It is your responsibility to ensure that people do what the scriptures teach. You will have many opportunities to gently guide people to do what you have taught them. When you learn this together, you will be a much stronger congregation, able to rejoice at the power of God's word.

ACTION ASSIGNMENT

1. Think about your experience with church discipline.
   (Choose one case from your experience to answer the following questions.)

   What was the primary motive of the leaders? Was it love for the person or concern for the purity of the church or something else?

   _____

   _____

   What actions were taken in the process of discipline? (Be specific)

   _____

   _____

   _____

   From what we have learned from the scripture, were the actions Biblical? _____ Explain why or why not.

   _____

   _____

   _____

2. Why do you think it is so difficult for believers to take the first step in Matthew 18?

   _____

   _____

   _____

3. What is the result when this step is overlooked?

   _____

   _____

   _____

4. Look at the six problems under "wrong process." Reflect on the list. Which have been most common in your church, and what has been the result?

_____

_____

_____

_____

5. What specific action can you take as a leader to help your people follow the scriptural commands for discipline? (Note: The higher your position of leadership, the more control you will have in this area. However, each person can do something to contribute to growth in this area.)

_____

_____

_____

_____

_____

When will you do this? _____

Chapter Thirteen
THE LEADER AND CHURCH ADMINISTRATION

Pastor Frank stands before the congregation and clears his throat, as he prepares to make the announcements. He holds several small papers in his hand, which he shuffles back and forth as he reads. "The ladies will hold their meeting this afternoon at 3:00. Is that time correct?" He waits while the chairlady answers the question from the audience. Then he continues, "The crusades which we announced last week will be canceled due to some circumstances which made it impossible to continue. All the youth should meet briefly after the service in the sanctuary. Also, the men are to meet in the sanctuary. Well, that can't work, so the youth will meet outside. Okay, now let's see…" He strains to read the writing on the paper, "The baptism which we were going to have this evening will be postponed, because the water is too high in the river. We will announce when we are going to do it again. Now, whoever is to lead the final song, please come, and lead us." With that he sits down, dropping a couple of the papers, which he quickly stuffs into his coat pocket.

Does Pastor Frank love Jesus? Absolutely! Is he going to heaven? Absolutely! Will he grow a strong church? Absolutely NOT! Why? His administrative skills are very weak.

At the word "administration" most church leaders wrinkle up their faces and look like they have to go to the dentist to have a tooth pulled!

Administration may not be the most exciting activity in leadership, but it is still crucial. If you are a strong leader but a poor administrator, many things will not go well in your leadership. Administration is weak in many otherwise strong churches. My goal in this chapter is to help you do the work of administration effectively.

First, what is administration? To administer is to, "manage or supervise the execution, use, or conduct of" or "to manage affairs." For our use, administration is *the management needed to carry out the vision.* Vision provides direction, but without adequate administration, vision will never materialize. Administration includes details like planning, organizing, writing letters, setting goals, and filing that are necessary to implement the vision God has given you. This is in contrast to the more "spiritual" aspects of ministry like praying, preaching, and evangelizing.

THE PRIORITY OF ADMINISTRATION

Many people look at administration as a non-spiritual activity that is at best endured and often totally overlooked. I want to change that perception by showing you the value of administration as it relates to leadership.

ADMINISTRATION PROVIDES NEEDED STRUCTURE

Administration provides the structure and order that vision requires. Administration is the engine that gets the vision moving. Vision without administration will never work well, and will remain a dream in the mind of the leader. Vision paints a picture of the destination, while administration provides a map of the journey. Administration is the flesh on the skeleton and without the flesh your dreams are useless!

ADMINISTRATION PROVIDES NEEDED GROWTH

Good administration enables a leader to experience both personal growth and organizational growth.

Personal Growth

Through effective administration the leader can do more in less time, with fewer resources. This allows the leader to continue growing in the areas of his or her strength. Growing people learn to organize and discipline themselves. They plan and schedule their lives to do the most important things. A life in order will be a growing life, and growing leaders produce growing organizations.

Every leader must have some administrative skills. The leader who is weaker in administration needs enough ability to manage the organization through well qualified people.

Organizational Growth

A well-administered church will attract more people and higher levels of people. People are attracted to a place where they find order, purpose and a clear sense of direction. Even people who themselves live confused lives aren't attracted to a church where there is confusion, where plans are made at the last minute and often fail for lack of adequate preparation. This was Pastor Frank's problem. All other things being equal, people prefer a church that is well administered, rather than one led by Pastor Frank!

Good administration also attracts a higher level of people. People with strong leadership qualities will not stay with a church where things are in chaos. They live an organized life, work in places where there is order and structure, and expect things to be well done in the church. Without good administration, these people will soon be seeking another church home. Pastor Frank has already lost them! When they leave he comments, "They weren't really committed anyway!"

Many groups or churches never succeed because of poor administration. While administration is a spiritual gift, all leaders can develop some proficiency in this art. A good secretary can provide valuable assistance in this area. As an organization grows, people more gifted can be enlisted to assist.

SPIRITUALITY IS NO SUBSTITUTE FOR ADMINISTRATION

Spiritual anointing and passion are needed to attract people, but when they find inadequate planning, order, or follow-up on things needing attention, they will leave.

Having emphasized the importance of administration, let me clarify that administration cannot replace relationships with people. I don't want to imply that all it takes for a successful church is good administration. Good administration with poor people skills will also fall short. A proper balance is required.

This chapter is directed to pastors and those in top leadership positions; but applicable to all leaders. It will lay a foundation to keep growing in this area of administration.

THE PROCESS OF ADMINISTRATION

What is the process of administration? There are three major areas that a pastor or key leader should focus on: **OUTLINE, ORGANIZE, and OPERATE.** Outline deals with plans, organize involves people, and operate examines the process.

OUTLINE DEALS WITH PLANS

A significant part of administration involves planning, outlining what you want to happen. We looked briefly at this issue in chapter four on goals, but it also relates to administration.

Plan Your Goals

Goals should be set for every area. The method of setting goals has been explained in chapter four, but a few additional points need to be noted here.

When the goals have been set, publicize them! This is a part of sharing the vision with the people. Don't hesitate to remind people continually. Yes, some may fail, but if they have been well made most will be accomplished and will be an encouragement to the people.

This is a frightening step, because it really puts our leadership on the line. In a recent year I set a goal to reach 365 people for Christ as a church, one person every day. Although convinced that we could do it, saying it was challenging! But I shared the goal with people and continually reminded them of the goal. I put a chart in the church, and in my office I put signs that read: "365!"

You will also need to evaluate your goals as a leader, and rectify any problems that have developed. Set a time on a monthly basis to look at your goals and see how far you have progressed. If you are not on schedule, determine what needs to be done to succeed.

Plan Your Program

After the goals are set, put dates on them. This involves making a program of events, a church calendar. This includes a long-term and a short-term program.

A long-term program

The long-term program deals with a whole year of activities. This program should be made before the beginning of the year

The long-term program is essential for proper planning. Why?

1. It avoids conflicts of scheduling.
2. It helps meet your goals. If you don't put your goals on the calendar, they are unlikely to happen!

Of course, some changes will be made in the course of the year, but this provides an excellent framework for coordinating activities.

How do you do it? Get a relaxed time to sit down with your goals, a calendar, and any other schedules that might affect your planning. For example, you may have a denominational calendar to consider.

Start putting activities on your calendar in pencil so that you can easily make changes as necessary. If you have certain things which happen on a regular basis, put them in your calendar first. For example, the ladies may have a fellowship monthly on the first Sunday afternoon, or you may have a week of prayer every third week of the month. Then begin placing other events on the calendar, beginning with major items such as fundraisings or crusades. Go through the year and see what works well and what doesn't. Some things which you should consider as you plan:

- Holidays. You may want to use some for special events; also consider enjoying a holiday without church activities!
- School schedules. This will affect youth activities, and may also influence times when it is difficult to raise money!
- Weather patterns that can affect outdoor meetings and baptisms.
- Your denominational calendar.

Space out major events so that people won't be overloaded. Allow time to raise finances for projects that require money.

A short-term program

The short-term program covers 1-3 months and involves schedules for preaching, leaders of the services, ushers, and

243

other routine events. The larger your church grows, the more important this program becomes to keep things running smoothly. Make sure the people on the program are informed of their responsibilities!

If you are inviting visiting speakers, be sure to inquire about their availability before putting them on the program. Speak to them or write a letter inviting them to come, with the appropriate details on times and expectations.

ORGANIZE DEALS WITH PEOPLE

The administrator should not only make plans for the church, but must organize the people to work well together. Appropriate structures must be established to carry out the vision. This includes establishing a leadership structure, choosing and appointing leaders, and empowering people to help carry out the vision. Since this structure will vary from one style of church government to another, I will provide only general guidelines that can be adapted to your particular situation.

Organize your leadership structure

The first area that should be organized is the leadership structure: how leaders are appointed and the levels of accountability in the church. In many churches these are specified in the constitution or bylaws. In such cases you only need to know the administrative structure and implement it.

In other churches, particularly new ones, the structure has not yet been determined. When a church or ministry is small, it is tempting to think that these issues are not important. But the leader should be looking ahead and laying a solid foundation for the future. It is important to ask questions about the structure of the church. Will the pastor alone run the church? Will there be a council or board? How can the pastor be replaced? How will leaders be chosen? Replaced? What are the qualifications and the lines of accountability?

These must be answered BEFORE PROBLEMS ARISE! In the heat of problems it becomes very difficult to answer these questions. Many churches do not foresee difficulties in these areas, only to discover serious problems. Therefore, it is wise to establish the structure of the church early.

Write down how your church will be organized

If you belong to a denomination, this may already be provided for you in the constitution or bylaws. If any flexibility is given to the local church, you will need to think about those areas. Answer the questions above. Seek counsel from other church leaders or leaders in similar organizations. Find out what has worked well, and what they would do differently.

Develop an organizational chart

An organizational chart is a graphic drawing of how different positions in the church relate to each other. It can help greatly in understanding lines of accountability in the church. It clearly shows which person or group is responsible to whom. It must be clearly understood, especially by the leaders.

Look below at two simple organizational charts. In chart "A" the pastor is clearly in a position above the church board. His voice is final! In chart "B", the church board has authority over the pastor.

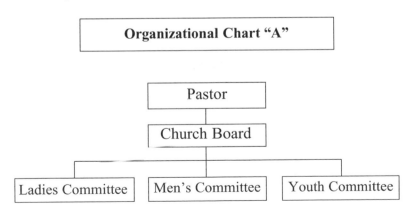

Organizational Chart "A"

Pastor

Church Board

Ladies Committee | Men's Committee | Youth Committee

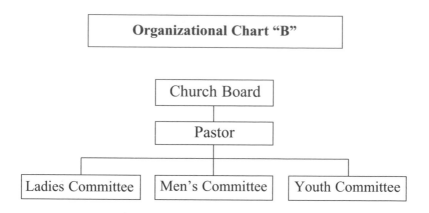

Your church structure might have a 'board' 'council' 'session' or other term to describe the top administrative body.

Our objective here is not to argue the merits of each system, but to say that the relationship between the different leadership organs in the church should be clearly understood by everyone involved.

Organize your leaders

Once the leadership structure is established, the leaders must be chosen. The method of choosing leaders will depend on the organizational structure you have chosen. Some churches give the pastor almost total control; others give the power to the council or the people.

Many times when I teach about this concept a participant will ask, "What is the best way?" The Bible doesn't state, "Thou shall appoint leaders by elections" nor does it say, "The pastor shall appoint leaders of his choice." In many instances in scripture leaders are appointed; in other cases, the people are given a voice in the process. (See Acts 6:1-6 and Acts 14:23 for two different methods used in the early church.)

If given a choice, I prefer to select leaders by appointment in a young church, while allowing more input from the members as the church grows and matures. The top leadership (pastor and/or council) should always retain the right of final approval of leaders chosen by the members. For example, the ladies might choose leaders among themselves, subject to approval by the church leader(s). As a pastor I might know something about someone that would disqualify her, while the others may not be aware of that issue. Even in a situation where the church members have the power to select their leaders, a wise pastor will influence the process with good teaching about what to look for in a leader.

In chapter eight we looked at how to choose leaders. Here I will focus on two groups commonly found in churches, elders, and deacons. Since these offices are generally the highest, special care must be taken in the selection process.

Elders and deacons

Look first at the Biblical qualifications for elders and deacons found in 1 Timothy 3:1-13, Titus 1:6-9. God has given clear instructions about the type of persons selected for these offices. When God says family life should be in order, don't ignore the potential leader's family life! It is easy to think a certain person is so spiritual that we overlook important aspects of his life.

When choosing an elder or deacon, don't look only at education, economic status, or prominence in the community. A true elder is already providing "pastoral" care to people, in formal or informal ways. Do people visit his home for counsel and prayer? Does he visit others to counsel and encourage? Does he connect well with people and have their confidence? If these are not happening before you call him, don't expect miracles afterwards!

Deacons should likewise already be actively involved in practical service. A good way to spot a deacon is to watch for people that arrange seats, organize food to be served, and remember to bring towels to the baptism. A person with the gift of serving will be easy to spot, if you are watching keenly.

247

Organize your committees

When the leadership structure is established and leaders have been chosen, in most cases they will be grouped in committees. Committees exist to share the work and spread responsibility. They allow a small group of people to focus on a specific aspect of the vision, and help to carry it out. A committee can think specifically on missions, or on finances. Another may deal with the special needs of the widows. When committees are functioning well under the direction of the pastor and top leadership in the church, much can be accomplished. A wise leader will learn to work through committees.

Determine what committees are required for the smooth operations of your church. Make sure that there is a demonstrable need for them. Don't establish committees just to give people something to do. Make sure that there is a clear objective and that the committee will actually facilitate the growth and involvement of others. As a church grows, remember that some committees may no longer be needed. Abolish them!

Since committees form the "core" of the church structure we'll use the word **CORE** to give guidelines on using committees effectively.

C̲ALL THEM

The method of calling will depend on your church structure. When calling people to serve, consider their gifts, spiritual maturity, availability, and willingness. Don't call them outside their gifts, above their spiritual maturity, past their availability, or beyond their willingness. Re-read this paragraph and reflect on its implications for your organization!

O̲RGANIZE THEM

Having chosen your committee members, organize them. This involves several steps.

1. Give them their purpose, lines of accountability and limits of authority

This should be done in writing as they begin their work. Explain clearly the job of each committee, the person or board to whom they are accountable, and the limits of their authority. For example, you might tell the youth committee that they are responsible for planning all the youth functions, subject to approval by the elders.

2. Choose officers

Generally this will be a chairperson, a secretary, and a treasurer. In some cases a vice-chairman and assistant secretary will also be needed.

3. Help officers understand their roles

Never assume that everyone understands what their roles should be. Make sure that you clearly inform the officers of their roles. I have used the following "job descriptions" for officers.

Responsibilities of the Chairperson:

1. Call the meeting
2. Present the agendas to the group
3. Guide the discussion and ensure that satisfactory decisions are reached.
4. Oversee implementation of the decisions.

See *Appendix G* for a sample training session for chairpersons.

Responsibilities of the Secretary:

1. Accurately record everything significant which happens in the meeting
2. Write the official correspondence.
3. Maintain the file in good condition.

See *Appendix H*, "The Work of the Secretary of a Committee" which can be used to train secretaries. See also *Appendix I* for a sample of how minutes can be taken.

Responsibilities of the Treasurer:

1. Collect and disburse the money of the group as per the directions of the committee.
2. Keep accurate records of all income and expenses.
3. Provide reports of the finances as required.
4. Maintain a bank account if needed.

See chapter fourteen for more details about financial record keeping.

RELEASE THEM

After choosing and organizing the committee, release them! Often committees are appointed, but then the church leader keeps doing the job. Pastor Peter told the missions committee to plan for the crusade. A few days later he met the chairman on the road and told him, "Oh, by the way I met a friend of mine yesterday and invited him to be the speaker at the crusade, and he will come with his own equipment. I also talked to the printer about the posters." When this happens, committee members become frustrated and lose interest. They need the freedom to do their work. They will make some mistakes, we all do! So let them learn. Support them!

One aspect of releasing committees is public recognition of the committee members to the rest of the church/organization. Let others know who they are and what they are responsible for. Recognize them publicly for their good effort.

Releasing them does not mean that no oversight is required. They are accountable to the pastor or a board. They may need some training to be more effective. They will need some correction as they learn from mistakes. Do it and do it well! But don't do their work.

EVALUATE THEM

Appoint the members of the committee. Give them their assignment. Make sure their boundaries are clear. Establish accountability. Release them to do their work. Then evaluate, to ensure that the work is being done. The pastor or the responsible person should meet regularly with each chairperson for review, problem solving, encouragement, and sharing of the vision. The pastor may occasionally meet with the entire committee, but this should become less and less necessary.

OPERATE DEALS WITH PROCESS

We will now look at the third component of the administrative process, operate. This deals with the actual process of administration, and will review some of the areas we have already examined and add more flesh to others.

Let's look at the word "O.P.E.R.A.T.E."

Organize

This word has already been used in this chapter. First we looked at the need to organize the structure of the church then to organize the committees. These dealt specifically with organizing people.

There is still much work to be done by the leaders of the local church that involves organizing. Temporary committees are essential for specific short-term assignments. Major events such as community outreach efforts require much organization.

Offices need to be organized, with an adequate filing system. When someone comes to the office and asks for a baptismal card, and you dig through a mound of paperwork muttering, "I know that file is somewhere here!" the person waiting will observe that you need help with administration!

Organization deals with your personal life as well. Having a diary and sticking to it is important. Decide when you will be in the office, and when you will do visitation. Use your priorities to plan your schedule. Let your people know when you are available.

Organizing is not a one-time event; it is a necessary process at all stages of growth. As the church grows larger, more organizing will be needed.

Plan

Plan is another prominent word in administration! Planning is a key ingredient in the whole administrative process and bears repeating here.

Planning requires time and effort. It will not happen without a conscious decision. Too many church leaders fail to plan, and chaos results. In his book on Christian management Peter Wiwcharuck asks, "God's great universe is operating according to a strict plan. Is there any excuse why your "universe" should operate as an accident evolving from conflict and confusion?"[53]

Planning includes getting permits, publicity, preparing budgets, inviting and confirming speakers, and many other things. Look at the events in your calendar. Set a time early enough that you can plan for each event. The larger the event, the earlier the planning should begin. If you have a board meeting, schedule time to plan for that meeting. If you have a seminar scheduled, set a time to invite a speaker or prepare the teaching for that seminar. This may seem tedious (and it is!) but the results are well worth the effort. Remember, "He who fails to plan, plans to fail."

Employ

As your church or organization grows, it will become necessary to hire others to help carry out the vision. If you aren't yet at that stage, keep working on the vision! Your vision and goals should be big enough to eventually require others to assist you. Employing people is a serious business, and Christian organizations have their share of problems related to employment.

Let's look at several keys to successful employment.

A. Find the right person

The person you employ will either build you up or tear you

---

[53] Peter Wiwcharuck, *Building Effective Leadership* (Three Hills, Alberta: International Christian Leadership Development Foundation, 1987) p. 180.

down. Be extremely careful in selection. Maxwell says that in a small organization the person that you hire is even more crucial than in a large one. If you have a staff of 10 and one person is bad, you have a problem with only 10%. But if you have only two people and one is bad, you have a problem with 50% of your staff! So, make sure the first person you get is good!

> Look for the best person that you can get for the job

Always look for the best person available for the job. Go for true leaders, not just someone looking for a job. Not everyone who is "available" will do the job! Think before you hire. What kind of person do I need? Have a picture in your mind before trying to choose the person. Think about the personality needed for the job as well as the skills and spiritual gift required. If you seek an accountant, look for a melancholic. But if you need a receptionist or evangelist, don't employ a Maxwell lists his "top 20" personal requirements in a potential staff member: Positive Attitude, High Energy Level, Personal Warmth, Integrity, Responsibility, Good Self-Image, Mental Horsepower, Leadership Ability, Absence Of Personal Problems, People Skills, Sense Of Humor, Resilience, Track Record, Desire, Self-Discipline, Creativity, Flexibility, Sees 'Big Picture', Intuitive.[54]

B. Establish job descriptions

Job descriptions must clearly state the expectations of both parties involved in an employment agreement. It can help alleviate misunderstandings, and also provides some accountability between the church and the employee. It also provides legal protection for both parties. It becomes increasingly important as more people are added to the staff.

---

[54] Maxwell, *Developing the Leader Within You*, 186.

Even volunteer positions, such as secretaries of committees, will benefit from a clear, written description. We cannot just assume that everyone knows what is expected of them and how they are supposed to work.

There are formal and informal job descriptions. Formal job descriptions include: starting date, monthly salary and benefits, accountability, method of terminating the agreement, vacation time, working hours, and the work expected to be accomplished.

See *Appendix J* for sample appointment letter and terms of employment between an employer and employee.

C. Communicate
Communication is a key issue in relating to staff. Many problems in work relationships arise because of communication breakdowns. What should you communicate?

Dreams

Share your dreams with each staff member. If they lack the vision, their work will just be a job, not a ministry. They should understand how their job fits into the big picture, and why it is crucial to the vision.

Expectations

What do you expect from the person? Be specific. Give training where required. Don't expect a new person to know how you want everything done. Even if they have done a similar job for someone else, they will need to learn how to work with you. Make your expectations clear from the beginning. Tell them how and when you will evaluate their performance.

Failures

When a person has failed, tell them! Speak the truth in love. Many times administrators fail to communicate clearly when expectations haven't been met. This only leads to frustrations on both sides. Talk about it, review your expectations, and agree together on steps of change.

D. Reward

Employees need incentives to stay highly motivated. Think of how you can reward the type of behavior and work that you desire. Maxwell says, "The things that are rewarded get done." A small bonus, a gift, some time off, public recognition, a note of thanks for a job well done will all go a long way to encourage productivity and high morale. These things don't all cost money, but they do take a deliberate effort on your part as a leader.

E. Evaluate

Regular evaluation helps everyone rise to a higher level. As an employer it is crucial that every member of your team has a regular evaluation. This should be done at least annually and preferably every six months. It is important to review the job description with the employee and assess his/her performance in different areas of work and work related behavior. This can be done by having different staff members evaluate one another, or for the employee to do a self-evaluation. I have used the evaluation form in *Appendix K,* requesting staff persons to fill out the form, and rating their performance in the appropriate areas. When we meet, we exchange our papers, read through them, and then talk! This takes courage, but on several occasions my employees have told me they appreciated my willingness to sit and talk with them, because it made them better workers and stronger people.

F. Release appropriately

Sometimes a worker doesn't measure up to expectations. This may be an issue of not doing assigned work properly, or it may be character or attitude issues. It is difficult in Christian settings to release a worker, but it will sometimes be necessary. Remember that as the leader, you are responsible to keep the best staff possible for the growth of the organization. When you keep an incompetent person, you are hurting the organization and the person. That puts the issue in a different light! When it needs to be done follow these three "do's":

- **Do it carefully**
Make sure the issues are clear. Pray, talk, and get counsel. Ask yourself if you have done everything possible to develop this person. Has the worker understood what is lacking in their performance? Has he or she been warned adequately? Releasing someone should be the final resort, not the first step of action.
- **Do it personally**
Sit and talk with the person. Don't give him a letter as he leaves the office! You may need to write a formal letter of termination for your records, but have the courage and courtesy to face the person. Let him vent any anger or bitterness to you as the leader.
- **Do it quickly**
Once you have decided that someone needs to be released, do it quickly. Don't delay. Pay the person appropriately and release him or her. It is better to pay a month's salary and release the person, than to have him stay and drain the morale of the whole organization.

*R*ecord

Keeping records is an important part of administration. Record keeping should start early and continue throughout the life of the church. Keeping records does three things:

- It provides an accurate record of what is happening in the church.
- It enables needed things to be found easily.
- It allows others to understand what is happening or has happened.

Our goal in keeping records is to preserve important information for future leadership. Perhaps this is why many pastors don't see much need of keeping records; they have no plans to work themselves out of a job! As long as they can understand and remember things, they see no need for the time to maintain records. But they will one day leave their position of leadership, and would be wise to prepare for it!

Every church should have a system of keeping records. This is commonly done with some type of filing system. Every committee or board in the church should keep a file. In addition, records should be kept of other activities in the church. For example, files for baptisms, dedication of children, deaths, marriages, moveable property, finances, and membership help maintain the records accurately. Files for reporting to your denomination and for correspondence are also necessary.

Records of the church should be kept in a safe place, preferably not under the pastor's mattress! Even if the pastor doesn't have an office, the church records should be separated from his personal papers. Build a cabinet to store them as soon as possible.

Correspondence is an important part of recordkeeping. Letters belong to the organization, not the writer. A copy should be filed. Photocopying is appropriate, or if you are using a computer, print an additional copy.

Attend meetings

Meetings are important because they bring minds together to discuss issues and make decisions that will benefit the whole group. Much time is devoted to meetings. This can be time well spent, or it can be wasted time.

What can you do as a leader to make a meeting successful?

• **Be prepared**

Before the meeting determine the agenda. What are the most important issues? What will be needed ... a report, a letter, or a file? Make sure the minutes of the last meeting are ready. Read them to recall what things have been done, and what has not been done from the previous meeting.

- **Keep the meeting moving**

Determine how much time should be allotted for the meeting and budget that time to ensure that the necessary business is covered. Much time is wasted talking about insignificant issues, leaving insufficient time to tackle more important matters. If no consensus is reached, and the decision is not urgent, table it until the next meeting. Move on to the important things. Allow enough time for members to express differences of opinion, but when everyone is in agreement don't waste time. Ask, "Is there anyone who does not agree?"

- **Make decisions**

Your goal is to make decisions whenever possible. Don't allow the discussion to go around and around without reaching a decision. If no conclusion can be reached, you may agree to decide it at the next meeting, but whenever possible make a decision. Agree on what is to be done, when it is to be done, and who is to do it.

Take time

One of the great needs in administration is time. It takes time to administer well. Many pastors fail to invest the time needed to administer, feeling that their time is better spent in prayer or witnessing. While, administration is not the primary calling of the pastor, he should set aside a reasonable amount of time to accomplish it. Perhaps one morning per week would be a good place to start. That's the time to sit and plan, write letters, organize the work, and prepare for meetings. As the work grows some of this can be delegated to another person gifted in administration, but make sure that enough time is given to administrative issues.

Evaluate

In administration, like so many other areas in leadership, evaluation is essential. "Where have we been, how have we done, what went right, what went wrong?" are all important questions. Strive for continual improvement. Ask God to strengthen you in your weak areas.

Continually examine the administrative structure of the church, to ensure that it serves the needs. As the church grows, the structure should be re-examined. Will it allow us to keep growing? What changes are needed?

Others can help you in this area. Ask for feedback about how you are doing. As a pastor, I met weekly with a group of people to evaluate the Sunday service. We looked at how well we kept time, how the music and worship was led, how the equipment functioned, how visitors were welcomed, and many other areas. This might be seen as a waste of time, but we were evaluating for excellence, always striving to improve.

THE PITFALLS OF ADMINISTRATION

What are the problems that we encounter in administration?

NOT DOING ENOUGH!

A common problem among church leaders is that they simply don't do enough administration. Perhaps they haven't been trained to do it and it doesn't come naturally, or they do not understand the importance of administration.

Take time for administration. Learn how to administer. Go through the steps methodically. It may seem like drudgery, but with practice it will become more familiar and you will improve. Every leader who desires to grow in this area can become proficient enough to take his church or organization to a higher level.

LACK OF DELEGATION

Delegation is an area of administration and people development that we have not discussed much, but in which many leaders are weak. Delegation is working through others; enabling them to help accomplish the task. Until we learn to delegate, our church/organization will not grow beyond a "one-man show." Ask yourself, "What am I doing that others could/should do?" "Who can do it?" "What training do they need?" This is an issue of equipping, which is a key part of your role as a leader.

Often leaders fail to delegate because they don't think the job will get done as well as they could do it. This may or may not be true, but it's not wise! When a leader insists on doing everything himself, he will never reach his full potential. When he delegates, he can focus on other areas that may bring a greater return to the organization and take him to a higher level. Management experts recommend that when someone else can do a job 80% as well as you can do it; it's time to delegate. Let others develop also, and together you will accomplish more.

Delegate.
Daily.
Diligently.
Deliberately.

A sign in my office reminds me: Delegate. Daily. Diligently. Deliberately.

Consider this wisdom from J. Oswald Sanders, "A one-person office can never grow larger than the load one person can carry." And, "Failing to delegate, the leader is caught in a morass of secondary detail; it overburdens him and diverts his attention from primary tasks. People under him do not achieve their own potential. In some cases, insisting on doing a job oneself is a result of simple conceit."[55]

It's not always easy to let others do things that we know how to do and requires that we have a long range vision. Maxwell says, "If you want to do a few small things right, do them yourself. If you want to do great things and make a big impact, learn to delegate."[56]

---

[55] Sanders, *Spiritual Leadership*, 138.

[56] John C. Maxwell, *Developing the Leaders Around You* (Nashville: Thomas Nelson, 1995) p. 173.

Take a moment and evaluate yourself in the area of delegation. How can you delegate more effectively?

PERSONALIZED ADMINISTRATION

A final pitfall is what I call "personalized administration." By this I mean administration that is done in such a way that others can't follow. A treasurer may record the church finances on a torn piece of paper he keeps in a drawer at home. He can tell you about every piece of paper, but no one else can make any sense out of the scraps. If filing is done carelessly, the person who did it may be able to find what is needed, but no one else has a chance!

In a well administered church/organization, another leader can step in, see what is happening, and move forward. Always build for the future. Lay a foundation that will endure, and will be usable to others.

CONCLUSION

Church administration is a crucial part of your leadership, and you can do everything required for you to be a good administrator. Even if it is not an area of your giftedness, your effort to improve will take you to a higher level as a leader. Do the work. Sweat the details. The results will reward you! Start with the action assignment and move forward from there.

261

ACTION ASSIGNMENT

1. In what areas are you currently involved in administration?

2. As a leader, think about how much time you give to administration.
Circle the most applicable description: Not nearly enough, barely enough, enough, too much. What is the result?

3. Think about your church/organization as a whole. What value is placed on administration or organization? Circle the most applicable description: Not nearly enough, barely enough, enough, too much. What is the result?

4. Examine the administrative structure in your church/organization by answering the following questions. You may need to inquire if you are unaware of some answers.
    a. Who chooses leaders?

    b. Who is the primary decision maker? (This could be a person or committee)

    c. What committees exist?

d. To whom are the committees accountable?

e. Who is responsible to keep the official records?

f. Does your church have a constitution and/or bylaws?

g. Is there an organizational chart?

h. Who determines the short-term program?

5. Think about the committees in your church. Are they functioning well or just there on paper? Are the members released to do their assignment? Are they well chosen and properly equipped? Spend a few minutes thinking about those issues and then answer the following question by circling the most appropriate response: From your perspective, how would you rate the usefulness of committees in your church? (Not useful at all, somewhat useful, very useful)

What can you do that would strengthen the role of committees in your church?

When will you do it?

6. Look at your notes at the acronym O.P.E.R.A.T.E. (organize, plan, employ, record, attend meetings, take time, evaluate) Which of these areas is most relevant to your needs right now as a leader? _____ In the area that you have chosen, write three short paragraphs on another paper. In paragraph one, put in your own words the teaching related to that area. In paragraph two, write your experience (successes, failures, observations) in that area. In paragraph three, write what you have done and will do to strengthen your administration.

Chapter Fourteen
THE LEADER AND FINANCES

I listened intently as Pastor Frank poured out his heart to me. "I'm behind in my rent, and the landlord is coming every day to get his money. The church hasn't paid my allowance for two months. I have borrowed money to survive, but now I don't know where to turn." His face reflected his frustration, and his worn out clothes spoke of his suffering. Frank represents many pastors who have a sincere heart to serve God, but struggle greatly in the area of finances.

It has been my observation that as many as 80% of God's people are living in financial bondage, including leaders like Pastor Frank. This is displeasing to God, and very frustrating to the individuals involved. Surely this is not God's plan for believers.

Churches are always crying, "There's not enough money." Why? Is it because God planned for His Kingdom to be poor? Does He desire that pastors be among the most poorly paid people in society? Is it in His heart to see programs delayed for lack of resources? No, a thousand times no!

What's happening? Why is there not enough money in the church? I believe that there are two primary reasons:

LACK OF VISION

Many times a lack of money is simply a reflection of a lack of vision in the leader. As we noted in chapter three, money flows towards vision. When a vision is clearly stated and accepted by people they will be motivated to give towards the vision. Followers need a vision that is compelling enough that they want to be involved and are willing to sacrifice for it! When this vision is not clearly stated or accepted by the followers, there will be reluctance to give and financial problems may result.

The vision needs to be large enough to inspire sacrificial giving. Although the church treasurer may be concerned about having enough money to pay all the bills and meet the budget, members are not likely to get excited about simply maintaining the church. Share a larger vision. "Let's give generously so that after we have paid our expenses, we will be able to finance the outreach event in our community to bring people to Jesus."

LACK OF OBEDIENCE TO THE WORD

A second reason many churches and ministries lack money is a failure to obey the Word of God. This may come through ignorance of the Word or willful disobedience, or both.

Who is to blame? Is it the economy? The government? Not enough donors? No! "Everything rises and falls on leadership." These are problems that church leaders must wrestle with and solve. It's a part of leadership.

Before we go to the details of what a leader should do in the area of finances, let's examine a scripture that will underline the importance of finances in the life of a leader.

Luke 16:10, 11, *"Whoever can be trusted with very little can also be trusted with much, and whoever is dishonest with very little will also be dishonest with much. So if you have not been trustworthy in handling worldly wealth, who will trust you with true riches?"*

Note carefully two things that Jesus is saying here. First, you can't expect more, if you don't properly handle the little that you have. If you do not faithfully handle a few coins, why should God give you more? He is not a fool! You need to ask yourself if you have faithfully handled what God has given you. Be faithful in the little things, and then pray for more.

Secondly, Jesus says that if we don't properly handle material wealth we cannot be trusted with more important things that He calls *"true riches."* Material wealth is not "true" wealth; it will not survive the test of time. It can be stolen or lost. Spiritual leaders are entrusted with the souls of men and women that are worth far more than earthly currency. Therefore, a leader that isn't living according to the Word of God in his finances will never experience God's fullest blessing on his ministry! Many leaders I've talked with believe God should make an exception in their case because they are in real need. But God does not make exceptions to His Word. When we are preaching and teaching, but living in financial bondage, it portrays a bad picture of the God we serve.

So, what should leaders do concerning finances? There are three things every leader should do to make a significant change in every church.

LEADERS SHOULD OBEY GOD'S PRINCIPLES OF FINANCES IN THEIR PERSONAL LIVES

In every area of leadership, it is vital that what we say and do lines up, and the area of finances is no exception. We are to be *"examples to the flock."* (1 Peter 5:3) We are to obey the Word before we teach others.

Ezra gives us this model to follow when it comes to God's Word. Ezra 7:10, *"For Ezra had devoted himself to* *the <u>study</u> and <u>observance</u> of the Law of the LORD, and to <u>teaching</u> its decrees and laws in Israel."* Ezra took three steps with the Word: he studied, he observed, and he taught it to others. Without study, we won't know what to do. Without doing, we are not qualified to teach. Without teaching, we cannot help others!

- Don't teach before you have studied!
- Don't study without obeying!
- Don't do without teaching!

Let's apply these principles to leaders and finances.

STUDY THE WORD

A leader should have a good understanding of what the Bible says about money—and it has plenty to say. Get a concordance and look up references on money, wealth, work, and possessions. You'll be amazed at how much the Word says about money. Proverbs alone has over 125 verses that deal with finances.

Many leaders are simply ignorant of what the Bible teaches about money. Most Christians have only heard messages about giving and tithing, and nothing more. Yet, there is much more the Bible says about money. Tithing is only one aspect of honoring God with our money.

As you study the Word, read other Christian books about finances. My book, *7 Keys to Financial Freedom,* is a result of my study of the Word on this subject. Many other good books are available. Take advantage of them.

OBEY THE WORD

After understanding what the Word teaches about finances, begin to practice what you learned. Knowing what to do and doing it are two different things! *"Do not merely listen to the word, and so deceive yourselves. Do what it says." "Anyone, then, who knows the good he ought to do and doesn't do it, sins."* (James 1:22; 4:17)

Before the church will change in the area of finances, we as leaders must start living the Word of God in the area of finances. We already have too many preachers pounding the pulpit about tithing who aren't tithing. Other leaders demand tithes from their people, but do not give what they have promised to the denominational leaders above them! No wonder the church is in confusion about money! WE NEED EXAMPLES! Be that example to others about money.

LEADERS SHOULD TEACH GOD'S PRINCIPLES OF FINANCES IN THEIR CHURCHES

Jesus said that we are to go into the entire world and make disciples...teaching them to *"obey everything I have commanded you."* (Matthew 28:20) Did he teach about finances? Yes! More than about heaven or hell! Any pastor who doesn't teach what Jesus taught about money is disobeying this command!

Somehow, pastors have developed a bad attitude about teaching about finances. In my early years as a pastor, I really struggled with this issue. I taught about many things but I didn't want to mess with people's finances! I was afraid to be seen as greedy for money and preaching for my own benefit. This went on for several years until I finally realized this was doing more harm than good. I realized that God's Word is for us to obey and is for our good. If His word teaches about money, and I withhold that from people, they will miss the blessing that God wants to give them. Furthermore, I will suffer as a pastor, because the people are walking in disobedience and I'm not teaching them! But if I teach them and they follow God they will receive His blessings. They will benefit, the church will benefit, and yes, the pastor will benefit. What's the problem with that? So, I started teaching!

If you are a pastor, realize that your responsibility is to make sure people are taught. Often, pastors don't want to preach on this subject, so they invite a visitor to come and preach about giving. If the pastor is not willing to live and teach about finances, a sermon by a visitor will be of little value. So, take courage! Get your life in order, and then teach people what God says.

What should you teach people?

TEACH PRINCIPLES OF EARNING, GIVING, AND MANAGING FINANCES!

Your teaching should be a well-rounded approach to finances. People need to understand the spiritual nature of finances and how it affects our spiritual lives and testimonies. They need teaching on the right and wrong ways of earning money, and on Biblical principles of giving, saving and budgeting.

My book, *7 Keys to Financial Freedom,* was designed for this purpose. In fact, I developed the teachings for my church and later put them in writing! I am grateful that it has been a tremendous blessing in many churches. One pastor used it and saw an immediate increase of 50% in the income of the church.

Teaching must be done repeatedly, especially in the area of finances. Some people will hear the message and make a change, but soon revert to their old habits. Others need to hear the message two or three times before they accept it. If some are not yet ready to accept all of it, give them time and come back to it again. The same church that saw a 50% increase in income after the teachings needed a reminder after a few months because their giving started going down again. Follow-up teaching is needed for lasting life change. You may need to have a yearly series of teaching on finances to keep people walking in obedience.

TEACH ABOUT SUPPORTING THE PASTORS

Let us look at financial support for pastors, because it is such a difficult and sensitive area for teaching. Many pastors suffer needlessly because they are not willing to teach their people what the Word teaches about God's plan for supporting the leadership in the church. Pastors tend to avoid this altogether, or go to the opposite extreme and preach it all the time as though it is the only financial issue God cares about! Pastors should find a healthy balance.

Before teaching or preaching on this area, the leader should check his heart and motives carefully. It must not be done out of personal bitterness, pain or greed for money. Search your heart and ask God to open your eyes to your deepest motives. If any impure motives are present in your life, let God set you free before you teach on this subject.

As I look at the Word of God, I'm convinced that most churches are not following His plan for financing the ministry. Is it God's plan that pastors should earn less working for the Kingdom than they would in the world? I believe not. Is it God's plan that pastors need to have other jobs to support their family? I believe not, although for some time it may be a necessity. On the other hand, is it God's plan that the pastor lives in luxury and wealth, far above the standard of his congregation? Again, I believe not.

I understand the motives of many bi-vocational pastors who have started churches with a genuine heart for the people. Their favorite verse was "freely you have received, freely give" and this verse justified their refusal to accept money from the church. Yet, this approach almost always leads to financial weakness in the church. Paul tried it in Corinth and later apologized to the church. *"How were you inferior to the other churches, except that I was never a burden to you? Forgive me this wrong!"* (2 Corinthians 12:13) Ironically, this church had difficulty recognizing his apostleship. Maybe it is also time for you to apologize to your church!

271

The area of support for church leaders is so neglected and misunderstood that we need to look at several scriptures on the subject.

1 Corinthians 9:9-12, *"For it is written in the Law of Moses: "Do not muzzle an ox while it is treading out the grain." Is it about oxen that God is concerned? Surely he says this for us, doesn't he? Yes, this was written for us, because when the plowman plows and the thresher threshes, they ought to do so in the hope of sharing in the harvest. If we have sown spiritual seed among you, is it too much if we reap a material harvest from you? If others have this right of support from you, shouldn't we have it all the more? But we did not use this right. On the contrary, we put up with anything rather than hinder the gospel of Christ."*

SEVERAL PRINCIPLES CAN BE DRAWN FROM THESE VERSES:

a. It is right for the worker to "eat" from the work.
Everyone eats from the work of their hands. Why do some think that it is degrading for a man of God to receive his income from the church? This scripture makes it clear that it is right for the person who gives his time and energy to the work of the church to be supported by the church.

b. It is right for those who are ministered to spiritually to give material things (money) to the minister.
Paul says clearly that those who sow spiritual seed have a right to receive material fruit from their labor. He expected that those who received this ministry would give to support the worker.

c. Only the minister has the right to refuse this support.
In the case of the church at Corinth, Paul did not receive income from the church. However, he insists that he had the right, and we have already noted that he apologized to them for not exercising this right. It is never the right of the people to refuse to give support

272

to their leaders. When a minister does it, he should have a good reason and do it for a limited time only, or it will be detrimental to his life and to the people, as Paul's experience demonstrates.

Galatians 6:6-8, *"Anyone who receives instruction in the word must share all good things with his instructor. Do not be deceived: God cannot be mocked. A man reaps what he sows. The one who sows to please his sinful nature, from that nature will reap destruction; the one who sows to please the Spirit, from the Spirit will reap eternal life."*

Here it is commanded that listeners share with their instructors. What are the "good things" they are to give to the teacher? Is it to say, "Thank you for the message, God bless you?" No, Paul is speaking of material things or finances!

The law of sowing and reaping is not a message to sinners telling them to repent of the evil seeds they have sown. It is a message to the church that they should not be foolish in the way they support the minister! The way they sow into his life will determine what God will give to them. The implication of this verse is that a church that fails to give support to the minister is sowing to please the "sinful nature."

1 Timothy 5:17-18, *"The elders who direct the affairs of the church well are worthy of double honor, especially those whose work is preaching and teaching. For the Scripture says, "Do not muzzle the ox while it is treading out the grain," and "The worker deserves his wages."*

Is it clear yet? God expects his ministers to be supported, not by faith, but by the people of faith! Here the suggestion is that they are worthy of a double salary.

These verses are from the New Testament; the Old Testament is filled with examples of how God expected the people to provide for the priests and Levites. Time after time the nation of Israel rose and fell on this principle…as soon as the people stopped supporting the ministers, they would go back to their homes, the work of God would be neglected, and sin would continue to increase. With revivals, there was always an accompanying increase in the support of the ministry. (See 2 Chronicles 30-31 for one example.)

So, check your heart and motives, study the Word and then teach people what God says about supporting the work of the ministry.

LEADERS SHOULD ESTABLISH GOD'S PRINCIPLES OF FINANCES IN THEIR ORGANIZATION

A third thing leaders should do concerning finances is to ensure that God's principles regarding finances are practiced in their organization. What should a leader do to establish good organization in the area of finances? Let's talk about M.O.N.E.Y!

MONITOR

It is the responsibility of the pastor or leader to monitor what is happening with the money in the church. God has placed him over the church to guide and care for the flock. Finances are an important indicator of what is happening in the church.

This does not mean the pastor should have his hands on the money; that is not wise! If the pastor is actually counting or handling the money it can lead to abuse or suspicion. But he should not be so distant that he is not aware of what is happening. God will hold him accountable for how he handles the resources of the church, and his vision and direction will determine how they are used.

There should be some method of reporting to the leader. This can be weekly or monthly, but the pastor must be informed of the status of finances in the church and know when problems are present.

ORGANIZE

The leader needs to maintain a good system of organizing the finances. These principles are primarily for a church, but also apply to an organization. A good financial system will include at least three aspects:

A Working Budget

A budget is a projection of income and expenses for a given period, normally yearly. When well planned, it can reduce potential friction concerning financial management.

When preparing a budget consider the following:

* **Your past**

Look at income and expense records for the past year. It will give you a guideline to develop a future budget. If you have records for more than a year, it will be even more helpful. Don't let the past kill your faith, but let it bring realism to your projections.

* **Your goals**

Your vision and goals will determine several things in your budget. First, it will affect your income targets. If you plan for the church to double in number, the income should significantly increase. Your goals will also affect your priorities and particular expenses. If you are planning a major crusade, you will need to budget for that. If you are emphasizing discipleship and leadership development, you must allocate more money for those aspects.

When budgets are properly done, many time-consuming decisions can be handled quickly by the board or delegated to a person. For example, if you agree that this year you will spend a certain amount on the Sunday School program, tell the chairperson of that committee the amount budgeted, and ask him/her to work with it. The committee shouldn't need to write a letter to the board requesting for a box of chalk! Remember to release people to do their work.

- If the income exceeds or falls below the expected amount, the budget should be changed accordingly.
- Having a budget will keep you from falling into the trap of making decisions by asking, "Is there money in the bank?" Decisions should be based on the budget, not only on the availability of funds.

Accurate records

There is no excuse for church records written on the back of a wrinkled envelope kept under the bedcovers of the treasurer! Every church can afford a simple cashbook and a petty cash voucher!

When the church is small, these records don't need to be elaborate, but they should be clear and easily understood by anyone picking up the cashbook. It should contain a record of all income and expenses of the church and the balance on hand, both in cash and in the bank.

The records should enable the treasurer to prepare regular financial reports for the pastor, church council, or church. As the church grows, the system may become more complex to meet the demands of the church. A professional accountant can assist in setting the books in order.

See *Appendix L* for samples of a simple cashbook and reporting forms.

Internal controls

Every church, no matter how small, should establish a system of internal controls. Internal controls are simply a way of controlling the finances and making it more difficult to cheat in handling the money. They safeguard the money of the church, and eliminate needless temptations to those who handle the money.

This is difficult for us as believers, because we trust our brothers. Unfortunately, we can all tell stories of good "brothers" who stole money from the church. Many times the church leaders contributed to the problem by not having internal controls. A mentor advised me that when it comes to money, "It's not a matter of trust, but wisdom."

Here are six practical tips for internal controls that will help to establish a good system in your church.

- **Separate duties**

  Make sure that financial duties are clearly separated. Let one person handle the cash, and another keep the records. Let the persons responsible for counting the money be different from the ones that record the money. They should keep their own record of what they counted. Persons who receive cash should not have access to the accounting records. This can be confirmed with the treasurer's records.

- **Never allow one person to be alone with uncounted money**

  Realize that money is a powerful source of temptation! Don't allow any person, including yourself, to be alone with money that is uncounted. Think of how the tithes and offerings are collected, recorded, and banked. From the time they are collected until they are recorded, no person should be alone with the money. To allow this is an open door to temptation.

- **Confirm accounts regularly**

  No matter how much you trust the treasurer, check the accounts regularly. This can be regular (monthly, quarterly) or on a random basis, but make sure there is a day of accounting. Confirm the amounts in the cashbook with the actual cash and the amount in the bank with the bank statements. Check petty cash vouchers to confirm the amounts spent agree with the cash book entries, and that they are valid expenditures.

- **Change positions regularly**
  Anyone can be tempted over time with finances, and wisdom means that rotation of persons handling the cash will reduce temptation. Don't wait for trouble to arise, plan for regular changes.

- **Use a bank account**
  Bank accounts are much safer than handling everything in cash, yet many small churches are without a bank account even after several years of existence. In a bank, records of deposits and withdrawals are easily confirmed; two signatories can be required for any transactions, and the money is kept in a safe place. Of course, some cash is necessary, but it can be withdrawn from the bank and records kept of how it is spent.

- **Keep clear written records**
  All financial transactions should be clearly recorded in writing. Signatures should accompany every transfer of money from one person to another. If two deacons collect and count the money and give it to the treasurer, the treasurer should sign that he received the money. When money is paid to someone for travel expenses, let him sign a petty cash voucher. Even the pastor should sign for any money received.

Develop a system that meets your needs. Make it practical, not too complicated. Include a working budget, accurate records, and internal controls.

NOTIFY

A third aspect of good financial organization is to have a system to notify the people of what is happening in the church finances.

Biblically, I don't believe this is required. Scripture assumes that when people give to the Lord, they have finished their responsibility and relinquished all control over how the money is spent. However, because it will protect your integrity, it is wise to inform people. Openness in financial issues also encourages people to give more cheerfully to the work.

You may choose to notify people monthly or quarterly. At least provide a yearly report of all income and expenses in the church. Allow time for people to make comments, ask questions, and give suggestions. If you have done everything in a godly manner, you have nothing to fear!

ENGAGE FAITHFUL PEOPLE

Faithful people are needed in handling money, and great care should be taken when giving someone that responsibility. In small churches this person will probably be a volunteer rather than "employed." In larger churches, an accountant or administrator may handle the finances. The most important person in this regard is the treasurer or accountant who is entrusted with keeping the finances of the church. Others may be involved in collecting and counting the money. The same principles apply to all of them.

A corrupt treasurer doesn't help anyone! Even Jesus had this experience! *"But one of his disciples, Judas Iscariot, who was later to betray him, objected, 'Why wasn't this perfume sold and the money given to the poor? It was worth a year's wages.' He did not say this because he cared about the poor but because he was a thief; as keeper of the money bag, he used to help himself to what was put into it."* (John 12: 4-6)

I'm comforted to know that even Jesus had some financial struggles in His organization!

Tips for choosing a treasurer. (Or how to avoid a Judas in your church!)

- **Choose based on character first, not occupation**
  Too many times in the church we choose a "professional." Later, his *profession* doesn't match his *expression*,

and we find our accounts in a *recession* and the church in *depression*! Persons who are professional account-ants or auditors may be a good choice, but make sure that they meet the other qualifications first.

- **Look for Faithfulness**
  The treasurer must be faithful in attendance, in his/her commitment to the church, and generally in life. Remember Luke 16:10, *"Whoever can be trusted with very little can also be trusted with much..."*

- **Identify a person who is good with details**
  A good treasurer should be good with details, neat, and orderly. Look for someone with strong melancholic strengths!

- **Look for a controlled tongue**
  The treasurer will have inside knowledge of many aspects of the church. It is important that he/she will not disclose to others how much money a needy person was given, or how much the secretary is paid.

- **Find a person who is teachable**
  A person who thinks he knows it all is dangerous in any area, but especially when it comes to money. He/she may need training in how to keep the books. If he/she knows the technical part, you may still need to teach more about the Word of God concerning finances. Help them understand that their work is not to make decisions about money, but to implement them! This is a common misconception among people who handle money.

- **Look for someone who is accountable**
  The treasurer is accountable to the church for how the finances are managed. He should be willing to recognize the appropriate authority. If he is accountable, he will gladly produce reports in a timely manner.
- **Choose one who understands Biblical principles of finances**
  It is important that the treasurer understands (or is ready to be taught) the Biblical principles of finances. He needs to recognize that he is a steward, not the owner of the church money. He needs to be aware of the danger of borrowing, and other Biblical principles.

YIELD NOT TO TEMPTATION!

Money produces subtle temptations to leaders. Let's look at three.

The temptation to minister to get money.

We all need money and can be tempted to serve for money. We are tempted to give more attention to wealthy contributors than to poor widows. We think about how someone else is building a house, while we are still renting. We sometimes preach to please people and win their financial support, instead of preaching the message God has for them. For the Christian leader, this is a heart issue dealing with the love of money. Consider the following verses:

1 Peter 5:2 *"Be shepherds of God's flock that is under your care, serving as overseers—not because you must, but because you are willing, as God wants you to be; not greedy for money, but eager to serve;"*

1 Timothy 6:10, *"For the love of money is a root of all kinds of evil. Some people, eager for money, have wandered from the faith and pierced themselves with many griefs."*

281

To avoid this temptation… Remember your calling

You are not called to receive, but to give. God has called you to shepherd the flock of Christ, not to receive from the flock.

The temptation to manipulate to get money.

Many times the need for funds in the church is so great that the leader is tempted to use any available means to get them, even manipulation. How does this happen?

1. Through producing guilt

There is a real danger to manipulate people to give out of a sense of guilt. The leader may say, "Every committed member should give $20, so everyone that wants to be known as a "committed member" digs into his pocket. Not willingly, but because of guilt.

Think about the methods your church uses to raise funds. Do you encourage joyful, willing giving, or do you try to manipulate people? Consider what the following verses teach about the motive for giving.

1 Corinthians 16:2, *"On the first day of every week, each one of you should set aside a sum of money in keeping with his income, saving it up, so that when I come no collections will have to be made."*

2 Corinthians 8: 3, 4 *"For I testify that they gave as much as they were able, and even beyond their ability. Entirely on their own, they urgently pleaded with us for the privilege of sharing in this service to the saints."*

2 Corinthians 8:8-12, *"I am not commanding you, but I want to test the sincerity of your love by comparing it with the earnestness of others. For you know the grace of our Lord Jesus Christ, that though he was rich, yet for your sakes he became poor, so that you through his poverty might become rich. And here is my advice about what is best for you in this matter: Last year you were the first not only to give but also to have the desire to do so. Now finish the work, so that your eager willingness to do it may be matched by*

your completion of it, according to your means. For if the willingness is there, the gift is acceptable according to what one has, not according to what he does not have."

Do people under your leadership give from a cheerful heart or because of guilt?

2. By encouraging giving to receive

It is good to encourage people to give, and the Bible clearly says that there is blessing when we give. But there is a danger when a leader begins to encourage people to give in order to receive. I have heard preachers say, "If you give $5 now, God will give you $10 in return." This is a dangerous motivation. If we are not careful, we will teach people to give to get. This is not a godly motive but a selfish one. We should give out of love for God and obedience to his commands. When we do that, we will also receive his blessings, as the *result* of obedience, not the *purpose*. We should give to be like Jesus!

What is the result of encouraging people to give in order to receive? It may increase short term giving, but won't produce Christ-like generosity.

To avoid this temptation... remember that God is the provider.

The temptation to misuse money

When a leader has control of money, he will be tempted to misuse it. This can come by trying to divert some of it to his own pockets (which can be as subtle as using the church envelope to write a letter to your mom!); or by diverting money given specifically for one project to another.

Paul recognized this danger and responded in 2 Corinthians 8:20-21, *"We want to avoid any criticism of the way we administer this liberal gift. For we are taking pains to do what is right, not only in the eyes of the Lord but also in the eyes of men."* He "went the second mile" to avoid any criticism of how he was handling the money. He wanted not only to avoid the temptation but also any suggestion of the same. He was wise!

To avoid this temptation... Remember we are accountable to God.

Romans 14:12, *"So then, each of us will give an account of himself to God."*

Hebrews 13:17, *"Obey your leaders and submit to their authority. They keep watch over you as men who must give an account. Obey them so that their work will be a joy, not a burden, for that would be of no advantage to you."*

Jesus is the One to whom we must give an account. The money we handle in His Name is a sacred trust, and we must not become careless with it.

CONCLUSION

The way a leader handles money is critically important. He should study and obey God's principles; teach them to people, and establish them in the church. Then finances will be a blessing to the leaders and the followers.

Take a few minutes to do the action assignment before going on to the next chapter.

ACTION ASSIGNMENT

1. On a scale of 1 to 10 how would you rate your personal obedience to God's Word in the area of finances?

   What do you need to change to improve?

2. What steps have you taken to study what the Word says about money?

   What more do you need to do and when will you do it?

3. What teaching has been done in your church in the last year about finances?

   What needs to be taught and when will you do it?

4. Write several sentences that describe your church in regards to finances. (This may be positive or negative.)

5. Refer to the three temptations mentioned when dealing with money. Which of the three temptations do you struggle with most?

   What can you do to overcome this temptation?

6. Rate your church in the following areas: (mark the most applicable column)

Area	Not existing	Poor	Fair	Good	Excellent
Budget					
Accurate Records					
Internal Controls					

7. What changes in the area of finances will you make in your church as a result of having read this chapter? (Be specific and give dates.)

Chapter Fifteen
THE LEADER AND HIS BOARD

A young pastor steps out of Bible School ready to challenge the world. But after his first board meeting, he is ready to resign! An older pastor feels that God wants to make some changes at the church, but knows that the board will resist any new moves. What can he do?

Many pastors wish they could do away with their boards, and run the church alone! And some boards are looking for ways to get rid of the pastor! (Your "board" may be called a "council" or "committee" or another name, but it is the top leadership group in the church.) But think for a moment about what could happen if the pastor and his board worked well together. Several positive things would happen. First, the board would provide *good counsel* for the pastor. Board members can bring their wisdom and different perspectives to the issues facing the church, and after discussion godly decisions can be reached. It is always dangerous for one person to have too much power. *"Plans fail for lack of counsel, but with many advisers they succeed."* (Proverbs 15:22) Second, the board provides *moral support* in leadership. There is much strength when a pastor can say, "The board and I have agreed...." The board can help the pastor not to feel so alone in ministry. A final benefit is that a healthy board can help *carry the load* of the pastor. The weight of responsibility pastors carry can be shared with the members of the board. They can pray together and think deeply about the issues facing the church. So although many pastors and boards struggle to have a healthy relationship, it should be a relationship that will benefit both parties.

What can a pastor do to promote healthy board relationships? Here are three tips for pastors to achieve smooth relationships with their boards.

CHOOSE THEM CAREFULLY

Many churches have stagnated because the wrong people are in leadership. Often people are chosen for leadership because they have money, education, or status in the community. But they are spiritually carnal and will keep the church from growing. In one church a treasurer was chosen because he was a professional accountant. He kept the records well, but always resisted the pastor's leadership and caused a lot of struggle in the church.

What should you look for in choosing board members? We already looked at the process of choosing leaders in chapter eight. However, let's focus on several factors that are especially relevant for board members.

LOOK FOR SPIRITUAL MATURITY

Not perfection, but maturity. Spiritual maturity should be evident in the person's attitudes, his personal walk with God, his family life, and his finances. Maturity is also evidenced by spiritual reproduction, transferring life to others. Spiritually mature leaders are not seeking power and position. They have shown commitment to the local church through faithful attendance and regular giving.

288

LOOK ALSO FOR PERSONS THAT ARE GROWING

Some believers reach maturity but stop growing. Growth should be a continuous process in a leader, since this determines the growth of the church. Growing people are reading, attending seminars, and asking questions that help them grow.

LOOK FOR PEOPLE THAT THINK

Not everyone in the church is able to think and analyze problems. Anyone can recognize a problem, but leaders think of solutions. Don't choose people on the board who will just say "yes" to every proposal; you need people to help carry the mental load with you and challenge you if you are going in a wrong direction.

> Many pastors make the mistake of copying the political model of choosing leaders and choose only "yes men" to work with them on the board.

Many pastors make the mistake of copying the political model, and choose only "yes men" to work with them on the board. Pastor, you can't afford someone just to rubber stamp your ideas; you need a man of discernment who will lovingly rebuke you if you are heading in a wrong direction! *"Better is open rebuke than hidden love."* (Proverbs 27:5) If you find that already you choose people who aren't thinking, ask yourself the tough questions, "Am I too threatened by people with different opinions? Am I able to admit that I don't have all the answers?"

Jesus was very careful when He chose his "board" of 12 disciples. He spent time in prayer before calling them. The men He chose didn't look like strong leaders, but He shaped them into a powerful group that would change the world.

What should you do if you already have the wrong people on the board? This takes much wisdom and depends on how leaders are appointed and removed in your local church. You should first try hard to work with those leaders with the tips that follow, before making radical changes. If they don't respond, replace them over time with others that meet the qualifications.

UNDERSTAND THEM COMPLETELY

After choosing the board, it is crucial that as a pastor you learn to understand your board members well. Many problems arise in relationships simply due to a lack of understanding.

What should you understand about each board member? At least three things are important. First, understand the *spiritual gift* of the board member. His spiritual gift will greatly affect the way he sees priorities and problems in the church. If his gift is evangelism, he may want to see a lot of money spent on crusades. If he has a gift of mercy, he may want the church to develop ministries to the orphans and street children. If his gift is teaching, he may get excited about planning seminars for the members. Can you list the spiritual gifts of each of your board members? (Look back at the list you made in *Appendix F to see if you used any of their names.)*

Second, understand the board member's *personality or temperament.* We looked at this topic in chapter nine, and I encourage you to review that information about personalities. Here they are in brief: Choleric (strong, aggressive, leader), Sanguine (Outgoing, people person), Phlegmatic (easy going, relaxed, quiet) and Melancholic (introverted, organized, with attention to details). The temperament of your board member will explain why he/she is aggressive and dominant, or hardly says a word! You need to learn to connect with each of them in different ways.

Finally, understand *the level of influence* of your board member. Leadership is influence. It is important to understand how much influence each board member has. Probably, there is one member of your board who influences all the others. You would be wise to spend extra time with him, sharing your vision and your heart for ministry. Some members may have influence in different areas, and you need to recognize who they influence.

Jesus understood His disciples. He knew that Peter was quick to talk, but He also saw that Peter would become the "rock" of the church. He understood Thomas' need to see the evidence. Jesus did not relate to each of them the same, but dealt with each one according to his needs. He didn't spend equal amounts of time with each of them, but focused on those who had the most influence.

The more you understand your board members, the more likely you can work well with them. It takes time and effort to know them well, but the positive returns are worth the price!

At the same time you should help the board members understand you. Open your heart to them; share your vision and dreams. Let them know your goals, and don't be afraid to disclose your weaknesses to them. (They know them; they are just waiting to see if you will admit them!)

EQUIP THEM THOROUGHLY

A final tip for pastors to work well with their boards is to focus on equipping each board member for ministry. Even when you choose the right persons and know them well; don't assume that they don't need further equipping. We have already observed from Ephesians 4:11-12, that your primary job as a pastor is to *"equip the saints for the work of ministry."* The pastor is to be a coach, not the star player! Your role is to ensure 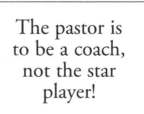 that the members are equipped to do what God expects them to do. This equipping should begin with those closest to you in leadership, your board. Pastors often hesitate to do this because they are intimidated by these men who might be older, richer, or more educated. Take courage, it is your God-given task and He will enable you to do it well!

Equipping must be a deliberate effort; it will never happen by accident. You must have a vision to equip the board, and share this vision with them. They might be reluctant at first, but if your heart is right they will soon respond. You might begin by simply sharing a short scripture and some thoughts with them at the beginning of your meetings. Choose a scripture that talks about spiritual leadership like 1 Peter 5:1-5; 1 Timothy 3:1-13; Luke 22:24-27. When the board is ready for more formal training, take one meeting a month for more in-depth study of these passages. Make that a special meeting for equipping instead of business. Teach them about spiritual gifts, personalities, and other subjects that will make them more effective leaders.

Another way that you can equip your board members is to provide books, tapes and other resources. This might be difficult financially, but it is a worthy investment that will result in tremendous growth. Look for seminars or training that you can attend with your board members that will encourage you all to grow together. Discuss what you are learning, and what it means for the church. Use this book as a resource to train your leaders.

Equipping calls for intense commitment from the pastor, in terms of time and energy. But in equipping, you multiply your ministry instead of adding. The results will be worth the effort. Jesus was a master equipper. He poured His life into His disciples. He taught them formally on the mountain. But He also took the opportunities of life and ministry to do most of His teaching. He modeled ministry to them and then gave them opportunities to do the work of ministry. He encouraged them, rebuked them, walked with them, and shared His heart with them. He is our model.

These tips provide a starting place for building relation-ships with your board members. When you and your board are working together as a team and growing spiritually, your church will be transformed. You will be able to do things that you never dreamed possible. May God strength-en you and your board to fulfill His calling for you.

ACTION ASSIGNMENT

Take time to reflect on the persons who serve on your board and answer the following questions about them:

	Name	Spiritual Gift	Personality	Influence Level (on scale of 1 to 10)
1.				
2.				
3.				
4.				
5.				
6.				
7.				
8.				
9.				
10.				
11.				
12.				

With which board members do you have the strongest relationship?

With which board members do you have the weakest relationship?

What can you do to strengthen these relationships? (Be specific and put a date when you will do it.)

Think about your job to equip these persons. What is your strategy and when will you begin? (Be as detailed as possible.)

Epilogue

Congratulations, you've persevered to the end! If you have done the action assignments, you have already experienced great changes in your life. I want to assure you that much more is ahead. The world is crying for leadership! Will you rise to the challenge and give yourself afresh to fulfill God's purposes for your life? He is calling you to develop all the potential He has placed within you and to use your gifts, abilities, and passions for the building of His Kingdom. The King stretches forth His hand and places it on your head as you kneel before Him. "Go, My child and lead. Do it in My way and for My glory. And as you do, I will use you in even greater ways than you have imagined. Much more is ahead of you. I will give you the wisdom you need to rise to every challenge I place before you. The task is great, but I have given you my Spirit to accomplish the task. Go in Jesus' name and lead as He led."

Will you take a moment right now to quietly bow in His presence and commit yourself anew to Him, asking Him to speak these words deep into your spirit? Go ahead, He's waiting for you!

May God bless you and take you to greater heights in leadership for His glory!

APPENDIX A: MY IDENTITY IN CHRIST
(Available for download on website)

Instructions: Stand erect in front of a mirror and repeat this statement morning and evening for 30 days. Say it out loud and believe it! Mark the box at the bottom when you complete each day.

I, _____, am uniquely created by God as a wonderful person. I am a significant person because Christ died for me and called me to be His child.

My sins are forgiven and I am a new creation in Christ, the old has gone and the new has come. I am completely forgiven of my past and made righteous. I am free from all condemnation of sin. I am chosen by Jesus Himself and am a child of God. I have been richly blessed with every spiritual blessing in Him. My God has supplied all my needs. My body is the temple of Christ and His Spirit and His life dwell in me.

I have been created with enormous potential to do great things for His Kingdom, and God has wonderful plans for my life. I am His workmanship, created to do good things. God has created me for His pleasure and He delights in my life. I am a one-of-a-kind person and no one can take my place. I have a good self-image and respect myself as a special creation of God. I am created to be a success and daily developing to become all that God created me to be. Nothing is impossible with God, and through Christ I can do all things. I do not have the spirit of fear, but of power, love and a sound mind.

Because He lives in me, my life is a reflection of all that He is and all that He possesses. I am changing from glory to glory.

I discipline my *mind* to take every ungodly thought captive. I am a person with a good, positive attitude towards myself and others. I choose to see the best in life. I choose to only read or see that which is positive and Godly.

I am a focused person with clear *goals* for my life. I am willing to work hard to reach my goals, and to overcome every obstacle. I am a leader, and will positively influence everyone I meet. I treat my *body* with respect; eating and exercising properly to keep it fit for life. I am energetic and healthy.

I respect others around me and treat every person as a special gift from God. I am called to serve others with my gifts and abilities, and will do so cheerfully. I am sensitive to their needs, and I go the second mile for others.

I recognize the power of *my tongue* to bring life or to destroy, and I will not let unwholesome talk come out of my mouth. I speak the truth always, and use my tongue to build others up. I find the good in others and compliment them genuinely. I consciously forgive those who wrong me, and extend God's grace to those who are weak.

I use my time well and discipline myself to be prompt. I recognize that my days are numbered, and that this day is a preparation for eternity. Therefore, I will use every moment to the fullest to fulfill my God-given destiny.

Morning: These are the qualities of the winner God created me to be. Today is the first day of the rest of my life, and it is wonderful!

Evening: Tonight I'm going to sleep wonderfully well. I will dream powerful, positive dreams. I will awaken energized and refreshed, and tomorrow's going to be magnificent!

(References Psalms 1:1-3; 34:9-10; 139:14; 149:4; 147:11; Proverbs 3:24-26; Jeremiah 29:11; Zephaniah 3:17; Romans 5:1, 8:1,17; 1 Corinthians 3:16; 6:19; 2 Corinthians 3:18, 5:17; 1 Peter 2:9,10; Ephesians 1:3, 4; 2:6,10; 3:12; 4:29; Philippians 2:5, 4:19; Hebrews 4:16; 1 Timothy 1:7)

1	2	3	4	5	6	7	8	9	10	11	12	13	14	15	16	17	18	19	20	21	22	23	24	25	26	27	28	29	30

(This material was adapted from writing by Zig Ziglar, and Neil Anderson)

APPENDIX B: TIME EVALUATION CHART
(Available for download on website)

Time	Day 1		Day 2		Day 3	
5:00 AM						
5:30 AM						
6:00 AM						
6:30 AM						
7:00 AM						
7:30 AM						
8:00 AM						
8:30 AM						
9:00 AM						
9:30 AM						
10:00 AM						
10:30 AM						
11:00 AM						
11:30 AM						
12:00 PM						
12:30 PM						
1:00 PM						
1:30 PM						
2:00 PM						
2:30 PM						
3:00 PM						
3:30 PM						
4:00 PM						
4:30 PM						
5:00 PM						

TIME EVALUATION CHART

Time	Day 1		Day 2		Day 3	
5:30 PM						
6:00 PM						
6:30 PM						
7:00 PM						
7:30 PM						
8:00 PM						
8:30 PM						
9:00 PM						
9:30 PM						
10:00 PM						
10:30 PM						
11:00 PM						
11:30 PM						
12:00 AM						

TIME EVALUATION CHART

Time	Day 4		Day 5		Day 6	
5:00 AM						
5:30 AM						
6:00 AM						
6:30 AM						
7:00 AM						
7:30 AM						
8:00 AM						
8:30 AM						
9:00 AM						
9:30 AM						
10:00 AM						
10:30 AM						
11:00 AM						
11:30 AM						
12:00 PM						
12:30 PM						
1:00 PM						
1:30 PM						
2:00 PM						
2:30 PM						
3:00 PM						
3:30 PM						
4:00 PM						
4:30 PM						
5:00 PM						

TIME EVALUATION CHART

Time	Day 4		Day 5		Day 6	
5:30 PM						
6:00 PM						
6:30 PM						
7:00 PM						
7:30 PM						
8:00 PM						
8:30 PM						
9:00 PM						
9:30 PM						
10:00 PM						
10:30 PM						
11:00 PM						
11:30 PM						
12:00 AM						

Time	Day 7					
5:00 AM						
5:30 AM						
6:00 AM						
6:30 AM						
7:00 AM						
7:30 AM						
8:00 AM						
8:30 AM						
9:00 AM						
9:30 AM						
10:00 AM						
10:30 AM						
11:00 AM						
11:30 AM						
12:00 PM						
12:30 PM						
1:00 PM						
1:30 PM						
2:00 PM						
2:30 PM						
3:00 PM						
3:30 PM						
4:00 PM						
4:30 PM						
5:00 PM						

Time	Day 7					
5:30 PM						
6:00 PM						
6:30 PM						
7:00 PM						
7:30 PM						
8:00 PM						
8:30 PM						
9:00 PM						
9:30 PM						
10:00 PM						
10:30 PM						
11:00 PM						
11:30 PM						
12:00 AM						

303

APPENDIX C: PRIORITIES: THE THREE "R'S"

The Pareto Principle works in every area of your life. Complete the following section on the 3 "R's." You can do this for family, business, or ministry depending on the position you are evaluating.

A. Required (What is required of me?)

1. _____   4. _____
2. _____   5. _____
3. _____   6. _____

B. Return (What gives the greatest return to my organization?)

1. _____   4. _____
2. _____   5. _____
3. _____   6. _____

C. Reward (What do I most enjoy doing?)

1. _____   4. _____
2. _____   5. _____
3. _____   6. _____

Based on the above, what should be your highest priorities?

1. _____   4. _____
2. _____   5. _____
3. _____   6. _____

What things that you are now doing should you reduce or eliminate from your schedule?

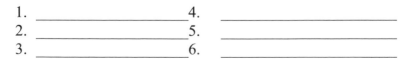

1. _____   4. _____
2. _____   5. _____
3. _____   6. _____

APPENDIX D: PRIORITIES: TIME EVALUATION

Complete the time evaluation sheet (*Appendix B*) for one week. You only need to record the time you spend in ministry/work. Then use the codes below to evaluate each 30-minute time segment. Use the priorities you established in *Appendix C* to determine the correct number. Put the number from the following list that best describes that 30-minute activity in the space next to it on the chart.

(1) Requirement   (2) Return   (3) Reward   (4) All Three
(5) None of the above

Now, total your numbers in the space below. Remember that each space represents 30 minutes, so divide the number of 1's by 2 to get the total hours.

Total number of 1's _____   Number of hours _____
Total number of 2's _____   Number of hours _____
Total number of 3's _____   Number of hours _____
Total number of 4's _____   Number of hours _____
                 Total hours evaluated   _____
How many hours were 2's and 4's? _____
What percentage are these of the total? _____
(Ideally 80% of your ministry time should include high return of 2's and 4's)

Also reflect on your time evaluation sheet as you answer the following questions:

1. What are your top 5 to 8 time wasters?

2. What are the top 5 things you can do to better control your time usage?

3. Do you control your time, or do you allow your time to be controlled by the dictates of others?

What can you do to improve in this area?

APPENDIX E: PRIORITIZE PROGRAMS

Instructions:

Step One: List your programs in the first column (1 to 6). Then go to the next column and identify which programs give the greatest return to the organization. Put a '1'. Do the same for the second and third one in that column. List the top three only. Go to the next column and identify which ones are closest to the heart of the people. Again give only the top three. Continue with the last two columns.

Programs	Greatest return to the organization	Closest to the heart of people	Closest to the heart of the pastor/top leader	Closest to the heart of God
1.				
2.				
3.				
4.				
5.				
6.				

Step two: Evaluate. Look for the programs that have numbers in each column. This indicates a high priority program. In some cases the program might be a high priority for the leader but not the people. This means that more communication of the vision is needed. If it is a high priority for the organization, but not the leader, the leader should consider delegating or resigning! If it is high with God, but low in other areas, the leader should seek to change himself and the people through prayer, Bible study, etc.

Step Three: Rewrite your programs in order of priorities

1. _____
2. _____
3. _____
4. _____
5. _____
6. _____

APPENDIX F: PRIORITIZE THE
PEOPLE AND MONEY

List the top 10 people in your organization, with their gifts and in which ministry area they are currently. Then, if needed write changes that you propose for them.

	Name	Gift	Ministry	Proposed changes
1.				
2.				
3.				
4.				
5.				
6.				
7.				
8.				
9.				
10.				

Money. List the top five programs in your organization with the amount of the budget allocated to each.

	Programs	Amount of money	% of Budget
1.			
2.			
3.			
4.			
5.			

Do you spend 80% of the budget for the top 20% of the programs? If not, what adjustments need to be made?

APPENDIX G: CHAIRPERSON'S TRAINING

(This training session will give general training for the person leading a committee or group meeting. The following one relates to the work of the secretary and keeping minutes. Recognize that there are different expectations in different locations. Adapt the information to your setting as needed.)

IMPORTANCE OF THE CHAIRPERSON

"Everything rises and falls on leadership." The success of your committee/ministry will depend on your ability to lead them. If the committee is not working well together, it is your job to find the problem and fix it. If morale is down, it is your responsibility to boost it. Your vision, your commitment, and your passion will, more than anything else, determine what will be done.

Therefore...
• Get a servant's heart.
• Get growing.
• Get God's vision for your group.
• Get moving!

RESPONSIBILITIES OF THE CHAIRPERSON:

1. Call the meeting

If you don't call for a meeting, there will be no meeting! It is your responsibility to ensure that your committee is meeting as often as needed. Don't adjourn without setting the date and time for the next meeting.

Communicate to the office by the deadline if you want the meeting to be put in the bulletin. You may also call or write your committee members if they need a reminder.

2. Present the agenda to the group

The chairman should bring the agenda items to the meeting and present them to the committee. This usually includes: Reading and confirming the previous minutes, signing the minutes, matters arising, new agenda items that you prepared in advance, and any other business as needed.

3. Guide the discussion and ensure that satisfactory decisions are reached

Your role is to guide the group in the discussion process. Be careful that you don't dominate the meeting. Allow each member to have input, especially on major decisions. It is good to sell your vision to the group, but make sure that they are really buying into it before you start moving. If they need time to think about it, allow them to do that.

4. Oversee implementation of the decisions

Decisions are often made by the committee that are to be carried out before the next meeting. You are responsible to ensure that this happens. If you delegate tasks, make sure they have been completed in a timely fashion.

5. Keep the office informed of what is happening in your group

This may be done through submission of the minutes or a scheduled meeting with the person to whom you report.

TIPS ON LEADING A MEETING

A. Be prepared

Before the meeting determine the agenda of the meeting. What issues need to be dealt with? What are the most important issues? What will be needed to present ideas? (If you need a report, a letter, or a file, bring it.) Make sure the minutes of the last meeting are ready. Read through them ahead of the meeting and know what items need to be discussed from the previous meeting. When possible, learn ahead of time what has been done and what has not been done from the previous meeting to minimize this reporting time.

B. Keep the meeting moving

Allot a certain amount of time for the meeting, and budget that time to ensure that the necessary business is covered. Much time is wasted talking and talking about insignificant issues, and then there is not enough time for more important matters. If no consensus is reached, and the decision is not urgent, table it until the next meeting. Move on to the essential things. Allow enough time for members to express their opinions, but when there is agreement don't waste time. Ask, "Is there anyone who does not agree?"

You will build trust with the members if you start *and* end on time!

C. Make decisions

Our goal in a meeting is to make wise decisions. Don't go around and around without a decision. If no conclusion can be reached, postpone the decision, but whenever possible make a decision. Agree on what is to be done, when, and who is to do it. The secretary can help you in this, since all decisions are to be accurately recorded in the minutes.

APPENDIX H: THE WORK OF THE SECRETARY OF A COMMITTEE

The work of the secretary is very important. When properly done, it will result in lasting records that can be easily followed by others. This service for the Lord will be rewarded.

The responsibilities of a secretary are to:
1. Record minutes of all meetings held by the committee.
2. Write official letters and correspondence for the committee.
3. Keep the file updated and organized

Minute taking
This is your most important function. The purpose of minutes is to keep an accurate and permanent record of the committee meeting. Without minutes everyone depends on his or her own memory.

Well-kept minutes make it easy to follow the decisions of the committee and allow others who come later to understand the important actions.

SOME DO'S AND DON'TS FOR WRITING MINUTES:

1. Record all persons present, the place and time of meeting. Normally the secretary is the one taking minutes. If someone else is doing it, put "taking minutes" next to name.
2. Write a title for each minute. This helps to quickly find a particular item later. The title should summarize the issue being discussed. For example, "Min. 4 Youth Outing" or "Min 3 Monthly fellowship" It is helpful if the title is underlined.
3. Make sure that the issue is introduced properly. Write for those who are NOT there. Ask yourself, "Could someone who was not there understand what went on?" For example, "The chairman reported the need to collect

312

money from all the mothers." Or, "A letter from the pastor was read requesting all members to attend the leaders retreat."

4. Record all decisions, and who is responsible to carry out the action. For example, "After discussion it was agreed that the chairman would write a letter to the principal." Or "Sister Johnson will contact the pastor about this issue."

5. Use complete sentences as you summarize the points discussed. Don't list points.

6. You may want to take rough notes in the meeting and then rewrite them later. If so, do it quickly before forgetting many things, and place the minutes in the file.

7. Leave a wide margin on the left side so that the minutes can be read after filing.

8. See sample for format. (*Appendix I*)

Writing official letters
1. Use church letterheads when appropriate.
2. Make copies for the committee members, for the file, and the church council (or board).

Keeping the file
1. The file should be kept in the church office except during meetings.
2. File papers and minutes in the order that they are received.

APPENDIX I: SAMPLE MINUTES

MINUTES OF _____ CHURCH
(Council, designated committee)
MEETING HELD ON _____ (date) at
_____ (location)

PRESENT: ABSENT:
1.   , Chairman   1.
2.   , Secretary   2. , with apology
3.
4.

AGENDA:
1. Confirmation of last minutes
2. Matters arising
3. (Any other agenda item)
4. A.O.B. (Any Other Business)

The meeting was opened with a prayer by _____ (person)
at _____ (time)

Minute 1 Confirmation of previous minutes.
The minutes of the meeting of _____ (date) were read by
(person). (After a few corrections) _____ proposed and
_____ seconded that they were a true copy of the minutes. (If major corrections are needed insert them here. For
example, "It was noted that in Min. 3 the following should
be added: All agreed to pray about the issue.")

Minute 2 Matters Arising (This comes from the previous
minutes and is only for issues that needed further action.
Ideally this should be a brief part of the meeting and should
not repeat what was discussed in the other meeting.)

a. (Give the title of the minute from the previous minutes.)

Summarize the action taken or not taken and any resulting decisions by the committee. For example, "The chairman reported that the permit has been approved and picked up."

b.

Minute 3 (other agenda item)

Summarize the discussion of the group, especially who brought the issue, any decisions agreed upon, and who is responsible to follow up the issue.

Minute 4 A.O.B. (This can include any last minute issues that are raised by members after the chairman has finished his agenda.)

1.

2.

3.

(Having no other business) the meeting was closed with a word of prayer by _____ (person) at _____ (time).

The above minutes were confirmed on _____ (date left blank until confirmation).

Chairman _____ Secretary _____

APPENDIX J: SAMPLE APPOINTMENT LETTER
AND TERMS OF EMPLOYMENT

Re: APPOINTMENT

Following our interview with you on _____ I am pleased to inform you that you have been appointed to the position _____. Your job description will be as follows:

(List the job description point by point)

Any other duties as assigned by _____.

Accountability. You will be directly responsible to _____.

Please read the enclosed "Terms and Conditions of Employment" and if agreeable to you sign them and return one copy to us.

I look forward to your favorable response.

Yours in Christ's service,

(Employer)

Sample Terms and Conditions of Employment

Note: (This is a sample only and should be adapted to fit your organization's needs.)

This agreement is entered into between _____ (employee) and _____ (employer).

The following terms and conditions apply:

EMPLOYMENT-Employment begins on _____.
-A probationary period of 90 days will apply, concluding on _____, with continued employment being contingent upon mutual agreement.

SALARY -Monthly salary shall be _____, inclusive of housing allowance, payable at the end of each month (if other benefits are included, add them here).

MEDICAL -A yearly medical benefit of _____ shall be available for the employee, spouse, and children. It is payable upon presentation of receipts for medical treatment.

REVIEW -Salary and benefits shall be reviewed in _____ (month) of each year.

WORKING HOURS -Normal working hours are 8:00 a.m. to 5:00 p.m., with a one hour lunch break, Monday-Friday and from 8:00 a.m. to 1:00 p.m. on Saturday.

HOLIDAYS -Annual paid holidays will be any holiday officially recognized by the government.

LEAVE -Annual paid leave is ____ working days commencing at the end of six months employment, after approval in writing by _____. (Optional) In addition the employee may request _____ personal "off" days. Any "offs" beyond the five days will be deducted from the employee's annual leave.

TERMINATION -This agreement can be terminated by either party with a written notice of 30 days or compensation of the same, except in the case of gross neglect of duty, or behavior incompatible with our Christian Testimony. In such cases, the agreement can be terminated in writing with immediate effect and without compensation.

The above details are understood by and agreed to by both parties:

Employee Signed: _____ Date: _____

Employer Signed: _____ Date: _____

APPENDIX K: STAFF EVALUATION FORM

Name: _____

Date of evaluation: _____

Part One: To be competed by the employee and employer.
(Assess each on a scale of 1-10)

1. Attitude (Do you possess a positive attitude towards work, other staff, and customers/members?): _____
   Comments:

2. Quality of work (Is your work excellent?): _____
   Comments:

3. Quantity of work (How much do you accomplish in a day?): _____
   Comments:

4. Relationships with other staff members. (How well do you get along with the rest of the staff?) _____
   Comments:

5. People skills (How well do you relate to others? Do you attract people to yourself? Do they see you as a warm and friendly person? Do you smile a lot?): _____
   Comments:

6. Timeliness (How well do you do at getting to work on time?) _____
   Comments:

7. Time management (How well do you utilize your time at work?): _____
   Comments:

8. Personal Growth (Are you growing to your full potential?): _____
   Comments:

9. Member satisfaction (If you were the only person representing us to our members, would they have a good impression of us?) _____
   Comments:

10. Ideas. (Do you think of ways of improving your job or the ministry?) _____
    Comments:

11. Understanding and supporting our vision and values.
    _____
    Comments:

Part Two: To be completed by the employee only. Give your answers to the following questions.

1. In what areas of your work are you very satisfied about your job?

2. In what areas are you frustrated? (This could include job assignments that you do not like, or areas in which you are not performing well, etc.)

3. In what areas do you need to improve? If so, what can be done to improve them?

4. What would you like to spend more time doing?

5. Is your job description clear for you? (Do you understand what is expected of you?)

6. Is your salary adequate to meet your basic needs? Mark the one that best applies. (Not at all, barely, sufficient, more than enough)

7. Do you have needs that should be addressed by your employer that are not currently considered? Explain.

8. Do you have any suggestions that would make us more effective in ministry or more pleasant for you?

9. What do I (employer) do that motivates you?

10. What do I do that discourages you? (Causes you to lose morale)

11. What goals do you have for the coming year, and how can I help you to reach them?

12. What is the most helpful thing for me to know about you, to truly understand "the real you?"

Signed: _____ Date: _____

APPENDIX L: SAMPLE CASHBOOK AND REPORTING FORMS

SAMPLE CASHBOOK FOR HOLY GHOST CHURCH

Cash

Date	Transaction	In	Out	Balance
	Balance c/f			0
Jan. 2	Tithes	5000		5000
	Offerings	500		5500
Jan. 3	Money banked		5000	500
Jan. 5	Envelopes purchased		100	400
Jan. 9	Tithes	4000		4400
	Offerings	600		5000
Jan. 10	Money banked		3000	2000
Jan. 11	Crusade publicity		800	1200
Jan. 11	Sunday School books		200	1000
Jan. 11	Discipleship books		500	500
Jan. 17	Tithes	2000		2500
	Offerings	200		2700
Jan. 18	Money banked		2000	700
Jan. 24	Tithes	1000		1700
	Offerings	100		1800
Jan. 31	From Bank	9500		11300
Jan. 31	Pastor's Salary		10000	1300
Jan. 31	Headquarters' support		1100	200

Bank

Date	Transaction	In	Out	Balance
	Balance c/f			0
Jan. 3	From cash	5000		5000
Jan. 10	From cash	3000		8000
Jan. 18	From cash	2000		10000
Jan. 31	To Cash		9500	500

Financial report for Holy Ghost Church

January 20_____

Balance C/F   0.00

INCOME:

	Tithes:	12,000
	Offerings:	1,400

Total income   **13,400**

EXPENSES:

Salary	10,000
Headquarters	1,100
Office expense	100
Crusade	800
Discipleship	500
Sunday School	200
Misc.	0

Total expenses: **12,700**
Income/loss for period   **700**

Balance C/F		700
Cash balance:	200	
Bank balance	500	
Total	700	

APPENDIX M: RECOMMENDED BOOKS/RESOURCES FOR YOUR CONTINUED GROWTH

Anderson, Neil. *The Bondage Breaker.*
Barna, George, *The Power of Team Leadership.*
Blanchard, Ken et. all. *The Generosity Factor.*
Blanchard, Ken et. al. *Leadership by the Book.*
Blanchard, Ken. *The Heart of a Leader.*
Blanchard, Ken. *The Secret.*
Briner, Bob et al. *More Leadership Lessons of Jesus: A Timeless Model for Today's Leaders.*
Byler, Jon. *The Art of Christian Leadership.*
Byler, *The Heart of Christian Leadership.*
Byler, *Use that Gift.*
Byler, *Authority.*
Byler, *The Purpose Driven Church Bible Study Guide*
Byler, *7 Keys to Financial Freedom.* For any of these items Contact the author at Jon@LeadersServe.com
Covey, Stephen. *The 7 Habits of Highly Effective People.*
Eims, LeRoy. *Be the Leader You Were Meant to Be.*
Finzel, Hans. *The Top 10 Mistakes Leaders Make.*
Finzel, Hans. *Empowered Leaders.*
Foster, Richard. *Celebration of Discipline.*
Haggai, John Edmund. *Lead On!*
Hendricks, Howard. *Teaching to Change Lives.*
Hunter, Jim. *The Servant.*
Hybels, Bill. *Courageous Leadership.* (Great book especially for pastors.)
Jacobs, Donald. *From Rubble to Rejoicing.*
James M. Kouzes, and Barry Z. Posner, *The Leadership Challenge*
Kreider, Larry. *The Biblical Role of Elders for Today's Church*
Kreider, Larry. *Authentic Spiritual Mentoring*
LaHaye, Tim. *Why You Act the Way You Do.* (Great book for understanding yourself and others; explains the temperaments)
Lencioni, Patrick. *The Five Dysfunctions of a Team.*
Littauer, Florence. *Personality Plus:How to Understand Others by Understanding Yourself.* (Great book on temperaments.)
MacDonald, Gordon. *Ordering Your Private World.*
Marshall, Tom. *Understanding Leadership.*
Maxwell, John C. and Donovan, Jim. *Becoming a Person of Influence.*
Maxwell, John C. *Developing the Leaders Around You.*
Maxwell, *Developing the Leader Within You.*
Maxwell, *The Success Journey.*
Maxwell, *Failing Forward.*
Maxwell, *Priorities, the Pathway to Success.* (Video Presentation)

Maxwell, *The 21 Irrefutable Laws of Leadership*
Maxwell, *There's No Such Thing as Business Ethics.*
Maxwell, *Partners in Prayer.* (A guide to developing a lay prayer ministry in the church. See also the video, *The Pastor's MVP.*
Maxwell, *The 21 Most Powerful Minutes in a Leaders' Day.* (Biblical examples of the 21 Laws)
Maxwell, *Thinking For a Change.*
Maxwell, *The Leadership Bible.* (Great Bible with all sorts of insights on leadership. NKJV)
Maxwell, *The Winning Attitude.*
Maxwell, *Injoy Life Club,* Leadership tape series, Out of production but see Web resources below for more information.
Meyer, Joyce. *Battlefield of the Mind.*
Meyer, Joyce. *How to Succeed at Being Yourself.*
Meyer, Joyce. *A Leader in the Making.*
Munroe, Myles. *Becoming a Leader.*
Munroe, Myles. *Understanding Your Potential.*
Pollock, David. *Church Administration the Dollars and Sense of it.*
Sanders, Oswald. *Spiritual Leadership.* (Classic reading on Christian Leadership)
Silvoso, Ed. *Anointed for Business.*
Smith, Ken. *It's About Time.* (Good book on time management.)
Swarr, Sharon. *Transform the World.* (Business and mission.
Tennyson, Mack. *Church Finances for People who Count.*
Veith, Gene. *God at Work* (On vocation)
Warren, Rick. *The Purpose Driven Church.*
Warren, Rick. *The Purpose Driven Life.*
Wilkinson, Bruce. *The 7 Laws of the Learner.* (Excellent for Teachers. Also available as a video series.)
Wilkinson, Bruce, *Teaching With Style*, video series. (Excellent for teachers)
Wilkinson, Bruce, *The Prayer of Jabez.*
Wilkinson, Bruce, *Secrets of the Vine.*
Wilkinson, Bruce, *The Dream Giver.*
Ziglar, Zig. *Over the Top.*
Ziglar, Zig. *Staying Up, Up, Up in a Down Down World.*

Web resources
(Visit our website for these links)

http://www.ncd-international.org, The home for Natural Church Development. They operate on the premise that a healthy church will grow and have tools to measure the health of a church in 8 key areas.

http://www.pastors.com, Rick Warren's *Ministry ToolBox* is a weekly newsletter full of tips, links, and articles to help you in your ministry. (also has many other resources for pastors, free sermons, etc.)

www.walkthru.org. Walk Through the Bible has many seminar and resources for training teachers.

http://www.carey.ac.nz/leadership/default.htm, Online Leadership Letters by Gordon Miller. Excellent reflections and advice for pastors. Written from New Zealand but deals with transcultural principles of church leadership and growth.

http://paul-timothy.net/ Training resources for pastors and church planters in multiple languages.

www.gpn.tv/videos/collections Many resources for pastors and leaders. Many John Maxwell tapes available for listening online. (Audio tapes/CD's of Maxwell available for purchase at www.growingattitudes.com

www.assess-yourself.org Free online tests to measure spiritual gifts, character, love for God, Worldview, and obstacles to growth.

www.lared.org A ministry devoted to teaching Biblical principles especially to business persons. Downloadable teaching material in PDF format and audio content.

http://www.world-map.com Provide free *ACTS* magazine and the book *Shepherd's Staff* to leaders in developing nations.

http://sgai.org/resources/audio/index.php Audio teachings by Malcolm Webber.

http://www.testcafe.com/ Free online tests for IQ, personality and emotional intelligence.

http://www.highiqsociety.org/iq_tests/ Free intelligence test.

http://bible.crosswalk.com/ Free online Bible study tools and resources.

http://www.ocafrica.net/ OC Africa publishes *The Church Leader in Africa* which can be viewed online.

Free email newsletters on leadership

Leadership Magazine. Free magazine by Pastor Gregg Johnson. Available in email format or hard copy, http://www.missionchurch.com/magazine/subscribe.htm Archived issues with excellent material are available at: http://www.acswebnetworks.com/leadershipmagazine/archives

Leadership Letters, free email letter by Malcolm Webber, www.LeadershipLetters.org.

The Leadership Link, Resources and free email newsletter by Tim Elmore focused on young leaders. http://www.growingleaders.com.

Leadership Wired, free email newsletter by John Maxwell and Pastor's Coach, free email newsletter by Dan Reiland. http://www.injoy.com/newsletters.

Ministry ToolBox, a free weekly newsletter from Rick Warren full of tips, links, and articles to help you in your ministry. http://www.pastors.com.

Bibliography

Anderson, Neil. *The Bondage Breaker.* Eugene, OR.: Harvest House Publishers, 1990.

Blanchard, Ken. *The Heart of a Leader.* Washington: Eagle Publishing, 2002.

Barna, George. *The Power of Team Leadership.* Colorado Springs: WaterBrook Press, 2001.

Chironna, Mark. *Breaking The Boundaries of The Possible.* New Kensington: Whitaker House, 1996.

Covey, Stephen. *The 7 Habits of Highly Effective People.* New York: Simon & Schuster, 1989.

Douglass, Merrill. *Success Secrets.* Colorado Springs: Honor Books, 1997.

Elmore, Tim. *Mentoring: How to Invest Your Life in Others.* Kingdom Publishing House, 1995.

Finzel, Hans. *The Top 10 Mistakes Leaders Make.* Colorado Springs: Cook Communications, 2004.

Habecker, Eugene. *Rediscovering the Soul of Leadership.* Colorado Springs: Victor Books, 1996.

LaHaye, Tim. *Why You Act the Way You Do.* Wheaton: Tyndale House Publishers, 1984.

Lencioni, Patrick. *The Five Dysfunctions of a Team.* San Franscisco: Jossney-Bass, 2002.

Littauer, Florence. *Personality Plus.* Grand Rapid: Revel, 1992.

Mahoney, Ralph. *The Shepherd's Staff.* Burbank: World MAP, 2002.

Mason, John. *An Enemy Called Average.* Tulsa: Insight Publishing Group, 1990.

Maxwell, John C. *Be All You Can Be.* Colorado: Chariot Victor Publishing, 1987.

Maxwell, John C. *Developing the Leader Within You.* Nashville, TN.: Thomas Nelson, Inc. Publishers, 1993.

Maxwell, John C. *Developing the Leaders Around You.* Nashville, TN.: Thomas Nelson, Inc. Publishers, 1995.

Maxwell, John C. *Failing Forward.* Nashville: Thomas Nelson, Inc. Publishers, 2000.

Maxwell, John C. *Priorities, the Pathway to Success.* (Video Presentation) Atlanta, GA.: INJOY, Inc., 1999.

Maxwell, John C. *The 17 Essential Qualities Of a Team Player.* Nashville: Thomas Nelson, 2006.

Maxwell, John C. *The Success Journey.* Nashville: Thomas Nelson, 1997.

Maxwell, John C. and Donavan, Jim. *Becoming a Person of Influence.* Nashville: Thomas Nelson Publishers, 1997.

Molitor, Brian D. *The Power of Agreement*. Nashville: Broadman & Holman Publishers, 1999.

Munroe, Myles. *Becoming a Leader*. Bakersfield: Pneuma Life Publishing, 1993.

Munroe, Myles. *Understanding Your Potential*. Shippensburg: Pneuma Life Publishing, 1993.

Porter, Mark. *The Time of Your Life*. Kansas City: Walterick Pub, 1988.

Renner, Rick. *Who is Ready for a Spiritual Promotion?* Tulsa: Rick Renner Ministries, 2000.

Sanders, Oswald. *Spiritual Leadership*. Chicago: Moody Press, 1967.

Smith, Ken. *It's About Time*. Wheaton: Crossway Books, 1992.

Stevenin, Thomas J. *People Power: Tapping the Spirit of Quality Performance & Service in Your Organization*. Chicago: Northfield Publishing, 1996.

Wilkinson, Bruce. *The 7 Laws of the Learner*. Sisters, OR.: Multnomah Press, 1992.

Wiwcharuck, Peter. *Building Effective Leadership*, Alberta, Canada: International Christian Leadership Development Foundation, 1987.

Ziglar, Zig. *Over the Top*. Nashville: Thomas Nelson, 1997.

Ziglar, Zig. *See You at the Top*. Gretna: Pelican Publishing Company, 1982.

About the author

Jon Byler has a passion to see church leaders grow and develop into mature, Christ-like leaders. He is committed to developing a worldwide alliance of leadership training programs through his role as the International Coordinator of Global LEAD Alliance. He lived in Thika, Kenya for 13 years and currently resides in Lancaster, Pennsylvania, USA. He and his wife Loice are the parents of three children. He has experience as a pastor and has authored several books.

The Heart of Christian Leadership
7 Keys to Financial Freedom
Preaching to Change Lives, a homiletics textbook
Use that Gift, a study of spiritual gifts
Pits, Prisons and Palaces, a study of the life of Joseph
Steps to Maturity, a 10-lesson discipleship course
Free at Last, a study of deliverance
The Christian and Authority
A Church With a Purpose, A Bible Study Guide Series

About Global LEAD Alliance

Global LEAD Alliance is an international alliance of leadership development programs. These programs are efforts of local churches and focus on shaping character and leadership skills to develop a generation of leaders capable of fulfilling the great commission of Jesus Christ. Global LEAD Alliance is a ministry track of Global Disciples.

About Global Disciples

Global Disciples believes all unreached people should have the opportunity to choose Jesus, based on the Great Commission mandate. Through its strategic network, Global Disciples enables every part of the international body of Christ to do its part in developing locally owned, effective, and sustainable programs for discipleship, leadership development, and business-based mission models.

For more information about Global Disciples, Global LEAD Alliance, or to find supplemental materials from this book visit our website at www.GlobalDisciples.net, or contact us below.

Global Disciples
315 W James St., Suite 202
Lancaster, PA. 17603
Email: mail@GlobalDisciples.net

Tel 717.290.7550

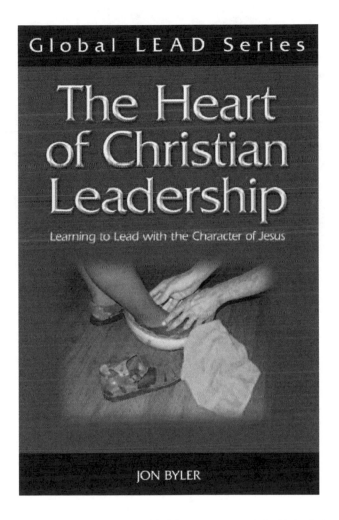

This companion book is available at www.GlobalDisciples.net